TEACHERS' WORLDS AND WORK

'Almost no-one, worldwide, c⟨...⟩ ⟨...⟩ ⟨...⟩ teachers' work
and teachers' professional lear⟨...⟩ ⟨...⟩hris Day. In this
magnum opus of a text, Profe⟨...⟩ ⟨...⟩ding and insight
into the core elements of teaching quality, such as ⟨...⟩ ⟨...⟩eacher resilience
and teachers' identity. Day's work is erudite, accessible and entirely up-to-date, but most of
all, it is deeply appreciative of who teachers are, what teachers do and why they do it.'

Andy Hargreaves, Brennan Chair in Education, Boston College, USA

'Early in this volume Chris Day writes: "We now live in a climate in which many teachers
struggle to teach to their best and well." For me, the book is a deeply committed investigation of why this is and how teachers in the contemporary world, both through their own
determination and through the creation of the right conditions in their schools and classrooms,
can challenge this climate. The vision is both realistic and humane, drawing as Day does on a
wide range of research, both his own and that of many other scholars. His great achievement
is to join together many different perspectives in order to integrate the insights into a holistic
portrayal of what it may mean to be a successful teacher in the twenty-first century.'

Ian Menter, Emeritus Professor of Teacher Education, University of Oxford, UK

'This book makes a significant contribution to understanding the complexities of the work
and worlds of teachers. It brings together the work, insights and contributions Chris Day
has made to the field of education in general and the teaching profession in particular over a
long and sustained career. *Teachers' Worlds and Work* helps us to make sense of how the complexities of teaching and being a teacher are connected to influence the design, development
and enactment of government and school policies, strategies and cultures. Day's voice as an
advocate for teachers and the teaching profession is strong and confident and, with a political
intent and an optimistic vision, it provides a voice for all teachers who are concerned with
what really matters for the teaching profession and what needs to matter to all those who are
concerned with enhancing their work and effectiveness in times of uncertainty, unrelenting
change and policy ambiguity.'

Judyth Sachs, Emeritus Professor, Macquarie University, Australia

Understanding what influences the quality of teachers' work across a career is key to building and sustaining their on-going commitment and effectiveness. *Teachers' Worlds and Work*
provides a new, research-informed consideration of key elements which independently and
together influence teachers' work and lives: policy and workplace conditions, teacher professionalism, identity, emotions, commitment and resilience, types of professional learning
and development, and the importance of the contribution to these made by high-quality
leadership. In bringing these elements together, the book provides new, detailed and holistic
understandings of their influence and suggests ways of building and sustaining teachers' abilities and willingness to teach to their best and well over their careers. This groundbreaking
text will be essential reading for teacher educators, teachers, head teachers and academics.

Christopher Day is Professor of Education at the School of Education, University of
Nottingham, UK.

Teacher Quality And School Development Series

Series Editors: Christopher Day and Ann Lieberman

TEACHERS' WORLDS AND WORK

Understanding Complexity, Building Quality

Christopher Day

Routledge
Taylor & Francis Group

LONDON AND NEW YORK

First published 2017
by Routledge
2 Park Square, Milton Park, Abingdon, Oxon OX14 4RN

and by Routledge
711 Third Avenue, New York, NY 10017

Routledge is an imprint of the Taylor & Francis Group, an informa business

© 2017 C. Day

British Library Cataloguing in Publication Data
A catalogue record for this book is available from the British Library

Library of Congress Cataloging in Publication Data
Names: Day, Christopher, 1943- author.
Title: Teachers' worlds and work: understanding complexity,
building quality / Christopher Day.
Description: Abingdon, Oxon; New York, NY: Routledge, 2017. |
Includes bibliographical references.
Identifiers: LCCN 2016057927 (print) | LCCN 2017022607 (ebook) |
ISBN 9781315170091 (ebk) | ISBN 9781138048591 (hbk: alk. paper) |
ISBN 9781138048607 (pbk: alk. paper)
Subjects: LCSH: Teachers–In-service training. | Teachers–Psychology. |
Effective teaching. | Educational leadership.
Classification: LCC LB1731 (ebook) | LCC LB1731 .D393 2017 (print) |
DDC 371.102–dc23
LC record available at https://lccn.loc.gov/2016057927

ISBN: 978-1-138-04859-1 (hbk)
ISBN: 978-1-138-04860-7 (pbk)
ISBN: 978-1-315-17009-1 (ebk)

Typeset in Bembo
by Deanta Global Publishing Services, Chennai, India

This book is dedicated to all teachers who strive always to teach to their best and well, regardless of country, culture or circumstance.

CONTENTS

FIGURES

TABLES

FOREWORD

Chris Day has written a virtual encyclopedia of what it means to be a teacher today, live in a school culture, and keep learning over time and working towards being a high-quality contributor. The one-line description is easy to write, but the complexities of teaching, learning, living in and outside one's school, and negotiating the professional and personal growth are complicated. And that is what this book is about – how to untangle and explain what it means to be a teacher over time in a school with the continuous struggle to stay current, stay connected to your students, and negotiate the connections between the professional obligations of being a teacher and one's personal life.

We learn about the changing nature of the times we live in and how it affects teachers all over the world. But what this book contributes is **how** policies, principals and practices are connected to teacher's work lives. Many have studied teachers, their motivations, their effectiveness and their development, but few have figured out and written about how all the changing conditions of teachers' growth and influences are connected. This book is unafraid to take apart, and put together again, all the complexities, relationships and pressures of being a high-quality teacher today!

We begin by learning about what these changes are including increased workload, pressures to learn and use digital technology, professional development on the complexities of increased knowledge.

How are these being handled? Who leads the professional learning? What is most important to know? Are teachers considered 'professionals' or are they merely 'technicians'. Are teachers involved in their own learning or is it mandated by others? What are the kinds of conditions that are created for teachers to learn and deepen their knowledge? All of these questions are examined by this book, from a variety of perspectives and authors.

The focus on teaching as 'emotional work' and the power of 'resilience' are critical ideas never before written about as to how they are connected to teacher quality, and the means to stay in teaching despite the pressures that exist. We learn about the growth of **commitment** as teachers learn new knowledge and skills and continue to face the challenges that are presented.

Teachers who are '**resilient**' learn to adapt to changing conditions, and they figure out how to balance the demands and challenges that come with being a teacher in today's world. Resilience is not just surviving, but figuring out how to stay positive, how to make teaching satisfying, and, most importantly, 'how to enhance collective efficacy and shared beliefs of professional control, influence and responsibility"(Day and Gu, 2014:11).

This discussion is priceless! It helps us understand why teaching is so complex and how resilience turns out to be a critical factor in understanding how teachers create, work, and learn to deal with complexities.

We learn also about the critical importance of principal leadership in helping facilitate teacher learning. The book serves as both a critique of a variety of phrases such as 'instructional leadership' and 'transformational leadership' and posits a more comprehensive view of how successful principals learn to work on personal, interpersonal and organizational levels all at the same time.

What makes this book so important is that we all learn – teachers, principals, academics and parents – that teachers' values and beliefs, the school culture and professional learning, and enlightened principal leadership and development all matter and all influence teaching, learning and leading. And if we are to have high-quality teachers, we must deal with not one thing at a time, but the complicated web of policies, leadership, support, trust and both the professionalism and emotional qualities that are present in teaching.

One of the most powerful ideas in the book is the discussion of the professional development of teachers, how it is organized, where the ideas come from, the tensions involved in gaining new knowledge and how teachers get involved in their own learning. And again we come to understand the need for commitment and renewal and the tug between compliance on the one hand and active engagement of teachers on the other – a significant theme throughout the book. It is about creating the conditions for learning both intellectually and emotionally, organizationally and personally, connecting to the head AND the heart and realizing that it is important to know how adults learn and participate in their own growth as teachers (and learners) in their own school culture. The pressures, tensions and necessities for continuous learning are presented to us, the readers.

Embracing the complexities of teacher's world and work is the essence of this extremely important book. Day has consulted many authors to analyse and understand the complexities of teaching, learning and leadership from both a policy, research and practice perspective. As readers we are well educated and can both learn and enjoy a fine contribution to our understanding of how quality teachers can be supported in a challenging world!

Ann Lieberman, Senior Scholar at the
Stanford Center for Opportunity
Policy in Education (SCOPE)

PREFACE

This book unpicks the complexities of the work and world of teachers. Its aim is to identify what teachers need for them to teach to their best and well, and what helps and what hinders them in this endeavour. I use the phrase 'to their best and well' throughout the book because, although it is important that teachers always teach to their best, it cannot be assumed that they will always do so or that this necessarily means that they will always teach well. Ideally, all teachers will strive always, whatever the circumstances, *to enable their students to reach for and achieve their full potential*. Yet, their willingness and abilities to do so will be influenced not only by the extent of their initial motivation and commitment – and this will vary – but also by present and future circumstance. On entry to teaching, for example, there will be some for whom teaching is a service, a passionate vocation; but there will be others for whom it is a career or even 'just a job'. Whilst there is no necessary direct cause-and-effect relationship between motivation and effectiveness, it is likely that there will be qualitative differences between the energy and commitment (arguably essential contributory elements to effective teaching) that teachers with different motivations and notions of service will give to their work. Sustaining these over time will be intellectually and emotionally challenging, whatever the strength of their initial motivations and commitment.

The discussions throughout this book do not assume that all teachers are unhappy 'victims' of policies that have 'technicized' or devalued their work to the extent that they have a sense of powerlessness in the face of 'neo-liberal' government agendas. Indeed, there is a considerable amount of empirical evidence that demonstrates that, given the right workplace conditions, this is far from the case. Nor does the book 'valorize' all teachers. While there are many who teach to their best and well, there are those who do not, and there are those whose willingness and abilities to do so fluctuates. At the same time, the book provides clear evidence internationally that for teaching to be effective over a career, teachers need not only acquire, apply and, where necessary, enhance their subject knowledge and classroom competencies, but that they also need to feel respected, valued and trusted; that, in addition to being assessed and judged, their motivation, commitment and capacities for resilience are necessary if the ambitions of standard-raising agendas are to be achieved. A wide range of research internationally suggests strongly that these are closely related to the extent to which their sense of professionalism and professional identity are nurtured, supported and, where appropriate, challenged.

In short, if we believe that all students have an entitlement to be taught by teachers who are equipped and committed to providing the best learning opportunities for all students, then we need to understand and acknowledge that teaching, at its best, can be both intellectually and emotionally engaging and intellectually *and* emotionally exhausting; and that students will benefit if their teachers have a strong sense of professionalism, professional identity, commitment and capacity for resilience, have access to a wide range of fit-for-purpose professional learning and development opportunities and benefit from positive school cultures, characterized by ethics of high expectations, care and achievement.

I originally intended to write this book as an updated version of *Developing Teachers: The Challenges of Lifelong Learning* (1999), which had been a culmination of my experiences and thinking, first as a classroom teacher, then as a teacher educator and local authority schools' advisor, and latterly as a university tutor and researcher. Instead, as I began to review events since then, and make sense of them, I found that policy interventions had continued at an accelerated pace and that, as a result, much had changed in the governance and curriculum of schools, the terms and conditions of teachers and their work, and the means of recording and judging their effectiveness. Over the same period, new research-informed understandings of schools, teachers and school leadership, had revealed more insights about why many teachers continue to be passionately, knowledgeably and skilfully committed to teaching over the whole span of their careers; why some do not; what makes the difference; and what helps and hinders teachers' willingness and capacities to contribute to their best and well, to the academic achievement and well-being of all the students they teach in the face of huge personal, intellectual and emotional challenges posed by changes in policy, workplace and social environments. I found, also, that although much is made, rightly, of the important contribution of regular, 'fit-for-purpose' opportunities for professional learning and development, they are insufficient in themselves to ensure that all teachers are able to teach to their best and well over a career, however well designed, differentiated and managed they may be.

As I sought to provide a holistic perspective on teachers' work and worlds, it also became clear that much research continues to focus upon investigating different elements of teachers' lives, work, and policy and social contexts as discrete entities. I found that, although such research contributes much that is of value in increasing insights, knowledge and understanding of aspects of teachers' work and lives, because many of the findings are contained within a particular individual's research focus and research discipline, it was not always possible to 'join the dots', to see connections between their findings or their implications for schools, teachers and students' worlds and work. How, for example, notions of teacher professionalism and professional identity influence teachers' commitment and capacity for resilience; how these might be strengthened or diminished by the quality of school leadership and professional learning and development; and how emotions run, like a thread, through every aspect of teachers' work and lives. As teachers pursue their work over the course of their careers, these are not experienced singly, as separate entities, but collectively and in different personal, professional and workplace contexts. How they are experienced will influence teachers' views and expectations of themselves and how they carry out their daily work. How well they are equipped, and remain equipped, to manage and mediate them in different phases of their teaching lives and in different policy and school contexts, will affect the quality of their work, and their willingness and abilities to be effective. Taken together, they provide a frame for understanding its complexity.

So, this grew into a book that identifies and examines key internal and external factors that influence teachers' growth, well-being and effectiveness. Separately and in combination, these create the complexities of teachers' work and worlds. Understanding these, and how each connects to and interacts with the others to influence, needs to be at the heart of the design, development and enactment of government and school policies, strategies and cultures if they are to succeed in raising standards, and building and sustaining high-quality teachers and a high-quality teaching profession. It is a book, therefore, that is concerned with what really matters to teachers and what needs to matter to all those who are concerned with enhancing their work and effectiveness in times of change.

The book is in two parts. The first part examines the policy and school structures, conditions and cultures and emotional contexts in which many teachers' work, and what is known about the influences that help or hinder their sense of professionalism, professional identity, commitment and resilience, all of which impact, directly and indirectly, upon their willingness and capacities to be 'effective' over a career. The second part focuses upon the kinds of professional learning and development that are known to be 'effective' and the importance of the contribution to these made by high-quality leadership. Essentially, the chapters seek to answer a series of questions, which will further understandings of the complexity of teachers' work and worlds in order to contribute to building and sustaining their quality.

1. What is the nature of teacher professionalism in times of change? (Chapter 1)
2. What part do professional identity and emotions play in teachers' willingness and capacities to teach to their best? (Chapter 2)
3. What qualities of *commitment* are needed to continue to strive to teach well and effectively? (Chapter 3)
4. How can teachers maintain a capacity for *resilience* in order to sustain their passion to influence learners and learning? (Chapter 4)
5. What orientations of individual professional learning and development are effective? (Chapter 5)

6. What kinds of collaborative learning and development are effective: learning as a social endeavour? (Chapter 6)
7. What part can *leaders* play in creating and nurturing organizational cultures where participants (teachers and students) feel safe to learn, re-learn and enhance knowledge and understanding? (Chapter 7)
8. What are the challenges and opportunities for building and sustaining teacher quality in the twenty-first century? (Chapter 8)

Whilst the chapters seek to acknowledge, unpack and examine the complexities of teachers' work and lives, and the challenges which they face, by charting the connections and interactions between the different parts, they move beyond identifying these towards suggesting ways forward for a healthy, productive, committed, resilient and effective teaching profession, which every country needs and to which every school student is entitled.

Reference

Day, C. (1999). *Developing Teachers: The Challenges of Lifelong Learning.* Hove, UK: Psychology Press.

ACKNOWLEDGEMENTS

I wish to acknowledge Ann Lieberman and Judyth Sachs, 'critical readers' of this book, for their considered and wise feedback and Hayley McCalla for her production of the many early drafts. Finally, I want to thank the many colleagues whose passion and commitment to teachers and teaching, learners and learning have influenced my thinking and practice at different times over my working life. Like the best teachers, they will never be forgotten.

The author and the publisher are grateful for permission to use copyright material from the following works in this book:

Clarke, D. and Hollingsworth, H. (2002). Elaborating a model of teacher professional growth. *Teaching and Teacher Education*, 18 (8):947–967, reprinted with permission from Elsevier.

Day, C. and Kington, A. (2008). Identity, well-being and effectiveness: the emotional contexts of teaching. *Pedagogy, Culture and Society* 16 (1):7–23, reprinted by permission of Taylor & Francis Ltd, www.tandfonline.com.

Day, C. (2009). Building and sustaining successful principalship in England: The importance of trust. *Journal of Educational Administration*, 47 (6):719–730, reprinted by permission of Emerald.

Day, C. and Gu, Q. (2009). Veteran teachers: Commitment, resilience and quality retention. *Teachers and Teaching*, 15 (4):441–457, reprinted by permission of Taylor & Francis Ltd, www.tandfonline.com.

Day, C. and Hong, J. (2016). Influences on the capacities for emotional resilience of teachers in schools serving disadvantaged urban communities: challenges of living on the edge. *Teaching and Teacher Education*, 59:115–125, reprinted with permission from Elsevier.

Day, C., Sammons, P., Leithwood, K., Hopkins, D., Gu, Q., Brown, E. with Ahtaridou, E. (2011). *Successful School Leadership: Linking with Learning and Achievement*. Maidenhead: Open University Press. Reproduced with the kind permission of Open International Publishing Ltd. All rights reserved.

Fielding, M. (2012). Education as if people matter: John Macmurray, community and the struggle for democracy *Oxford Review of Education*, 38 (6) December, 675–692, reprinted by permission of Taylor & Francis Ltd, www.tandfonline.com.

Gu, Q. and Day, C. (2007). Teachers Resilience: A necessary condition for effectiveness. *Teaching and Teacher Education*, 23:1302–1316, reprinted with permission from Elsevier.

Hipp, K. K., Huffman, J. B., Pankake, A. M. and Olivier, D. F. (2008). Sustaining professional learning communities: Case studies, *Journal of Educational Change*, 9:173–195, reprinted with permission of Springer.

Jackson, D. S. (2000). The school improvement journey: Perspectives on leadership. *School Leadership and Management*, 20 (1):61–78, reprinted by permission of Taylor & Francis Ltd, www.tandfonline.com.

Lai, E. (2014). Principal leadership practices in exploiting situated possibilities to build teacher capacity for change. *Asia Pacific Education Review*, 15 (2):165–175, reprinted with permission of Springer.

Lesser, E. L. and Storck, J. (2001). Communities of practice and organizational performance. *IBM Systems Journal*, 40(4):831–841, adapted with permission from IBM.

Mansfield, C. F., Beltman, S., Price, A. and McConney, A. (2012). 'Don't sweat the small stuff': Understanding teacher resilience at the chalkface. *Teaching and Teacher Education*, 28:357–367, reprinted with permission from Elsevier.

Robinson, Viviane M. J. (2007). *School Leadership and Student Outcomes: Identifying What Works and Why*, Vol. 41. Melbourne: Australian Council for Educational Leaders (ACEL), reproduced by permission of ACEL.

Sachs, J. (2016). Teacher professionalism: Why are we still talking about it? *Teachers and Teaching: Theory and Practice*, 22 (4):413–425, reprinted by permission of Taylor and Francis Ltd, www.tandfonline.com.

Wong, J. L. N. (2010). What makes a professional learning community possible? A case study of a Mathematics department in a junior secondary school of China. *Asia Pacific Education Review*, (11):131–139, reprinted with permission of Springer.

1

TEACHER PROFESSIONALISM IN CHANGING TIMES

These are changing times in education systems around the world. With the start of the new millennium, many societies are engaging in serious and promising reforms. One of the key elements in most of these reforms is the professional development of teachers; societies are finally acknowledging that teachers are not only one of the 'variables' that need to be changed in order to improve their national systems, but they are also the most significant change agents in these reforms.

(Villegas-Reimers, 2003, UNESCO, IIEP:7)

If teachers are the most significant change agents in the school, then understanding their work and lives and what influences these in contexts of challenge and change over a 30- or 40-year career is key to ensuring their on-going commitment and quality. Whilst researchers have explored what influences their willingness and abilities to teach to their best – they have done so in different, often segmented, ways. When we read an article, a research report or a book, we are likely to find a focus on, for example, the effects of policy change; the role of principals in shaping and leading school vision, direction and culture; teachers' moral purposes; professional identities; efficacy and agency; commitment and resilience; trust; school improvement and effectiveness; teaching as emotional work; continuing professional development; and professional learning communities, partnerships and network learning. All these are important in understanding teachers' work and lives, but are often unconnected in the literature. We rarely glimpse the whole. Yet, while each of these themes contributes knowledge about contexts, influences and conditions for teachers' growth independently, it is only by viewing them as inter-connected parts of the inner and outer landscapes which influence teachers that we may begin to understand the complexity of their worlds and work and through this, contribute to building and sustaining the quality of their work.

This book brings together and discusses a range of international research that has found that:

1. Teachers will have different motivations that cause them to enter teaching (as a vocation, career, as a job, as a part of a varied work portfolio), and so not all will be pre-disposed to devoting the *levels of commitment* that are regularly required to arouse, engage and sustain the interests, expectations and ambitions of their students.
2. Teachers will experience different learning and development needs during *different phases of their professional lives*.
3. How teachers feel about themselves – their sense of positive, stable *professional identity* – is associated with their perceived ability to be effective in the classroom.
4. Successful professional learning and development focuses upon building personal, interpersonal and organizational capacities through a combination of the *functional and the attitudinal*.
5. Teaching is an *emotional* as well as an intellectual pursuit. To be willing and able to teach to their best, teachers need emotional as well as intellectual support.
6. To meet the predictable and unpredictable challenges of classroom interaction, teachers need to have the *capacity to be resilient*. Such capacity is likely to fluctuate at different times and for different reasons or combinations of reasons during their careers.
7. The quality of whole *school leadership* and relationships between colleagues are key contributing elements to teachers' morale, job satisfaction, self-efficacy and quality retention.
8. Building and sustaining individual and collective *professional capital* is a key function of school leaders.

Changing work contexts

Policy

In beginning to address the twin concerns of understanding complexity and building quality, I was struck immediately by how much the policy and social landscapes in all countries had continued to change, and how the policy voice has become increasingly dominant in decisions about teacher and school improvement. We now live in a climate in which many teachers struggle to teach well. As they continue to meet everyday complexities of teaching and learning, and to fulfil their broader ethically driven educational purposes, they do so alongside increased pressures to meet the external demands of results-driven policies. Of course, it may be reasonably argued that this has always been the case. However, there can be little doubt that teachers in this century face unprecedented national pressures to comply with policy agendas through increasingly interventionist systems of surveillance of the quality of their work and its measurable impact on pupil progress and attainment. Take, for example, four central policy initiatives evident in a number of countries:

1. *Pre-service contexts*

   National policies now have a greater influence on the structures and cultures of pre-service, with governments changing the ways students are prepared for teaching. These represent a shift away from 'theory-and-practice' models in which universities played the lead role, to apprentice-like 'practice' models in which universities and the educational research that they produce, with some exceptions, are becoming minor players – at best junior partners – in school-led enterprises. 'Teach for America' and its equivalents in, for example, England, Sweden and Australia, and 'Schools Direct' and 'School Centred Initial Teacher Training' (SCITT) models in England illustrate the trend. The tacit message is that teaching is perceived as a craft best learned alongside other practitioners. Whilst there are differences between countries in the pace of change, the directions of travel towards models of school-led, university-supported pathways are similar.

2. *Teachers' work*

   Government policies internationally have resulted in the increasing deprivatisation of teachers' work. One of the consequences has been that what, how and how well teachers are teaching are scrutinized much more closely and their impact on pupils assessed more frequently, through, for example, the use of annual teacher performance management (aka appraisal), progress and attainment measures (requiring differentiated targets for students), curriculum continuity and progression between years of schooling (so that there is no repetition of content) and nationally defined teacher and school standards.

3. *Bounded autonomy*

   Government policies are ensuring that schools become both more autonomous in their management of the curriculum and resources whilst also more accountable to parents and government for students' well-being and academic attainments. In England, the transfer of responsibilities for education and education standards away from government is illustrated through the establishment of 'self-improving' school systems of 'Academies', 'MATs' (Multi-Academy Trusts), 'Chains' (large groups of schools often managed by private companies) and 'TSAs' (Teaching School Alliances, led by exemplary 'Teaching Schools' and 'National Leaders of Education' and managed by 'Executive Principals'). In short, schools have become quasi-businesses, corporatized, supported by business managers. Corresponding with these measures of distributed leadership at the national system level and increased autonomy at school level, there has been a tightening of control from the centre over the curriculum and the means of assessing student achievement, through national tests and examinations. In England and an increasing number of other countries, school quality is monitored and evaluated by means of an independent Office for Standards in Education (Ofsted), whose inspectors, working to a national inspection framework, publicly judge individual schools in four categories: 'outstanding', 'good', 'requiring improvement' or 'special measures'.

4. *Globalization of education standards*
    Well documented over a number of years now have been the 'rise and rise' of results-driven agendas in the public services in many countries. The leaders of most education systems believe now that they are able to judge accurately the standards of schools and the success attained by students, particularly in core areas of literacy, numeracy and science, against school standards and student performance in schools both within and between countries, as a result of the development of international tests by the Organisation for Economic Co-operation and Development (OECD) such as PISA, TIMMS and PIRLS. Such 'regimes of numbers' have, it has been reasonably asserted, become 'a resource through which surveillance can be exercised', and 'data become the resource for comparison' (Ozga, 2008:264, 267).

Teacher professionalism in testing times

For some time now, it has been claimed that the emphasis on corporate management, which produced many of the reforms illustrated in the previous examples, has resulted, over the last 20 years, in a sea change in the nature of professionalism. In 1996, for example, it was claimed that each teacher must be a:

> professional who clearly meets corporate goals, set elsewhere, manages a range of students well and documents their achievements and problems for public accountability purposes. The criteria of the successful professional in this corporate model is one who works efficiently and effectively in meeting the standardised criteria set for the accomplishment of both students and teachers, as well as contributing to the school's formal accountability processes.
>
> *(Brennan, 1996:22)*

More recently, Stephen Ball and others have described the system in terms of 'performativity' and associated this with oppressive, 'neo-liberal' environments that stifle teacher agency and creativity:

> The first-order effect of performativity in education is to reorient pedagogical and scholarly activities towards these which are likely to have a positive impact on measurable performance outcomes for the group, for the institution and increasingly for the nation, and as such is a deflection of attention away from aspects of social, emotional or moral development that have no immediate measurable performativity value ... Performativity is enacted through measures and targets against which we are expected to position ourselves but often in ways that also produce uncertainties about how we should organise ourselves within our work ... Performativity 'works' most powerfully when it is inside our heads and our souls. That is, when we do it to ourselves, when

we take responsibility for working harder, faster and better, thus 'improving' our 'output', as part of our sense of personal worth and the worth of others … Performativity is not in any simple sense a technology of oppressions; it is also one of satisfaction and rewards, at least for some. Performativity is a key mechanism of neo-liberal management, a form of hands-off management that uses comparisons and judgements in place of interventions and direction … The self-managing individual and the autonomous organisation are produced within the intricacies of performativity through audits, inspections, appraisals, self-reviews, quality assurance …

(Ball, 2012:31–32)

Standard setting for teachers as a means of judging their performance by those outside schools has become the norm in schools in many countries. Sachs and Mockler (2012) have claimed that performance management and performance cultures are now 'embedded in policies and practices of education and are especially evident around government interventions to impose professional standards on the teaching profession' (p. 33). Such performance cultures, they assert, can unduly emphasize technical aspects of teaching, reduce teachers' traditional responsibilities for exercising discretionary judgements in the classroom and erode trust:

First, at best they can make public the aspects of teacher practice and decision-making that are taken for granted; second … privilege, and more problematic is that they privilege the technical aspects of teaching to the neglect of the relational and teachers' ability to make professional judgements. Third … they serve to subvert teacher autonomy to the extent that teachers become implementers of policy rather than the arbiters of their own practice. Consequently, trust between the teaching profession, unions and educational bureaucracies erodes as they increasingly operate in a climate of surveillance and with a contradictory set of assumptions about the nature of teachers' work, and how that work is recognised and rewarded. These cultures reinforce a rational technical form of teacher professionalism rather than a transformative one.

(Sachs and Mockler, 2012:33)

In essence, these and other critics claim that policy trends have changed the nature of teachers' professional orientation to work (Leicht and Fennell, 2001). They are said to be becoming 'technicians' (Apple, 2008; Ball, 2003a) as existing professional identities, by which 'individual teachers negotiate and reflect on the socially situated aspects of their role' (O'Connor, 2008:118) are challenged by changes in expectations brought about by continuing new policy interventions. Groundwater-Smith and Mockler (2012) have pointed to the punitive influence of these measures on teacher workload and morale, their negative effects on teacher recruitment and retention and the distortion of the broader purposes of school education, illustrated by an increased emphasis in classrooms on 'teaching to the test', and the growth of a 'fallacious' notion of teachers as technicians:

It is our fear that the current standards regimes and the policy contexts out of which they grow have, at their hearts, a desire not to build an understanding of the complexity and nuance of teaching or to celebrate the diversity of teachers and learners, but rather to standardise practice, stifle debate and promise the fallacious notion of professional objectivity.

(Groundwater-Smith and Mockler, 2009:8)

Five consequences of policy reform for teachers' work and lives

There have been five important consequences for teachers' work as a result of the increased policy voice and the changes in the needs of students.

One consequence has been an increase in the demands on teachers in terms of workload and bureaucracy associated with ever more detailed, often standardized recording and reporting procedures. Close attention to, if not compliance with, these is now an integral part of teachers' work.

A second consequence relates to the management of teachers' professional learning and development (PLD). As the management of schools becomes more devolved, school principals have a more explicit responsibility for its funding, management, direction and quality; and they are held more directly accountable by government for ensuring its impact upon raising standards of teaching, learning and student attainments. Participation in PLD has thus become less of a choice that individual teachers make and more of a formal requirement, as part of their responsibility to contribute to their schools' improvement profiles.

A third consequence is that as the traditional isolation of teachers has diminished, so too have acts of collaboration between teachers and between schools become more normal. There are benefits in this, for example, sharing of practice, making public and transparent how teachers make decisions and judgements about practice.

A fourth consequence has been increased pressures on teachers to enlarge their classroom teaching and learning approaches. Within this, the increased availability of digital technologies has meant that many are having to adapt their traditional roles as 'expert' content knowledge holders to roles in which they become knowledge brokers and mediators, assisting students to make informed judgements about the quality and efficacy of the wide range of unfiltered masses of instantly available information.

A fifth, unsought, *consequence* has been the continuing reporting of teachers' negative responses to changes. For example, an analysis of 2016 survey responses from 4,450 teachers carried out by *The Guardian*, a reputable national English newspaper, found that 98% reported that they were under increasing pressure, 82% reported that their workload had become unmanageable and 75% reported that their mental health was adversely affected. Only 12% reported that they had a good work-life balance and 43% were planning to leave within the next five years. Such responses can be found among teachers in many other countries. In England, among a growing number of countries, there is now a crisis of teacher recruitment and retention – 79% of schools reported that they were struggling to recruit and retain teachers (Lightfoot,

2016). A similar situation exists in the USA, one of many other countries which report low teacher morale and problems of recruitment and retention (Johnson *et al.*, 2012; Boyd *et al.*, 2010; Allensworth *et al.*, 2009).

The meanings of teacher professionalism

In the context of these broad policy changes and their consequences, the meaning of teacher professionalism continues to be a topic of considerable debate, especially among academics in many countries who are variously concerned that such changes in national policy demands, particularly external inspection and regulated student assessment related to the achievement of success in particular areas of the curriculum, threaten its key components: qualification following a period of extended training, teacher autonomy and discretionary decision-making. Thus, ownership of the three essential components of professionalism – knowledge, autonomy and responsibility – identified in 2000 by Furlong *et al.* (2000) continues to be tested.

The ways in which reforms are affecting teacher professionalism have been illustrated in two relatively recent empirical cross-national studies. The first, a report of a cross-cultural study which investigated the impact of policy on the work of secondary school teachers in England, France and Denmark (McNess, Broadfoot and Osborn, 2003),[1] found that in England the perceived demand for delivery of 'performance' had 'emphasized the managerially "effective"' in the interests of accountability while ignoring teachers' deeply rooted commitment to the affective aspects of teaching and learning (McNess *et al.*, 2003:243). It drew attention to the increasing body of work, which illuminates the extent to which the social and emotional aspects of teachers' work – the emotional investment of self in others – causes them to be vulnerable to policy changes, which reduce opportunities for them to exercise creativity and develop caring relationships with their pupils (Nias, 1996; Acker, 1999; Hargreaves, 1994; Woods and Jeffrey, 1996).

In Denmark, though reforms are different, the availability of children's test results on the internet indicates further movement towards a performativity agenda. In terms of teacher professionalism (in England), the research suggests that the role of teachers as knowledge constructors has been eroded, that autonomy in classroom decision-making has become constrained, that teachers' roles have become more instrumental as their worth is judged principally on their success in complying with the demands of central agendas. In Norway, too, there is national testing, national measures for judging the quality of schools and increased competition between schools as privately financed schools are encouraged (Welle-Strand and Tjeldvoll, 2002). Similar changes have been reported in Finland (Rinne, Kivirauma and Simola, 2002) and Sweden (Lundahl, 2002). Subsequent literature continues to chart the inexorable increase in government demands for measurable indicators of teacher and pupil performance and regular reporting of standards in relation to these (e.g. Power, 2004; Castells, 1997; Apple, 2006; Ozga, 2008; Ball, 2012).

Sachs and Mockler (2012) argue that there are three kinds of such performance cultures:

> *regulatory cultures:* found in standards regimes, or initiatives which are concerned with codifying practice. Regulation, enforcement and sanctions are required to ensure compliance
>
> *developmental cultures:* represent a responsive form of accountability in that they seek to meet the interests of various stakeholder communities, teachers, parents and students. In terms of professional standards, they are profession-driven with the locus of control on the profession ... they seek to balance the needs of externally imposed accountability with the developmental needs of teachers
>
> *measurement cultures:* reflect a form of contractual accountability in so far as they have as their primary concern standards, outcomes and results. They are supported by government rather than teachers as they rely on a set of predetermined performance indicators that supposedly represent a form of objective measurement of teaching performance and student outcomes.
>
> *(Sachs and Mockler, 2012:35–36)*

It is not difficult to relate these cultures to the ways in which the meaning of teacher professionalism is defined through the orientation of one or other of these performance cultures in their schools.

Evetts' (2011) delineation between two discourses of professionalism provides a useful means of conceptualizing two basic broad orientations; the first, 'occupational professionalism', is in tune with the pre-reform era and the prevailing preference of teachers, teachers' associations and unions.

Occupational professionalism

> A discourse constructed within professional occupational groups and incorporates collegial authority. It involves relations of practitioner trust from both employers and clients. It is based on autonomy and discretionary judgement and assessment by practitioners in complex cases.
>
> *(Evetts, 2011:23)*

The second, 'organizational professionalism', supports the views of critics of government policy.

Organizational professionalism

> A discourse used increasingly by managers in work organisations. It incorporates rational – legal forms of authority and hierarchical structures in decision-making. It involves increased standardisation of work procedures and practices and managerial controls. It relies on externalised forms of regulation and accountability measures such as target setting and performance review.
>
> *(Evetts, 201:23)*

Taken to excess, promoting only forms of organizational professionalism would be 'likely to promote a limited conception of being a teacher' (Day, 1999:139), diminish 'teachers' self-confidence, creativity and the moral purpose that sustains them in ambiguous and difficult situations … [and] … corrode their ability to act with confidence and authority and weaken(s) trust' (Sachs, 2016: 423). However, although such organizational professionalism promotes performance cultures that are primarily regulatory, 'concerned with compliance and reporting', they can *be helpful* in that they

> may produce some shared baselines about learning outcomes and provide teachers with a common and shared language about practice … they can also help outsiders recognise the scope and scale of teachers' work, and provide a systematic approach for the recognition and reward of teaching rather than an individualistic one.
>
> *(Sachs, 2016:415)*

My own experience of research with schools in England and many other parts of the world also paints a more complex picture of the relationships between this larger, 'macro-level' perspective and how teachers and schools go about their business. I have found that not all schools and not all teachers feel themselves to be 'oppressed', unable to work within external system constraints and policy change, unable to fulfil their broader educational purposes, unable to find 'room to manoeuvre', unable to find satisfaction and personal and professional fulfilment from their work; and that those who overcome the challenges with which they are faced, who continue to strive to teach to their best and well, are often driven by strong moral, ethical and humanistic purposes.

Thus, whilst at one level government reforms appear to have changed what it means to be a teacher as the locus of control in an increasing number of jurisdictions has shifted from the individual to school principals and system managers, even in an era of such unprecedented reform being and behaving as a professional continues to be associated with having a strong technical culture (knowledge base); service ethic (commitment to serving clients' needs); professional commitment (strong individual and collective identities); and professional autonomy (control over classroom practice) (Etzioni, 1969; Larson, 1977; Talbert and McLaughlin, 1996); and there continue to be a number of writers and researchers who, whilst acknowledging the views of 'critical theorists' (e.g. Apple, 2006; Ozga, 2012; Ball, 2012), propose a more nuanced view of professionalism in which it is quite possible for teachers to be active agents, able to mediate reform and maintain an ethic and practice of care, commitment and a measure of autonomy. Reporting on data gathered through the 'Teacher Status Project' in England (Hargreaves *et al.*, 2006, 2007), Swann *et al.* (2010) found that 'teachers' thinking about their professionalism may be construed as consisting of an inner core of strong, shared beliefs and commitments … [e.g. the possession of expertise and a need to be trusted]; an intermediate set of coherent but contested components of professionalism … [e.g. definitions of autonomy]; and an outer layer of disparate elements which are generally highly disputed and which remain unintegrated into broader ways of thinking' (Swann, 2010:549). The extent to which they are able to enact these within different policy mandates will depend on the strength of their own values in each of these spheres and the collective values expressed in the cultures of the schools in which they work.

Professional capital

More than two decades ago, Hargreaves and Goodson proposed seven principles of professionalism, which provided an alternative to 'command and control' reform agendas. Today, these continue to be important 'markers' for those who teach and lead schools in the increasing number of 'self-improving' systems:

1. Increased opportunity and responsibility to exercise discretionary judgement over the issues of teaching, curriculum and care that affect one's students;
2. Opportunities and expectations to engage with the moral and social purposes and value of what teachers teach, along with major curriculum and assessment matters in which these purposes are embedded;
3. Commitment to working with colleagues in collaborative cultures of help and support as a way of using shared expertise to solve on-going problems of professional practice, rather than engaging in joint work as a motivational device to implement the external mandates of others;
4. Occupational heteronomy rather than self-protective autonomy, where teachers work authoritatively yet openly and collaboratively with other partners in the wider community (especially parents and students themselves), who have a significant stake in students' learning;
5. A commitment to active care and not just anodyne service for students. (Professionalism, they asserted, must in this sense acknowledge and embrace the emotional as well as the cognitive dimensions of teaching, and also recognise the skills and dispositions that are essential to committed and effective caring);
6. A self-directed search and struggle for continuous learning related to one's own expertise and standards of practice, rather than compliance with the enervating obligations of endless change demanded by others (often under the guise of continuing learning or improvement); and
7. The creation and recognition of high task complexity with levels of status and reward appropriate to such complexity.

(Hargreaves and Goodson, 1996:20–21, cited in Day, 2002:681–682)

These principles have been elaborated and refined in subsequent years and become articulated more recently through the concept of 'professional capital'. In an important contribution to re-conceptualizing professionalism, Hargreaves and Fullan (2012) propose that investment in professional capital is necessary if students are to be taught well, by teachers who are 'highly committed, thoroughly prepared, continuously developed, properly paid, well networked with each other to maximise their own improvement, and able to make effective judgements using all their capabilities and experience, (2012:3). They combine notions of 'human', 'decisional' and 'social' capital as constituting 'professional capital'.

Human capital focuses upon qualifications, experience and developing individual knowledge and skills.

Decisional capital is about the ability to exercise *wise judgements* in the unpredictable processes of teaching and learning in the classroom. It is 'the capital that professionals acquire and accumulate through structured and unstructured experience, practice and reflection' (Hargreaves and Fullan, 2012: 93). In relation to this, it has been noted that 'individual resources of efficacy, hope, optimism, and resiliency synergistically contribute' to an individual's positive psychological capital (Avery *et al.*, 2009:434). Yet, it must be acknowledged that, however committed they may be to their work with students, it is difficult for teachers to exercise wise judgements when, tired as a result of heavy workloads, feeling under-valued by others or grappling with externally imposed changes, these resources become diminished.

Social capital is built through frequent, productive interactions with colleagues within and outside the school – what Huberman (1995) termed 'sustained interactivity' – that focus upon teaching and learning, and through which trust is built. The quality of teachers' relationships with one another has been identified as being a key contributor to both teacher retention and school improvement (Bryk and Schneider, 2002; Leana and Pit, 2006; Day *et al.*, 2007; Tschannen-Moran, 2014). This concept of professional capital suggests that Evetts' (2011) notion of 'occupational' professionalism can be strengthened through sustained, critical dialogue, mutual trust and respect.

Hargreaves and Fullan (2012) cite Leana's (2011) examination of the relationships between human and social capital among teachers through which teachers with high social capital increased their students' mathematics scores by 5.7% more than teachers with lower social capital ,and that students within the higher performing group of teachers, students of teachers with both high human capital and high social capital, achieved the highest gains. Importantly, Leana found that so-called 'low ability' (low human capital) teachers were able to achieve as well as teachers of so-called 'average ability' if they 'had strong social capital in their school' (Leana, 2011:34).

> Teaching like a pro means continuously inquiring into and improving one's own teaching. It means constantly developing and reinventing in professional capital ... planning teaching, improving teaching, and often doing teaching not as an isolated individual but as part of a high performing team. It means developing shared professional capital within an organisation and community ... being part and parcel of the wider teaching profession and contributing to its development.
>
> *(Hargreaves and Fullan, 2012:22–23)*

Relationships, then, are 'important sources of social capital, defined as the potential and actual set of cognitive, social and material resources made available through direct and indirect relationships with others ... [and can lead to] ... teacher learning and changes in practice, collegial knowledge sharing, commitment to student learning ... improved student achievement ... [and] ... higher job satisfaction' (Bridwell-Mitchell and Cooc, 2016:7).

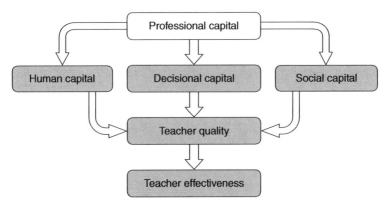

FIGURE 1.1 Hypothesized relationship between professional capital, teacher quality and effectiveness

Figure 1.1 illustrates how nurturing professional capital can lead to opportunities for teachers to teach to their best and well. Even so, we cannot assume a direct cause-and-effect relationship between teacher quality and teacher effectiveness.

Teacher quality and student attainment: a complex relationship

> There is considerable validity in the charges that tests don't reflect the whole child and don't tell us what we need to know; that the pressures on districts to cheat have increased dramatically, that some test-score improvement is just the result of narrow teaching. Nevertheless, tests are still the only widely available metric, and they hold a central place in policy debates, something that is not going to change in the near future.
>
> *(Payne, 2008:6–7)*

As government policies have become more evidence based, and as actions for school improvement have become more focused upon meeting government policy initiatives, so too the belief that better teaching will lead directly to increased student attainment results has become an unquestioned assumption. There is some evidence that this may well be so. For example, it has been claimed that

> Research shows that teacher quality is significantly and positively correlated with pupil attainment and that it is the most important within-school aspect explaining student performance.
>
> *(European Commission, 2007:3)*

Certainly, large-scale data sets produced, for example, by Rivers and Sanders (1996), Hanushek (2011) and Hattie (2009) all point to the difference that a 'good' teacher can make to increasing students' measurable attainments. Gladwell summarized this well:

Eric Hanushek, an economist from Stanford, has estimated that the students of a very bad teacher learn, on average, half a year's worth of material in one school year. The students in a class of a very good teacher will learn more than a year and a half's worth of material. That difference amounts to a year's worth of learning in a single year.

(Gladwell, 2008)

In a later paper, examining teacher quality as defined by student measurable performance outcomes, Hanushek (2011) found that in the United States there was considerable variation between the results of pupils taught by 'effective' and less-'effective' teachers:

[T]he average gains in learning across classrooms, even classrooms within the same school, are very different. Some teachers year after year produce bigger gains in student learning than other teachers. The magnitude of the differences is truly large, with some teachers producing 1.5 years of gain in achievement in an academic year while others with equivalent students produce only 1/2 year of gain. In other words, two students starting at the same level of achievement can know vastly different amounts at the end of a single academic year due solely to the teacher to which they are assigned. If a bad year is compounded by other bad years, it may not be possible for the student to recover.

(Hanushek, 2011:467)

Large-scale quantitative studies, whilst useful, are not, however, able to explain how or why teachers become 'very good' or 'very bad' in contributing to the progress and attainment of their pupils. They cannot tell us anything about the effects that different positive and negative workplace conditions and contexts may have on teachers' motivations, morale, sense of commitment, professional identities and capacity for resilience – all key contributors to teacher quality. It is important, for example, to distinguish between what teachers do in classrooms, how students learn and what students achieve in tests and examinations. In the USA Goe (2007) has argued that:

Standardised achievement tests were intended to measure student achievement and were not designed to measure teacher quality. It is difficult to sort out teacher effects (i.e. the contribution of teachers) from classroom effects (i.e. the contribution of peers, textbooks, materials, curriculum, classroom climate and other factors). It is difficult to obtain linked student-teacher data that makes it possible to connect specific teachers to student achievement test scores.

(Goe, 2007:2)

There is other research-informed evidence, also, which indicates that relationships between teacher quality and pupil attainment, and professional learning and development and student achievement are not quite as straightforward as they may seem. This different set of research evidence finds that becoming, being and remaining a teacher who teaches to their best and well over a career, in changing policy, workplace and life contexts, is beset with challenges and that not all students' learning and achievement will come about as a direct result of the quality of teachers and their teaching. Fenstermacher and Richardson (2005) have distinguished between *teacher* quality and *teaching* quality:

> Quality teaching could be understood as teaching that produces learning. In other words, there can indeed be a task sense of teaching, but any assertion that such teaching is quality teaching depends on students learning what the teacher is teaching. To keep these ideas clearly sorted, we label this sense of teaching successful teaching.
>
> *(Fenstermacher and Richardson, 2005:186)*

Questions, also, about the *stability* of teacher effects in terms of the power of their enduring qualities have been raised by Aaronson, Barrow and Sanders (2003). They found that on the basis of student test scores, of the teachers judged to be in the lower quartile of effectiveness in one year, only 36% remained in the following year and of those in the top quartile, only 57% remained in the following year.

Research has also found that contexts in which teachers work make a difference (Day *et al.*, 2007; Papay, 2011; Bryk *et al.*, 2010; McCaffrey, Sass, Lockwood and Mihaly, 2009).

> Teachers vary in the students they serve, the extracurricular duties they take on, the amount of time they have for planning ... Certainly some teachers are better able than others to accommodate the variety of stresses and strains they may face in their work. And to the extent that this is so, these differences may be due to differences in personal qualities ... We measure and track their value-added test scores but we do not measure their teaching loads, planning time, student absences, proportion of difficult to teach or resistant students, frequency of outside interruptions, access to text books or equipment of good quality.
>
> *(Kennedy, 2010:596–597)*

Difficulties in establishing causal rather than associative relationships between a teacher's work and student outcomes are reflected also in claims for direct cause-and-effect relationships between participation in PLD activities and sustained change in classroom practices. Whilst reports of this exist (see Chapter 5 and 6 for details), they are rare and often context and subject specific. Even teachers' characteristics (gender, age, qualifications and experience) have been found to have no statistically significant effects on students' measured outcomes (Kane *et al.*, 2008; Slater *et al.*, 2009).

Conditions which influence teacher learning, development and change

It is important to recognize that teacher change can be an extremely complicated and uncertain process and that the connections between teacher change and the standards of student learning are by no means straightforward. As a consequence of the continuing imposition of monitoring, inspection and public accountability systems, in addition to the increased intensification of work through added bureaucratic tasks directly associated with the performativity agenda, reforms engender high levels of uncertainty, instability and vulnerability for many teachers (Ball, 2003). As one author perceptively observes:

> [Y]ou get change by changing people, by developing them. People have to be convinced that there is some value in what you're asking them to do. People must have ownership over change, and that means change must be largely a bottom-up process, a voluntary process. You cannot simply issue mandates from on high and get real change in institutions as complex as schools. You issue mandates, you get compliance …
>
> *(Payne, 2008:193)*

As with students, teachers cannot *be* developed (passively). It is not only the quality of the learning experiences which are offered, but teachers' sense of ownership, relevance and (active) participation, and the contexts in which they are offered that will affect their willingness and capacities to learn. These will influence their sense of stable, positive professional identities, commitment and resilience which themselves will be associated with their sense of moral purpose and the contexts and conditions in which they work.

Kelchtermans' (1996) albeit small but nevertheless seminal study of the career stories of ten experienced primary school teachers revealed two recurring themes: striving for stability in the job and feelings of vulnerability to the judgements of colleagues, the principal and those outside the school gates, for example, parents, inspectors, media reports, which might be based exclusively on measurable student achievements. As vulnerability increased, they tended towards passivity and conservatism in teaching (Kelchtermans, 1996, cited in Day, 2002:688).

Change processes may be incremental (step-by-step, either at personal and/or organizational levels) or transformational (radical changes to existing beliefs and practices). Both are likely to contain a period of some uncertainty and disequilibrium for individuals. So, the *process of changing* needs to be supported over time – hence the importance of the school principal in establishing and growing school structures and cultures that support teachers' self-efficacy and agency. Figure 1.2 illustrates the dynamic influence of combinations of structures, cultures and supports on teachers' sense of agency and efficacy, and their willingness and capacities to engage in change.

Whether change is 'top-down', 'bottom-up', self- or other-generated, incremental or transformational, and whether a teacher's sense of agency and self-efficacy is relatively strong or relatively weak, it will be likely to involve loss and anxiety – loss because learning something new will involve 'unlearning' (e.g. deeply held beliefs and unexamined practices that may work against the development of new practices) and anxiety because, in the transition between the old and the new, new

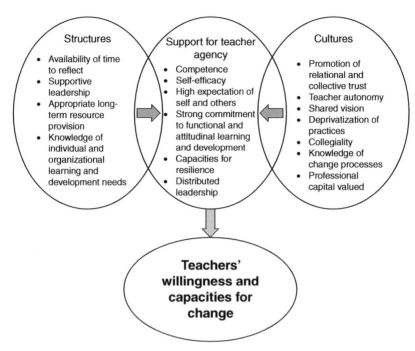

FIGURE 1.2 Organizational conditions for professional learning and change

practices may not work perfectly. So, changing will be a challenging process and may create in teachers feelings of loss and being de-skilled, at least temporarily. During this period, teachers who engage with changes that require them to question or challenge existing beliefs and practices are likely to need support.

Teaching and learning relationships: challenges of digital technologies

According to the English Government's Office for Science, 'Over the next 10 years, people's identities are likely to be significantly affected by several important drivers of change, in particular the rapid pace of developments in technology' (Government Office for Science, 2013:1). The implications for teachers of the well-documented increasing engagement of their students in digital technologies, such as video gaming, social media and the internet, are profound. Research findings from a range of sources have begun to coalesce around a number of key themes which have implications for students' school learning and, therefore, teachers' work in classrooms. Whilst space does not allow a comprehensive analysis of the literature (see also Day and Gu, 2011), the following drawn from the work of Gardner in the USA and Greenfield in England raise important issues concerning students and their learning, teacher change and teaching quality:

Attention spans

A survey of 400 primary teachers and 2,000 parents in England about children's reading habits found that 77% reported that the children experienced a 'significant decline in attention spans' and that they spent

> three times as much of their time on "onscreen" activity at home as they do reading traditional books. They are watching TV for 90 minutes per day, playing computers for 42 minutes and going online for 28 minutes, compared to 44 minutes a day reading.
>
> *(Pearson UK, 2011)*

Similar results of the increasing use of digital technologies were reported in an American survey of 2,000 secondary teachers (Greenfield, 2015: 27). These have implications for the way teachers plan their work and the roles they take in the classroom. They also suggest that teachers in general need to engineer learning opportunities, which stretch students' capacities to sustain their attention, so that learning becomes more engrossing and sustained, rather than 'dumbed down' into bite-sized fragments.

Empathy

Susan Greenfield, a neuroscientist, believes that 'It is through seeing others, or hearing their voices, that we can try to understand how they feel' and that 'too much time focused on the two-dimensional world of social networks may … be affecting young people's ability to empathise' (Greenfield, 2015:149). Similarly, Gardner and Davis (2013) found that, 'if we don't truly connect with others, we can't put ourselves in their shoes' and that, 'emotional risk is what brings us together' (pp. 104 and 119). This has profound implications, not only for those who promote the creative arts and humanities, in which the ability for students to empathize is a necessity, but also for the promotion of 'deep' as well as 'surface' learning by all teachers.

Deep learning (metacognition)

It has been claimed that computers are better suited to 'fast and shallow reading of short texts' and that this may 'reduce the mobilisation of cognitive resources … needed for self-regulation' (Ackerman and Goldsmith, 2011, cited in Greenfield, 2015:232). Gardner and Davis believe that:

> One of the big trade-offs between multi-tasking and "unitasking" … is that in multi-tasking, the opportunity for deeper thinking, for deliberation, or for abstract thinking is much more limited. You have to rely more on surface-level information, and that's not a good recipe for creativity or invention.
>
> *(Patoine, 2008, cited in Gardner and Davis, 2013:146)*

The challenge for all teachers, then, is to manage to combine the insistent policy demands to demonstrate annual improvements in teaching and learning in classrooms and in terms of quantifiable measures of increased levels of pupil attainment, with what Hargreaves and Fink (2006) defined as 'deep learning':

> Deep learning is often slow learning – critical, penetrative, thoughtful, and ruminative. It is learning that engages people's feelings and connects with their lives. It isn't too preoccupied with performance. It cannot be hurried. Targets don't improve it. Tests rarely take its measure. You can't do it just because someone else says you should.
>
> *(Hargreaves and Fink, 2006:53)*

Creative thinking

> Developing individual conceptual frameworks for understanding and interpreting the world also means encouraging individuals to have the confidence to question and deconstruct dogma and traditional views ... It is not a happy scenario to imagine a world peopled by individuals who have brilliant sensorimotor coordination, can multi-task and perform well in IQ tests, but who are incapable of reflective thought and understanding, let alone original ideas.
>
> *(Greenfield, 2015:259–260)*

In the USA, Gardner and Davis (2013) also reported that 'there is a distinction between youth's curiosity about different perspectives, experiences and practices on the one hand, and the focused, sustained attention that's required for deeper understanding, on the other ... [and] ... the ability to elaborate on ideas and engage in detailed and reflective thinking, as well as the motivation to be creative' (p. 88). Teachers are expected to engage all their students in learning that develops these qualities and skills at the very time when they appear to be at risk of declining. This makes their work more demanding.

The School Leadership Effect

> Diverse demands not only challenge the breadth of knowledge and skill possessed by a leader, but also test the adaptability and flexibility of his/her very sense of self, how leaders conceptualise themselves in relation to the multiple social roles they must perform.
>
> *(Hannah, Woolfolk and Lord, 2009: 169)*

It is likely that building and sustaining teachers' professional capital and capacities to engage with continuing professional learning and development will be successfully achieved when school structures and cultures provide the optimum environments for successful growth. Responsibility for creating and growing these learning cultures lies directly with principals. They are the key mediators of school improvement.

There are now more pressures upon principals to comply with so-called 'performativity' agendas, in which individual schools and countries compete to achieve higher ratings in test-driven league tables. Policy researchers (Elmore, 2004; Fullan, 2009) have expressed concerns, however, about the ability of externally generated reforms to produce changes in the quality of teaching, learning and pupil attainment. Some research carried out in so-called 'average' schools have suggested that although principals 'enact' (interpret and translate) rather than 'implement' policies, nevertheless policies themselves 'create circumstances in which the range of options available in deciding what to do are narrowed or changed, or particular goals or outcomes are set' (Braun *et al.*, 2010:549) and that mandated policies can compel principals to compromise their educational values (Hammersley-Fletcher, 2015). More recent research *in schools judged to be effective* in England, however, has found that successful principals use reforms as opportunities that they weave into existing processes of school improvement to create and sustain success in terms of a broad range of educational purposes, processes and outcomes (Day *et al.*, 2011).

One important change in the way many schools are led and managed, at least in part because of these contexts of social complexity and performativity, is that leadership has become a collective rather than an individual endeavour (Coleman, 2011). The increased numbers of people inside schools who participate in processes of culture shaping and reshaping and decision-making through distributed leadership provides strong evidence of this change. In a review of school leadership, Mulford (2008) argued that social relationships are an important resource, using the World Bank's definition of social capital as being 'most frequently defined in terms of the groups, networks, norms and trust that people have available to them for productive purposes' (Grootaert *et al.*, 2004:3, cited in Mulford, 2008:28). He distinguished three kinds of social capital – *bonding* (occurring within schools), *bridging* (occurring between schools) and *linking* (occurring between schools and their wider communities). The OECD (2004) suggests that 'bonding capital', defined by Mulford as occurring 'among work colleagues … being a valued part of a group' (p. 28), influences students and teachers' sense of 'belonging' and students' capacity of learning and academic performance (Feinstein, 2000; Field, 2005; Beatty and Brew, 2005; Hogan and Donovan, 2005). Significantly, in terms of school improvement, it is also 'directly related to their willingness and propensity to change …' (Louis *et al.*, 2005:198, cited in Mulford, 2008:29). School leadership, once the preserve of a few, has thus become reconfigured as a preserve of the many.

Principals themselves, however, are subject to a range of energy-testing experiences that are 'part and parcel' of their own worlds and work. Over the last twenty or more years, like their teachers, they have experienced an increase in multi-tasking and work longer and more unsocial working hours as they attempt to manage successfully the expanded number of duties placed upon them. The range and number of stakeholders with whom leaders must now interact externally on a regular basis has also increased enormously – a by-product of the age of public accountability and performativity. This is at least, in part, because of government reforms that call for more transparency and, in part, because there are more emotional demands on schools resulting from the changing needs of increasingly socially and economically fragmented societies. A survey in England, for example, (Angle *et al.*, 2007) showed that only 7% of secondary heads, like many of their teachers, perceived that they had any time to engage in interests outside of their work. Effective principals, research suggests, need to possess strong and clearly articulated educational values and exercise a greater range of strategic and interpersonal qualities and skills than ever before. In this context, it may be argued that the qualities necessary for school principals are now very similar to those required of business managers where, it is claimed, 'The new generation of managers should be recruited for their social and personal skills' and where attributes to look for should be 'honesty, openness and lack of resistance to change' (Cooper, 2016).

Responsibilities for teacher learning

Investment in professional learning and development is a responsibility of both individual teachers as professionals and the school. A range of research internationally on the leadership of effective and improving schools, points to their key focus on creating school-wide structures and cultures that enable and reinforce teachers' learning and development (Robinson *et al.*, 2009; Day *et al.*, 2011; Lieberman, 2010). In such schools, in addition to serving policy and organizational needs, variations in individual learning and development needs within and across each professional life phase are recognized and no single individual or group learning needs are ignored. However, building the kinds of trusting and trustworthy relationships that ensure that learning becomes not simply a series of 'add-ons' to their work in classrooms, but an integral part of teachers' everyday expectations and realities, takes time. Such in-school, informal learning opportunities are often forged through a myriad of shorter and longer interactions that occur, for example, through time for individual and shared reflections on practice, the exchange of information and ideas or curriculum materials with those who perform similar roles or/and who share similar personal and social characteristics, norms and values or experiences, and school-wide discussions about relevant research findings. Bridwell-Mitchell and Cooc (2016) examined the features of these informal relationships, finding that a combination of individual traits (e.g. demographics), organizational (e.g. structures and cultures) and informal social contexts (e.g. community features) together contribute to a sense of collegiality and provide access to social capital, and that there were different levels of informal learning relationships in terms of their strength, density and closure:

> *Strength* refers to the level of attachment between individuals. *Density* is the proportion of possible interactions that have actually occurred between the individuals. *Closure*, which is related to density, is how much individuals who are indirectly connected by third parties are also directly connected to each other.
>
> *(Bridwell-Mitchell and Cooc, 2016:8)*

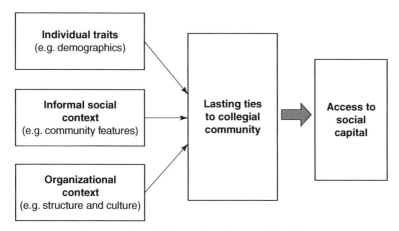

FIGURE 1.3   Conceptual model for teacher ties to collegial community

Source: Bridwell-Mitchell and Cooc, 2016:9

Figure 1.3 illustrates how the combination of individual traits, organisational contexts and informal social contexts together may contribute to a sense of collegiality and provide access to social capital.

The authors concluded that formal restructuring (e.g. of roles and responsibilities) in schools needs to be accompanied by the creation of opportunities for teachers to develop '*strong, overlapping, and mutually reinforcing relationships among the colleagues with whom they already tend to interact*' (Bridwell-Mitchell and Cooc, 2016:16).

Trust in schools

Trust and trustworthiness are essential components of social capital. In a multi-disciplinary review of the theoretical and empirical literature on trust spanning four decades, Tschannen-Moran and Hoy (2000) highlighted the need to pay attention to trust, particularly in terms of change. They found that trust is:

- a vital element in well-functioning organisations;
- necessary for effective cooperation and communication;
- the foundation for cohesive and productive relationships;
- a 'lubricant', greasing the way for efficient operations when people have confidence in other people's work and deeds; and
- a means of reducing the complexities of transactions and exchanges more quickly and economically than other means of managing organisational life.

(Tschannen-Moran and Hoy, 2000:549)

Conversely, distrust 'provokes feelings of anxiety and insecurity … self-protection by minimising (of) vulnerability … withholding information and … pretence or even deception to protect their interests' (Tschannen-Moran and Hoy, 2000:550).

Bryk and Schneider's seminal research (2002) on Chicago elementary schools found also that 'relational trust' (social capital) played a pivotal role in elementary schools that improved the reading and maths performance of their students over time; and a large-scale study in English primary and secondary schools (Day *et al.*, 2007) found statistically significant associations between the progress and measurable achievement of students and teachers' individual and collective commitment.

Investing in the functional and attitudinal

In successful schools, the enactment of professional learning and development encompasses both occupational and organizational professionalism. Referring to the work of Evans (2008), Sachs (2016) suggests that both orientations are likely to find expression in the kinds of professional learning and development activities available to teachers. In those schools the purposes and practices of PLD respond to the short-term, *functional* needs of the system, but also the more fundamental on-going *attitudinal* needs of teachers as professionals. Teachers' intellectual growth needs will be present in both the functional and attitudinal, though they are likely to be extended and deepened more in the 'attitudinal', since engaging in this is likely to require a greater breadth and depth of critical reflection on teachers' own stance in relation to professionalism, professional identity and commitment, and the policy and social contexts in which these are shaped. Where both *functional* and *attitudinal* needs are met, it is likely that this will contribute to fewer teachers leaving teaching, more remaining and, among these who do remain, more who are passionate about what they do, remain committed to teach to their best in educating the students they teach, have the capacity for resilience and are willing and able to teach to their best and well.

Defining professional learning and development

In 1999, I provided a definition of 'professional development' as:

> The process by which, alone and with others, teachers review, renew and extend their commitment as change agents to the moral purposes of teaching; and by which they acquire and develop critically the knowledge, skills, planning and practice with children, young people and colleagues through each phase of their teaching lives.
>
> *(Day, 1999:4)*

Whilst this definition implicitly encompassed both formal and informal (unplanned) learning and (planned) development, and implied a lifelong commitment by teachers to their ethical and moral purposes, it did not then take account, explicitly, of the emotional dimension of a teacher's work, a teacher's commitment, sense of efficacy, agency, professional identity and resilience – all necessary if teachers are to build and sustain the capacities to teach to their best. Nor did it address the differences between processes of professional learning and professional development. In this book, I seek to remedy this. Like Webster-Wright (2009), I challenge the dichotomy often made between *learning* (informal, often unrecorded, rarely monitored, through, for example, unplanned interactions with others, individual reflection in, on and about their work and the contexts in which it takes place) and *development* (formally constituted internally organised individual, group, whole school internally organized events and activities, attendance at external courses, often related to the improvement of teaching and learning and student performance, expected to result in change, and monitored through, for example, annual performance management). Rather, I acknowledge that teachers will learn through both these processes. However, the opportunities to engage in powerful learning informally depend not only upon chance meetings or the willingness and energy of individual teachers to engage in and learn from reflection. They also depend on the establishment of departmental and school cultures, co-operative and respectful teacher relations, and working conditions which provide opportunities for such informal learning and which encourage teachers to seek to pursue their core business of raising and maintaining standards of teaching, learning and achievement, in a range of classrooms, each of which has its own set of special challenges.

The following chapters address how informal professional learning and more formal professional development might take account more explicitly of the emotional dimension of teachers' work, teachers' commitment, sense of efficacy, agency, professional identity and resilience – all necessary if teachers are to build and sustain the capacities to teach to their best and well in contexts of national reform. They also provide examples of the cultures and conditions and the kinds of professional learning and development that are most likely to support these. The definition below, then, challenges the notion of a dichotomy between professional learning and development. It acknowledges that teachers learn in different ways, at different times and in different places, and as a result of different opportunities and experiences. It suggests that both professional learning and professional development are needed if teachers are to teach to their best and well.

Professional learning and development is:

The process by which teachers, as change agents, alone and with others:

- Extend their *emotional and intellectual career-long* commitment to the broader *ethical* and moral purposes of teaching *in contexts of national reform.*
- Review and renew their *sense of positive professional identity and professional capital.*
- Acquire and develop critically the values, *dispositions, qualities,* knowledge, skills, planning, practices and *capacities for the everyday resilience* needed to educate all children, young people and colleagues to their best *within and across* schools through each phase of their teaching lives.
- Engage in *functional and attitudinal* professional learning and development.

Conclusions

The changes in the educational landscapes of many countries over the last two decades have, as we have seen, led to increasing tensions between system leaders at national and local levels and many of those who work *in* classrooms. These tensions remain unresolved as education reform efforts continue in many countries in which standards of teaching, learning and students' attainments are enacted and expected to improve year-on-year. There is nothing wrong with that aspiration, of course. However, to assume that this is a simple matter of changing the governance of schools, upgrading the qualifications of school leaders and teachers and defining, applying and inspecting standards would be to misunderstand the complexities of teachers and their work and, in doing so, fail to adequately address how quality in teachers and teaching may be best built and sustained.

As policy voices grow ever more persistent, their effect on teachers' professionalism, professional identities, commitment and resilience and their work and lives need to be understood and acknowledged explicitly and, where policies are judged by the teaching profession to be detrimental to the continuing pursuit of high quality, challenged. Advances in *research* about teachers, the nature of teaching, the contexts and conditions in which they work, and what influences their willingness and capacity to teach to their best and well, have revealed much more about successful teaching as work which engages teachers' emotions as well as their intellect; the importance of well-being and job fulfilment; the need for all teachers over their careers to build and sustain their capacities commitment and for resilience; the increasing importance of school leaders in creating the conditions and opportunities for teachers' learning and development; and the importance to teachers' perceived and relative effectiveness of a positive, stable sense of professionalism and professional identity.

Note

1 This section is drawn from Day (2003) in Moos, L. and Krijsler, J. (eds.) *Professional Development and Educational Change – What Does It Mean to be Professional in Education?* Copenhagen: Danish University of Education Press, 2003, 45–67.

2

PROFESSIONAL IDENTITIES

Teaching as emotional work

How teachers perceive and enact their professional identity is an indicator and a key variable in their sense of professionalism, levels of commitment and capacity for resilience.

> Teacher professional identity ... stands at the core of the teaching profession. It provides a framework for teachers to construct their own ideas of 'how to be', 'how to act' and 'how to understand their work and their place in society'. Importantly, teacher identity is not something that is fixed nor is it imposed; rather it is negotiated through experience and the sense that is made of that experience.
>
> *(Sachs, 2005:15)*

Professional identity fashions teachers' expectations of themselves, what they perceive to be the expectations and perceptions of others from inside and outside the school, and their efficacy and agency, the strength of their beliefs that they can, or cannot, succeed in their work with pupils. In considering the role of professional identities in teachers' work, it is important to acknowledge that to teach to one's best will require an investment of the personal as well as the professional self. Many years ago, Kelchtermans (1993) proposed that the professional self, like the personal self, evolves over time and that it consists of five interrelated parts: i) self image: how teachers describe themselves though their career stories; ii) self-esteem: the evolution of self as a teacher, how good, or otherwise, they are as defined by self or others; iii) job motivation: what makes teachers choose, remain committed to or leave the job; iv) task perception: how teachers define their jobs; and v) future perspective: teachers' expectations for the future development of their jobs (Kelchtermans, 1993: 449–450, cited in Day, 2002: 682–683). Whilst such findings are persuasive, subsequent research suggests that the close involvement of the professional self in teachers' work (what I have called elsewhere 'the person in the professional' [Day and Gu, 2011]) needs to be located in 'professional identity' (values, beliefs, self-efficacy, agency), a broader concept that, as this chapter reveals, provides a more complex and nuanced picture of the individual and social complexities of teachers' work and lives. *How teacher identities are formed and whether and to what extent they are stable will, then, be the result of combinations of biographical, personal, professional, policy and workplace influences, and these are subject to change.*

Wenger (1998:149) suggests that there are five dimensions of professional identity:

> i) identity as *negotiated experiences* where we define who we are by the ways we experience our selves through participation, as well as the way we and others reify ourselves; ii) identity as *community membership* where we define who we are by the familiar and unfamiliar; iii) identity as *learning trajectory* where we define who we are by where we have been and where we are going; iv) identity as *nexus of multi-membership* where we define who we are by the ways we reconcile our various forms of identity into one identity; and v) identity as a *relation between the local and the global* where we define who we are by negotiating local ways of belonging to broader constellations and manifesting broader styles and discourses.
>
> *(Cited in Sachs, 2001:154)*

Professional identities are often 'less stable, less convergent and less coherent than … previously implied in the research literature' (MacLure, 1993:320). How reforms are received, adopted, adapted and sustained or not sustained, for example, will be influenced by the extent to which they appear to challenge what 'being a professional' means to individuals. Although what Jenkins (2004) terms 'primary' personal identities (for example, 'selfhood' or 'agency') are likely to be more resistant to challenge from the outside than others, even these are not always immutable when faced with consistent and strong pressures:

> In this particular internal–external dialectic, others hold most of the cards … Others' definitions of the situation become so dominant as to carry the day. Thus as alienation from others feeds back upon self-perception and reflexivity, individuals become alienated from themselves and their sense of selfhood.
>
> *(Jenkins, 2004:54)*

Negative emotions can develop among teachers, for example, when existing, preferred professional identities are called into question or their legitimacy is directly challenged (Burke and Stets, 2009). It does not necessarily follow that strong pressures from others always have entirely negative effects on teachers' professional identities. Whether they have a stable or unstable, positive or negative sense of professional identity may also be closely related not only to the ways they may respond to what they perceive to be positive and negative *external* influences, but also the strength of their *inner* motivations to teach. Recent research on motivations for choosing teaching as a career in the USA, Germany, Australia and Norway (Watt *et al.*, 2012) found that, regardless of country context, key motivations were intrinsic value, the desire to make a social contribution, and the desire to work with children and young adults. However, as Seligman noted, their 'work orientations' might differ:

> Scholars distinguish three kinds of 'work orientation': a job, a career, and a calling.
>
> You do *a job* for the pay check at the end of the week … It is just a means to another end …
>
> A *career* entails a deeper personal investment in work. You mark your achievements through money, but also through advancement … When the promotions stop … alienation starts, and you being to look elsewhere for gratification and meaning.
>
> A *calling* (or vocation) is a passionate commitment to work for its own sake. Individuals with a calling see their work as contributing to the greater good, to something larger than they are. The work is fulfilling in its own right, without regard for money or for advancement. When the money stops and the promotions end, the work goes on.
>
> *(Seligman, 2002:168)*

There should be no implication from this that teachers in one or other of these groupings will necessarily provide better teaching than others. It is reasonable to suggest, however, that within an overall common sense of professionalism, the nature of their commitments and their sense of professional identity will be different. Teachers' willingness and abilities to respond positively to a negative workplace, or to personal, student and policy demands, are likely to vary, depending upon not only the relative strength and intensity of the external challenges, but also their work orientations, the culture in the workplace and, within these, the strength of their intrinsic motivation (their values, beliefs, efficacy and agency).

The call to teach: moral purpose at the centre

> Teaching is unavoidably a moral endeavour … education (and schooling as a means to it) serves more expansive ends than scores of academic achievement, and thus the contributions that teachers make to the moral life of classrooms, to the moral lives that our … students lead, and to the character of our society, are critical.
>
> *(Sanger and Osguthorpe, 2011:570)*

Underpinning this review of the international literature on the role of beliefs in teacher learning and change, and running through Hargreaves and Fullan's (2012) concepts of human, social and decisional capital and teachers' sense of professionalism (see Chapter 1), is moral purpose (values and beliefs). An implicit part of every teacher's work in classrooms is the way they influence, through who they are and how they behave (their professional identities), students' self-perception, attitudes to learning, aspirations, relationships with others and understandings about the nature of society, and the possibilities for participation. Though it may not be an explicit part of teachers' responsibilities or conditions of work, there is little doubt that the best teaching is suffused with moral purpose. What Philip Jackson and his colleagues wrote more than 20 years ago is as true today as it was then:

> To anyone who takes a close look at what goes on in classrooms it becomes quickly evident that our schools do much more than pass along requisite knowledge to the students attending them (or fail to do so, as the case may be). They also influence the way those students look upon themselves and others. They affect the way learning is valued and sought after and lay the foundations of lifelong habits of thought and actions. They shape opinion and develop taste, helping to form likings and aversions. They contribute to the growth of character and in some instances, they may even be a factor in its corruption.
>
> *(Jackson et al., 1993:xii)*

Although teachers' concern for children is grounded in relationships, 'in the connectedness of teachers and learners' (Elbaz, 1990, 1991 and 1992:421), it goes beyond being responsive and caring for them to include a moral duty[1]. Many years ago, Sockett (1993) argued that

> The generic teacher does not just get people to learn within an educational endeavour, for teaching is an interpersonal activity directed at shaping and influencing (not moulding), by means of a range of pedagogical skills, what people become as persons through whatever it is that is taught ... As a teacher is one who helps to shape what a person becomes, so the moral good of every learner is of fundamental importance in every teaching situation ... I am describing a view of teaching as primarily moral (i.e. dedicated to an individual's welfare rather than instrumental (e.g. for economic reasons) or non-educative (e.g. for custodial reasons).
>
> *(Sockett 1993:13)*

Sockett's concern was with the moral rights and duties of a professional role and he defined four dimensions: *community* (which provides a framework of relationships); *knowledge or expertise* (with technique subservient to moral criteria); *accountability* (to individuals and the public); and *ideals*. To these four dimesnsions he added five major virtues intrinsic to teaching which are central to understanding its practice: *honesty, courage, care, fairness* and *practical wisdom*. Michael Eraut (1995), too, has argued convincingly that 'it is the moral and professional accountability of teachers

… [rather than the contractual] … which should provide the main motivation for their continuing professional development'. He suggested that being a professional practitioner implies

1. A moral commitment to serve the interests of students by reflecting on their well-being and their progress and deciding how best it can be fostered or promoted
2. A professional obligation to review periodically the nature and effectiveness of one's practice in order to improve the quality of one's management, pedagogy and decision-making
3. A professional obligation to continue to develop one's practical knowledge both by personal reflection and through interaction with others.

(Eraut, 1995:232)

From these perspectives, teachers are not only recipients of policy change initiated from outside their schools and classrooms, but also themselves *initiators of change.* Moral purpose in this sense is a natural ally of 'change agentry':

> Stated more directly, moral purpose – or making a difference – concerns bring about improvements. It is, in other words, a change theme … Moral purpose keeps teachers close to the need of children and youth, change agentry causes them to develop better strategies for accomplishing their moral goals.
>
> *(Fullan, 1993:12)*

Moral purpose is not a new concept, and the body of research relating to this continues to grow. Having a core moral dimension (Bogotch *et al.*, 1998) acknowledges that classroom teaching and school leadership at their best are more than the skilful acquisition, communication and application of knowledge and skills, that they go beyond technical solutions and include a sense of care and social justice for all members of the community (Beck, 1994; Noddings, 1992; Starratt, 1991). Hargreaves and Fullan's assertion reinforces the continuing importance of moral purpose to good teaching:

> When the vast majority of teachers come to exemplify the power of professional capital, they become smart and talented, committed and collegial, thoughtful and wise. Their moral purpose is expressed in their relentless, expert-driven pursuit of serving their students and their communities, and in learning, always learning, how to do that better.
>
> *(Hargreaves and Fullan, 2012:5)*

In a small-scale study of secondary school teachers' emotional experiences in Australia, O'Connor (2008:117) examined the caring nature of the teacher role, defining caring as primarily 'those emotions, actions and reflections that result from a teacher's desire to motivate, help or inspire their students'.

She explored 'how individual teachers use and manage emotions to care for and about students in their professional work' (O'Connor, 2008: 118). It is important to distinguish between *caring for* (teachers' professional duty to ensure, as best they can, the progress and achievement of all students) and *caring about* (genuine empathy and love for all students' well-being). There is a reciprocal relationship between 'caring about' and 'caring for'. Both are important to the quality of teaching and learning, teacher and learner.

In sum, many teachers' moral purposes, their values and beliefs, are embedded in their professional identities. They place principles of responsibility, care and justice, alongside their determination to ensure that all students leave their classrooms with the best possible life chances. Such moral purpose, at the heart of their professional identities, is essentially both an intellectual and an emotional commitment to care, to work for the 'betterment' of students.

Emotion and care in the construction of professional identities

> The ways in which teachers form their professional identities are influenced by both how they feel about themselves and how they feel about their students. This professional identity helps them to position or situate themselves in relation to their students and to make appropriate and effective adjustments in their practice and their beliefs about and engagement with students.
>
> *(James-Wilson, 2001:29)*

Teaching at its best is demanding work that requires not only teachers' cognitive but also emotional engagement. There are numerous studies that focus on teaching as emotional work (e.g. Schutz and Zembylas, 2009; Sutton, 2004; van Veen and Sleegers, 2006). Several researchers (Nias, 1989, 1996; Nias *et al.*, 1992; Hargreaves, 1994; Sumsion, 2002) have also noted that teacher identities not only are constructed from the more technical aspects of teaching (i.e. classroom management, subject knowledge and pupil test results) but also, as van den Berg (2002) explains, ' ... can be conceptualised as the result of an interaction between the personal experiences of teachers and the social, cultural, and institutional environment in which they function on a daily basis' (van den Berg, 2002:579, cited in Day, 2002:683). Zembylas (2005a) suggests not only that identity is not fixed or stable, and linked to personal lives, but that it is also negotiated in the context of relations at work. It is

> A polysemic product of experience, a product of practices that constitute this self in response to multiple meanings that need not converge upon a stable, unified identity *(Holstein and Gubrium, 2000)*
> This constant construction, destruction, and repair of boundaries around the constitution of self is fraught with emotions (Margolis, 1998) ... [which are] ... socially organised and managed through "social conventions, community

scrutiny, legal norms, familial obligations and religious injunctions" (Rose, 1990, p. 1). Thus, power and resistance are at the center of understanding the place of emotion in self-formation [professional identity].

(Zembylas, 2005a:24)

Arguing from a Foucauldian perspective, he provides a useful frame for understanding that

1. Professional identity is not fixed or immutable. It may change according to circumstance.
2. Professional identity formation involves the emotional as well as the rational self and requires the management of both by the individual.

There is a symbiotic relationship between professional and personal, cognitive and emotional influences on teachers' identities (Day, 2004; Kelchtermans, 2009), if only because the overwhelming evidence is that teaching demands significant personal investment of these.

Teachers' 'felt' sense of stable or unstable, positive or negative individual and collective professional identity is associated with their sense of professionalism, and is likely to affect their teaching behaviour and their management of the emotional tensions and inevitable vulnerabilities that are inescapable, everyday parts of their work. If, for example, alongside their content and pedagogical knowledge, they have strong moral purpose and direction, high self-efficacy, a strong sense of agency, motivation, job satisfaction and well-being, then their commitment to educating students to the best of their ability is likely to be high. When these are diminished then they are likely to become less effective.

The policy influence

National cultures, policies, individual school systems and cultures, colleagues and significant people outside the school all play important contributory roles to the ways in which teachers feel more, or less, confident about who they are as professionals, and the extent to which they see themselves as agents who may actively mediate, rather than victims who may only comply with external demands for change.

> Though teachers have their own ideas of what defines their professional identity and are capable of exercising their own agency, it is likely that these views will be influenced by the roles imposed upon them by various institutional bodies as well as those roles affirmed by other teachers with whom they share similar beliefs and practices.
>
> *(McDougall, 2010:682)*

The performativity agenda, coupled with the continuing monitoring and auditing of the efficiency with which teachers are expected to implement others' plans for the 'delivery' of curricula and approaches to teaching, learning and assessment, has five consequences which may reduce rather than increase teachers' willingness and capacity for resilience over the longer term. They may

1. threaten teachers' sense of efficacy and agency and well-being;
2. deplete their reserves of resilience (emotional energy);
3. reduce the time teachers have to connect with, care for and attend to the needs of individual students;
4. diminish teachers' sense of motivation, moral purpose and job fulfilment;
5. challenge teachers' substantive identity.

Reio (2005) examined the impact of mandated change by governments upon teachers' individual and collective professional identity, associating this with teacher emotions and, in particular, the effects upon their sense of vulnerability and subsequent disposition and willingness to engage in risk-taking in the classroom, arguably an essential part of high-quality teaching and learning. His research is one of only a small number that clearly discern 'the role of emotion in the identity-formation process when confronted with change' (Reio, 2005:992). An adaptation of his original conceptual model of the influence of reform on teacher identity, emotions, risk-taking and learning (Reio, 2005:992) is presented in Figure 2.1. It develops this by noting i) the effects of professional and contextual 'filters' that are likely to mediate the ways in which reforms are received and enacted by teachers, ii) whether they affect the emotional well-being of teachers, iii) how this may result in a sense of stable or unstable, positive or negative identity, iv) how teachers' sense of identity may itself impact on their sense of agency, commitment and resilience, v) how this may influence them in risk-taking in their teaching, and vi) the implications for the quality of teaching and learning associated with 'caring about' and 'caring for'. Finally, the model indicates key points in the process when opportunities for learning and development need to be provided.

Just as successful classroom teachers are those who care for the pupils they teach, so too sucessful leaders are also those who care for and care about their staff, for example, by constructing spaces that allow for dialogue and inquiry, diverse ideas and divergent thinking by listening and responding fully to their students and teachers, nurturing school cultures within which they experience a sense of being valued and respected (Kohn, 1996). Caring, from this perspective, becomes also a *fundamental organizational* value that helps determine a school's priorities and directs school decision-making. Without this, it is more likely that in practice teachers' initial capacities to 'care about' may become eroded over time.

This may affect their emotional commitment as their emotional work becomes emotional labour in which they maintain the outward appearance of caring for and caring about whilst in the relative privacy of their classrooms, abandoning the emotional 'capacity for connectedness' (Palmer, 1998:13), thus, reducing their

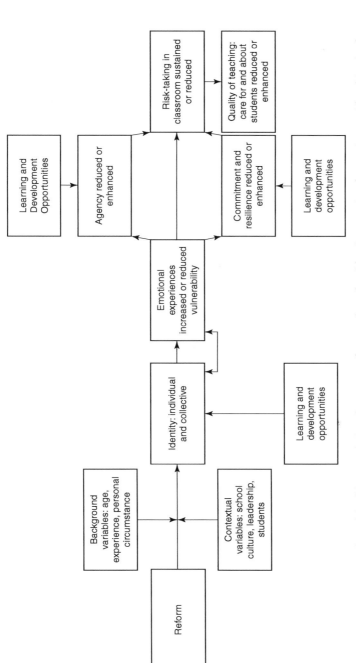

FIGURE 2.1 A conceptual model of the associations between reform and teacher identity, emotional experience, risk-taking in the classroom and the quality of teaching

Source: Adapted from Reio (2005:992)

investment in the intensity implied in 'caring for' their students. Hochschild (1983) researched service-related businesses (e.g. airline hosts) in which the conditions of employment demanded that employees showed only positive emotions to 'customers'. In these situations, employees were unable to exercise control over their externally expressed emotions because these were now controlled by their employers. She found that the higher the degree of emotional dissonance in their work (between emotions that employees displayed to others and those which they experienced), the higher the degree of felt depersonalization, stress and burnout. She named this phenomenon *emotional labour*. So, it is important for teachers to retain and sustain their sense of positive professional identity, well-being, commitment and capacity for resilience (first, to be aware when *emotional work* begins to turn into *emotional labour* and, second, to be able to manage, *and be supported in managing*, the emotions that are inherently a part of their work) if they are to optimize the opportunities for learning of every student. Emotions in teaching cannot be said to demand, as in Hochschild's (1983) research, the 'commercialisation of human feeling'. Unlike those participants in Hochschild's (1983) study who may be regarded as being involved in a series of short-term temporary service relationships with individuals, teachers are likely to be engaged in much longer term multiple social, emotional and intellectual relationships with individuals with whom they interact in classrooms.

As will be discussed in Chapter 3, teachers' engagement in their work, unsurprisingly, has been found to 'predict greater motivation ... increased productivity ... and higher rates of employee retention' (Kirkpatrick and Moore-Johnson, 2014:233). Sustained engagement, by definition, requires authentic caring relationships in which teachers are able to draw upon continuing reserves of emotional energy on a daily basis (Hargreaves and Fullan, 1992; Furu, 2007; Pyhältö *et al.*, 2011) as they seek to 'understand others, to have empathy with their situation, to feel their feelings as part of their own' (England and Farkas, 1986:91). All aspects of their values, qualities and behaviour will be under greater, more sustained and deeper scrutiny by students and so, for example, *the appearance of care* rather than care itself is likely to be identified by students and may influence adversely the nature of teacher–learner, teaching–learning relationships in the classroom.

Efficacy, agency and well-being

It has been claimed that there are close relationships between teachers' sense of efficacy, agency, well-being and professional identity:

> concepts of "identity", "agency" and "structure" are central in education and the learning of adults ... understanding agency in different contexts and times requires a focus on the dynamic interplay between (i) past influences and experiences, (ii) engagement with the present, and (iii) orientations towards the future.
>
> *(Eteläpelto* et al., *2013:57–58)*

This provides a compelling argument for acknowledging the dynamic relationships between identity, efficacy, agency and structure. In order to find the emotional as well as cognitive and even sometimes physical energy necessary to build and maintain a caring, positive, stable sense of professional identity through which they teach to their best and well, teachers need to be able to call upon their strength of moral purpose, and this is associated with the strength of their individual and collective efficacy and agency.

Personal and collective efficacy

A strong sense of self-efficacy is key to teachers' sense of positive professional identity. Efficacy has been defined as 'judgements about how well one can organise and execute courses of action required to deal with prospective situations that contain many ambiguous, unpredictable, and often stress, elements' (Bandura, 1982:122).

To rebound from setbacks and adversity, teachers need the strength of self-efficacy beliefs and, conversely, their sustained effort and perseverance in the face of difficulty will likely strengthen their sense of efficacy and result in a stronger sense of positive professional identity. Bandura further developed this construct by differentiating between *personal self-efficacy* (a self-assessment of one's ability to perform the task (i.e. confidence) and *outcome expectancy* (the expectation that performing the task will result in a desirable outcome' (Mintzes *et al.*, 2013:1202)). He identified four factors which contribute, positively or negatively, to personal self-efficacy – *mastery experiences* (e.g. knowledge of curriculum and pedagogies, for example, through lesson study, collaborative action research); *vicarious experiences* (e.g. external knowledge sources, observing other teachers); and the *physical and emotional state* of the individual (e.g. *job satisfaction/*fulfilment, sense of well-being, personal health, stress levels). He found that *personal efficacy* is a capability or capacity, not a fixed state. It is, therefore, subject to social influence. This is important because

> When faced with obstacles, setbacks, and failures, those who doubt their capabilities slacken their efforts, give up, or settle for mediocre solutions. Those who have a strong belief in their capabilities redouble their effort to master the challenges.
>
> *(Bandura, 2000:120)*

To these a fifth factor of organizational *culture* should be added (e.g. teacher–teacher relationships, trust, conditions for teaching and learning). Bandura pointed to the importance of *collective efficacy*, claiming that

> The strength of groups, organisations and even nations lies in people's sense of collective efficacy that they can solve their problems and improve their lives through collective effort … [and that] … Effective action for social change requires merging diverse self-interests in support of common goals …

> People who have a sense of collective efficacy will mobilise their efforts and resources to cope with external obstacles to the changes they seek. But those convinced of their inefficacy will cease trying even though changes are attainable through concerted effort.
>
> *(Bandura, 1982:143–144)*

Within these words, we can see not only the important role of school leaders in creating, building and sustaining collegial school cultures but also the complexity and challenges that they face in the potentially contradictory tasks of fostering professional capital in individuals, simultaneously seeking to pursue common, collegial, school visions, strategies and goals within an agreed consensus, and meeting externally initiated standards of performance. Advocates of PLCs (Professional Learning Communities) and other forms of within-school and school-to-school learning (see Chapter 6 for a more detailed discussion) rarely acknowledge the key roles played by personal, interpersonal and collective efficacy in meeting these challenges, their importance in forming and sustaining a positive, stable sense of identity and the need to manage them.

Agency

Efficacy is closely associated with 'agency', the enduring belief by teachers that they can 'make a difference' to students' learning and achievement by pursuing the goals that they value, taking account of, but not being dictated to by, circumstance.

> Within workplaces, people need professional agency in the construction of their professional identities and in the development of their work practices. We understand professional agency as being exercised in particular when professional subjects and/or communities exert influence, make choices, and take stances on their work and/or professional identities.
>
> *(Eteläpelto et al., 2013:57–58)*

The best teachers are often described as those who exercise 'agency'. Giddens' (1984) theory of structuration associates individual agency (for teachers, the assertion of their professional responsibility and competence to exercise autonomy through their exercise of discretionary judgements in classroom decision-making, what Hargreaves and Fullan [2012] have conceptualized as 'decisional capital') with a powerful belief that constraints of social and organizational structures and cultures can be, rather than simply tolerated, influenced by individual and collective action. In this view, far from being the 'victims' of, for example, a system which seeks to privilege 'performativity' and measurable student outcomes, through their individual and collective efficacy and agency, teachers are able to mobilize their educational beliefs, values, purposes and practices within this in order to assert broader moral purposes associated, for example, with attention to the personal and social education of their students (Biesta and Tedder, 2007).

Seen this way, teacher agency is part of a complex dynamic; it shapes and is shaped by the structural and cultural features of society and school cultures (Datnow, Hubbard and Mehen, 2002). In this context, policy mandates are adapted, adopted or ignored.

(Lasky, 2005:900)

Personal issues, workplace environments, external policy and student populations all place demands on teachers' energy. They are likely to present on-going and sometimes extreme challenges to their sense of individual and collective efficacy (self-esteem, self-image) and agency (values, beliefs, job motivation, task perception and future perspective). The extent to which they are able to manage to sustain these will be associated with whether they are more, or less, able to construct and sustain a positive, stable sense of well-being and health within the intellectual, social and emotional challenges of classroom life and changing school and policy contexts.

Well-being and health

Dewe and Cooper (2012:31) have noted that 'working life should offer (a) a sense of self-worth … (b) a greater emphasis in meaning and purpose … a focus on work that stimulates and challenges … and (c) an acceptance that good work is good health'. In a review of research which explores associations between teachers' health and well-being and student outcomes, Bajorek *et al.* hypothesized that 'an ill, stressed teacher with low job satisfaction would be unlikely to perform to the standard of healthy, unstressed teachers with high job satisfaction' (Bajorek *et al.*, 2014:11). They concluded that students taught by these teachers would be likely to achieve less than others. Bajorek and colleagues cited a number of research studies in support of these conclusions. For example, in Italy, Caprara *et al.* (2006) found that teachers' levels of self-efficacy and job satisfaction were associated with the overall academic achievement of students. Research by Dewberry and Briner (2007) found that 8% of variance in SATs (Student Attainment Test) results could 'be attributed to teacher wellbeing' (Bajorek *et al.*, 2014:11). In the Netherlands, Split *et al.* (2011) found that teachers' well-being, indirectly, had significant effects on students' emotional adjustment and academic performance. So, whilst individual research studies do not claim to find a direct causal link between teacher identity, health, well-being and students' academic performance, they reveal statistically significant associations.

Such research points strongly to the importance of teachers' sense of well-being and this suggests that conditions for teaching and learning in schools, and all PLD agendas, should address, either indirectly or directly, teachers' well-being and commitment needs. Luthans *et al.* (2006) suggest the development of 'organisational strategies that focus on (a) *risks* (identifying stress and positively intervening); (b) *assets* (building and improving organizational resources); and (c) *process* (developing adaptational effectiveness)' (Dewe and Cooper, 2012:128). The results of this research and research about associations between commitment and student outcomes (Day *et al.*, 2007) together provide a persuasive argument for the provision of *attitudinal* PLD opportunities that enable teachers' sense of positive, stable professional identity to be addressed, reviewed and nurtured.

The leadership influence

School leaders, as creators and custodians of school cultures, can have have a significant positive or negative influence on teachers' professional identities. Teachers' sense of professional identity can be influenced negatively, for example, by school cultures in which there is widespread fear of failure, excessive, critical scrutiny, low trust, and negative judgements by school leaders, government agencies and even the media. Their self- and collective efficacy can also be adversely affected by organizational norms that, for example, regulate their expression of emotional responses to the use of power to limit their agency and autonomy:

> When our feelings are trivialised, ignored, systematically criticised, or extremely constrained by the poverty of our expressive resources, this situation can lead to a very serious kind of dismissal – the dismissal of the significance to a person of his or her own life, in a way that reaches down deeply into what the significance of a life can be to the person whose life it is.
>
> *(Campbell, 1997:188, cited in Zembylas, 2003:122)*

In England, Day *et al.* (2007) found that teachers' perceived and measured effectiveness in terms of the progress and achievement of their students is influenced by how they are able to manage the interaction between personal, workplace and policy contexts (see Chapter 3 for a detailed discussion of these).

It is easy to see direct connections between individuals' capacity for self-efficacy, agency and professional identity, and indirect associations between teachers' professional identities and levels of teacher commitment, capacities for resilience and effectiveness within particular school cultures. Reforms from within or without the school that ignore, destabilize or erode core beliefs and values and threaten existing practices, and that are not led and managed with care by school leaders, can destroy teachers' sense of self-efficacy and agency, and destabilize and diminish their sense of stable professional identity.

Three identity scenarios

There are a number of frameworks for understanding the nature and constituent parts of professional identity: for example, a sense of subject matter expertise, positive teaching and learning relationships with students and classroom teaching skills (Beijaard *et al.*, 2000), and, more recently, the notion of a composite 'dialogical self' within which the influences – personal histories, patterns of behaviour and future concerns – are continuously negotiated (Akkerman and Meijer, 2011). Other research suggests that teachers seek and find their own sense of stability in different ways within what appear from the outside to be fragmentary identities. Common to all, however, is an implicit recognition that *being effective* requires teachers to maintain a sense of positive, stable identity, and that doing so is both an emotional and cognitive process that is likely to require them to engage in the managing tensions between several competing and potentially disruptive influences.

Here are illustrations of three broad scenarios,[2] identified by groups of teachers within and across different phases of their careers and in different school contexts, which required their attention in order to sustain a positive and relatively stable sense of self as teachers and their willingness and ability to be effective in the classroom (Day *et al.*, 2007; Day and Kington, 2008). In national research in England on variations in teachers' work, lives and effectiveness, analysis of interviews with 300 teachers over a three-year period identified three scenarios which challenged the stability of their professional identities. Teachers perceived that the confidence that they had in their existing professional identities, and thus their sense of self-efficacy, agency and well-being, was threatened when one or more influence (or combination of influences) dominated (such as personal crises, policy changes, pupil changes, school changes). Then, additional effort and emotional energy were needed to in order to manage a) each of the three influences and the interaction between them; b) critical events that threatened the stability of their existing sense of professional identity; and c) contradictions, tensions and conflicts within and between these various influences.

Scenario 1

Figure 2.2 shows an identity scenario that is relatively stable, with the three influences being held in balance. Thus, although there may be mild fluctuations within and between these from time to time, no action would need to be taken by the individual or school unless stability is negative, for example, if professional complacency were resulting in continuing ineffectiveness. Teachers in this scenario were identified as either a) likely to remain in teaching, or b) at risk of leaving the teaching profession because the stability they were experiencing was negative. The main characteristics of many, though not all, teachers in this scenario were the strength of their values and beliefs (moral purposes) and their high levels of agency, efficacy, motivation and commitment:

> I feel that I'm more committed and motivated than ever now that I have more time to spend on my work. Before, I had to split my time between work and children.
>
> *(Brenda)*

> I love working with children now as much as I did when I first started teaching. I can't imagine doing anything else.
>
> *(Martin)*

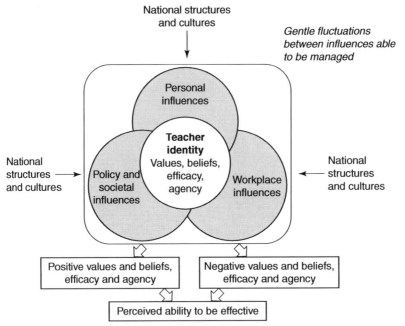

FIGURE 2.2 Scenario 1: influences in relative balance

Teachers experiencing Scenario 1 were also more likely to be positive about their well-being, work–life management and effectiveness, as Anna's story illustrates:

ANNA: POSITIVE (WELL-BEING AND WORK–LIFE TENSIONS)

Anna was a maths teacher of 13- to 14-year-olds in an urban, 11–16 mixed comprehensive school of 750 pupils from relatively advantaged communities. She had been teaching for four years and was originally attracted because she thought it was 'a valuable career' (teacher interview). The school was judged by Ofsted as 'an excellent school, in which very good teaching and first-rate leadership and management enable pupils to make very good progress'. Anna's husband had recently become a qualified teacher. She thought that this enabled him to fully understand what she experienced at work – 'it really helps when I've had a hard day' (teacher interview). This had a major impact on her sense of well-being and work–life balance because, together, they developed a routine, separating work and home time. Anna reported that they both kept certain nights and weekends free of work and this had helped her to improve her organization both at school and in her personal life.

In common with most (86%) of teachers in this scenario, Anna demonstrated a strong sense of efficacy, agency, commitment and emotional well-being, and her sense of stable and positive professional identity was strong.

Scenario 2

This scenario (Figure 2.3) comprised teachers for whom one of the three influences on identity dominated, depleting the reserves of energy needed to sustain the management of one or both of the other influences. In this situation, fluctuations were managed in the short term, depending upon the levels of teachers' motivation, commitment, self-efficacy, agency, support from colleagues, and leadership.

Many teachers in Scenario 2, like those in Scenario 1, tended to be highly motivated, as Carmelle's story demonstrates.

CARMELLE: DOMINANT (WORKPLACE INFLUENCE)

Carmelle was 51 years old and had been teaching for 29 years. She was the co-ordinator for maths and assessment with-year-old students in a rural primary school of 250 students. She had been originally attracted to teaching because of the opportunity to work with children and help to 'make a difference in their lives'. Carmelle had not been happy with the amount of pressure the previous head teacher had put on her and, as a result, her motivation had started to decrease. He had not been supportive and the way he spoke to the staff had been 'dreadful'. However, the school had recently gained a new head teacher, whom Carmelle reported as having a positive influence on her work. She reported that, as a result of this change in the working context, staff had started to work more collaboratively and relationships between members of staff had become more supportive, restoring her high level of motivation for her work.

However, a greater number of the teachers in this group than in Scenario 1 (52% v. 21%) expressed a negative view of their sense of efficacy, agency, well-being and management of work–life tensions (Day et al., 2007).

Scenario 3

In this scenario (Figure 2.4), two of the three influences on identity dominated. Charlie was a teacher who was being positively influenced professionally, but who was experiencing a negative workplace influence.

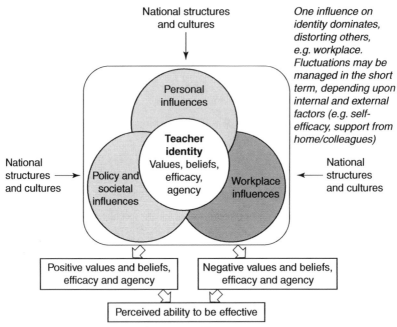

FIGURE 2.3   Scenario 2: one dominant influence

CHARLIE: NEGATIVE (DOMINANT PERSONAL AND WORKPLACE INFLUENCES)

Charlie was a 31-year-old principal with eight years' teaching experience, some of which had been in secondary and adult education. In spite of enjoying the new challenge of headship (professional), Charlie was depressed because his leadership/management role was distracting him from his teaching. He described this time as the lowest point in his career saying, 'It's my first headship and I'm finding it really difficult'.

In addition, the school student roll was falling, and several established members of staff were showing resentment towards changes Charlie was implementing in the school. Both of these issues were having a negative influence on his personal life, as he was having less time to spend with his wife and children out of school time.

Like Charlie, 70% of teachers in this group, unsurprisingly given the need to manage multiple influences, were more likely to be negative with regard to their well-being and work–life management:

> I've had to take some time off because it got too much, the teaching, workload, marking and my management role.

> *(Mary)*

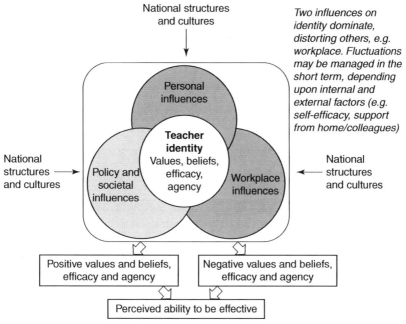

National structures and cultures

Two influences on identity dominate, distorting others, e.g. workplace. Fluctuations may be managed in the short term, depending upon internal and external factors (e.g. self-efficacy, support from home/colleagues)

Personal influences

Teacher identity
Values, beliefs, efficacy, agency

Policy and societal influences

Workplace influences

National structures and cultures

National structures and cultures

Positive values and beliefs, efficacy and agency

Negative values and beliefs, efficacy and agency

Perceived ability to be effective

FIGURE 2.4 Scenario 3: two dominant influences

Work does hinder my home life because I end up working most weekends and several nights in the week. I have no energy to do other things.

(Michelle)

Sustaining a positive sense of professional identity in Scenario 3 may, without support, lead to fatigue, exhaustion, cynicism and, eventually, burnout.

Exhaustion is characterised by a lack of emotional energy, and feelings of being strained and tired at work … whereas cynicism is reflected in indifference or aloofness towards work in general, and a disaffected or acerbic attitude towards students, parent or colleagues, as well as low organisational commitment.

(Soini et al., 2016:384)

Since energy is finite, depending on the amount required to manage one influence, it is likely to deplete the energy needed to manage the others.

There will be times over the course of a career when managing these influences requires relatively little attention, as in Scenario 1. The impact of any particular influence or combinations of influences in the scenarios presented will be mediated by teachers' internal strength of moral purpose and result in increased or decreased motivation, self-efficacy, agency, commitment, resilience, well-being, job satisfaction and effectiveness. However, the extent to which these grow or diminish in the different scenarios is also likely to relate to a) whether the dominant workplace influence has to be managed over a short, medium or long term (e.g. unsatisfactory relationships in the classroom, staffroom or home); b) individual biography (the strength of their vocation); c) the teacher's emotional resilience (vulnerability to stress of different kinds, and physical health); d) personal and professional support (e.g. leadership, colleagues, friends); and e) sense of efficacy, agency and well-being.

Conclusions

This chapter has discussed a range of research studies which, taken together, demonstrate that teaching is emotional work and that moral purpose, efficacy and agency are key parts of teachers' positive professional identities, important to their lives, well-being and effectiveness. Whether stable, positive identities are built and sustained will depend upon the extent to which teachers are willing and able to manage the interactions between the shifting positive and negative influences of personal biographies, culture, policy reforms, and individual and institutional values and practices.

We can see from these studies that the architecture of teachers' professional selves is unlikely to be uniformly stable over a career. At different times and in different personal, workplace and policy contexts, they may experience uncertainty about who they are, what is expected of them and how they are perceived as professionals. During these times, their willingness and ability to teach to their best and well may be adversely affected.

Finally, it cannot be concluded from this analysis of the nature of and challenges to professional identities faced by teachers that they are all 'victims' of a system that seeks only compliance. On the contrary, depending upon their individual dispositions, personal circumstances and workplace support, many teachers are well able to meet and manage what for others might be debilitating challenges. Teachers with a strong sense of moral purpose, efficacy, agency and positive, stable identity, working within school cultures which support, stretch and challenge them intellectually and emotionally and which build professional capital and self- and collective efficacy, are able to exercise agency and emotional energy in responding to all students' learning needs. Such teachers will be optimistic of success and will continue to believe – sometimes despite the short-term evidence to the contrary – that they *can* make a difference to students' motivations to learn, engagement in learning, and progress and achievement. As yet, successive government policies and reform strategies for raising standards have failed to address the key role that identity, like commitment, plays in teachers' willingness and ability to teach to their best and well. The evidence is that reforms which address key issues of professionalism, professional identity, commitment, teaching as an emotional as well as an intellectual enterprise, and processes of personal professional change are more likely to meet the standards-raising recruitment and retention agendas more efficiently and more effectively than current efforts which, though well intentioned, appear from empirical data to be failing to connect with the long-term learning and achievement needs of teachers and their students. The challenge, then, is not only how to achieve this but also how to sustain it in times of change and over a career.

Notes

1 This section (pages 28–29) is adapted from Day (1999), pages 14–15.
2 This section (pages 39–43) is adapted from Day and Kington, 2008:12–17, and used with the permission of the publisher.

3

VARIATIONS IN TEACHERS' WORK AND LIVES

Commitment as a key to quality[1]

There are few who would support a view that on-going PLD is not necessary if teachers are to

1. broaden and deepen their repertoires of knowledge and skills;
2. build their capacity to manage the inevitable changes in role expectations; classroom curricula and pedagogies, student-learning demands and the conditions of work which will occur over their career, and, alongside these, perhaps most important;
3. refresh, renew and sustain their motivation, commitment, sense of strong, stable professional identity, capacity for resilience and ethical and moral purposes so that they will be both willing and able to teach to their best and well.

There are few, also, who would disagree that most PLD opportunities should be physically embedded in schools, so that they should meet the direct (functional) needs of national and local policy initiatives, the classroom, the school and the department and, alongside these, the on-going professional (attitudinal) growth needs of the individual teacher.

So far, so good. Well, perhaps not so good because, as we have seen in Chapter 1, here the realities of context begin to muddy the achievement of such a consensus in practice. For example, although all would agree that when both the organization and individual teachers share responsibilities for PLD it is more likely that it will have a stronger and more lasting impact, many would agree also that not all schools are collegial 'learning communities' or are well led; that not all teachers always experience high degrees of professional motivation, commitment, resilience and moral purpose; that in some schools the PLD experienced by many teachers is narrowly focused on improving student test results; that systematic evaluation of its impact on teachers' motivations, commitment and well-being is rare

(Goodall *et al.*, 2005); and that, despite much investment over the years, there is not enough research-informed knowledge about how PLD may be responsive to the learning and development needs resulting from variations in teachers' commitment over a career.

I take commitment to mean a strong and enduring desire in teachers to make a positive difference to the motivation to learn, academic progress and the personal and social well-being of all pupils, whatever the circumstances, in the belief that this will, in the longer term, also contribute to the 'good' of society. Teachers who are committed are said to have a 'call to teach' (Hansen, 1995). They demonstrate a strong sense of moral purpose, self-efficacy, agency, care, optimism and hope rather than doubt, cynicism or pessimism. They are resilient in their determination to teach always to their best and well. Research has demonstrated that high levels of teacher commitment are associated also with pupils' measured performance in tests and examinations and that in each phase of their career, commitment can vary as a result of personal and contextual influences (see Chapter 2 for a detailed discussion of how these influence teachers' identity). For example, it demonstrates, counterintuitively, that levels of commitment are likely to be less for teachers in later phases of their careers and, within this group, that teachers in secondary schools are more likely than teachers in primary schools to experience lower levels of commitment (Day *et al.*, 2007).

A selected history of research on teachers' work and lives

Whilst, arguably, values and beliefs, efficacy, and agency are essential parts of all teachers' professional identities and are associated with their sense of professionalism, they can be strengthened or diminished at different times during the span of teachers' careers. Research has shown consistently that teachers' professional life phases are dynamic in nature and that the interaction between a range of influencing factors in their work and personal contexts are sophisticated and continuous processes that are not always predictable. These impact differentially on teachers' perceived and enacted effectiveness in different school contexts within and across the various phases of their professional lives. Recognition of these influences and their impact on teachers, in particular professional life phases, and the provision of informal and formal targeted support are necessary if teacher commitment and effectiveness are to be built, sustained and, where necessary, renewed.

Many years ago, researchers in England (Ball and Goodson, 1985; Sikes *et al.*, 1985; Nias, 1989), the USA (Lightfoot, 1983), Australia (Ingvarson and Greenway, 1984; Maclean, 1992), Canada (Butt, 1984) and Switzerland (Huberman, 1989) identified a number of key phases through which teachers were perceived to move in their careers. Kremer-Hayon and Fessler (1991), for example, proposed nine career-cycle stages: Pre-service, Induction, Competency, Building, Enthusiasm and Growth, Career Frustration, Stability and Stagnation, Career Wind-Down and Career Exit. The most authoritative and influential study of teachers' work lives (though not their effectiveness) was that of Swiss secondary school teachers by Michael Huberman (1988, 1995b). He found that they experienced five broad phases:

1. launching a career: initial commitment (easy or painful beginnings);
2. stabilization: find commitment (consolidation, emancipation, integration into peer group);
3. new challenges, new concerns (experimentation, responsibility, consternation);
4. reaching a professional plateau (sense of mortality, stop striving for promotion, enjoy or stagnate);
5. the final phase (increased concern with pupil learning and increasing pursuit of outside interests, disenchantment, contradiction of professional activity and interest).

Launching a career: a two-way struggle

Huberman characterized these first few years of teaching as a two-way struggle in which teachers try to create their own social reality by attempting to make their work match their personal vision of how it should be whilst, at the same time, being subjected to the powerful socializing forces of the school. This period was seen to be crucial in establishing novice teachers' definitions of teaching and their particular visions of how to behave as professionals. Their 'beginnings', he found, are likely to be easy or painful, depending not only upon their ability to deal with classroom organization and management problems, curriculum and pedagogical content knowledge, but also upon the influence of the school and staffroom cultures.

Stabilization, new challenges, new concerns

Following the initial 'beginner' and 'advanced' beginner period, a sense of teaching 'mastery' is likely to be established by most teachers. No longer novices, they are now accepted as experienced colleagues in the staffroom – feeling relatively secure in their knowledge of teaching practice and subject matter and comfortable with their identity as members of the particular school community. This sense of growing maturity is likely to be accompanied by some consolidation, refinement and extension of teaching repertoires and, possibly, involvement in a broader range of in-school and out-of-school educational developments as their vision of 'being a professional' and sense of professional identity evolves and broadens.

Reaching a professional plateau: reorientation or continued development

Huberman's research revealed that it is likely that 'trajectories in the middle phases of the career cycle (7–18 years) are more diverse than earlier or later ones' (Huberman, 1995b:197–198) and that this diversity is related to career advancement, school culture and the way in which teachers respond to the now well-established annually repeated cycle of students and colleagues which provides security but may, paradoxically, lack the variety, challenge and discovery of earlier years. It is a time when many teachers are likely to seek new challenges, either by taking new responsibilities in the same school or by moving schools for the purposes of promotion. However, it is a time, also, when responsibilities outside the school may begin to grow, whether these are related, for example, to ageing parents, growing families or deepening relationships.

In this phase, teachers may also experience mid-life crises and the beginnings of increasing levels of disenchantment caused by lack of promotion or role change, or diminishing levels of energy and enthusiasm. It is during this phase, also, that some teachers may seek opportunities to question the purposes and contexts of their work, to review and renew their intellectual commitments through further study either by participating in school, local education authority or district networks, or by participating in further degree work.[2]

The final phase

The final 10–15 years of a career is, theoretically, the phase of greatest expertise in teaching, albeit accompanied by the potential for increased personal health and family concerns. Yet, it may also be the time of greatest 'conservatism'. In Huberman's research, teachers in this phase complained more about the behaviour, commitment and values of students 'these days' and were sceptical about the virtues of change. They were unlikely to be a looking towards further promotion and were either serenely moving towards a 'satisfactory' career end or having to survive, dissatisfied, in an alien climate. Teachers in this phase could feel marginalized within the institution and embittered towards those whom they see as responsible for the condition of education and schooling and the declining standards of behaviour of the students they must teach. They might work hard in their core acts of teaching, but this would not necessarily be accompanied by the levels of enthusiasm, emotional and intellectual commitment necessary for achieving excellence.

Critical learning phases

Whilst this and other research have found that teachers experience different developmental phases, it is clear that they do so in different ways, at different times, according to different circumstances. Some research has suggested that these differences were in response to predictable events (Levinson *et al.*, 1978), whilst others focused upon work lives (Huberman, 1989), cognitive development (Oja, 1989) and life-cycle factors (Ball and Goodson, 1985). Other research has pointed to the importance of critical events in teachers' life and career histories and the current phase of development (Denicolo and Pope, 1990; Eraut, 1991; Gudmundsdottir, 1990; Leithwood, 1990; Sikes *et al.*, 1985; Oja, 1989; Ball and Goodson, 1985; Goodson, 1992; Huberman, 1989; Shulman, 1986). Research in England also suggested that '… cycles of accelerated development … whether prompted by internal or external factors, are likely to occur at any point in an individual's life' (Nolder, 1992). Nolder's empirical research over four years with secondary school teachers revealed that there were certain conditions which provided for development 'spurts'. These were variously described as 'critical incidents', 'dilemmas', 'landmark' or key events in an individual's life, around which pivotal decisions revolved. They provoked the individual into 'selecting particular kinds of actions, which led in particular directions' (Sikes *et al.*, 1985:57). These critical phases in teachers' professional biographies, it was claimed, represented 'the culmination of a decision-making process, crystallising the individual's thinking, rather than being responsible … [of themselves] … for that decision' (Sikes *et al.*, 1985:58). Individuals might be stuck at one level in some areas while more advanced in others (Watts, 1981).

In Canada, Ken Leithwood related teachers' psychological and career-cycle development to the growth of professional expertise. He claimed that this can be influenced directly by school principals (see Figure 3.1). In exemplifying the way that the dimensions of teachers' development were interrelated, he identified a direct relationship between reaching a professional plateau and stages 5 and 6 of development of professional expertise, suggesting that

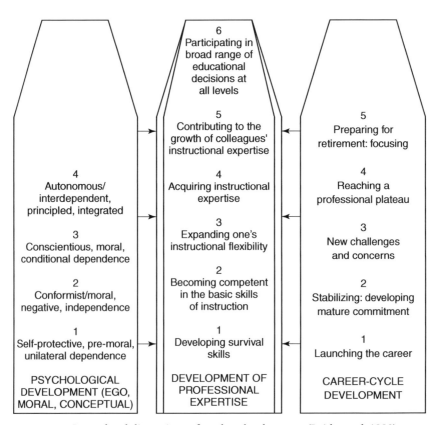

FIGURE 3.1 Interrelated dimensions of teacher development (Leithwood, 1990)

A significant part of the explanation for teachers perceiving themselves to be at a plateau is the failure, in many schools and school systems, to permit teachers greater scope to know and relate to multiple classrooms – to see and work with other teachers and their classrooms. Such challenges respond to the teacher's readiness to accept more responsibility and allow the school and school system to benefit from their accumulated expertise. Teachers who had experienced such challenges seem likely to enter their final career cycle stage either still in an expansionary frame of mind or at least as 'positive focusers'.

(Leithwood, 1990:81)

Whilst this multi-dimensional model may be used to inform the planning of teachers' career-long PD, it does not take account of fluctuations in their sense of efficacy, agency, sense of stable positive professional identity, the influence of emotional as well as cognitive factors, and the conditions in which they work.

Variations in teachers' work, lives and *effectiveness* in the twenty-first century

Findings from a national four-year national research project which investigated variations in the work, lives and effectiveness of 300 teachers in different phases of their careers, in 100 primary and secondary schools in England (VITAE),[3] provide an advance on this body of earlier research. Of the 300 teachers in different phases of their professional lives, almost all had entered teaching because they wanted to work with children and young people, to teach their subject, to make a difference; and most, but not all (74%), were still motivated and were sustaining their commitment and effectiveness – sometimes against the odds. The research (Day *et al.*, 2007) found that the commitment of teachers from both primary and secondary phases in their later years of teaching was more likely to be declining than those in their early and middle years and that primary school teachers were more likely to remain committed over their professional lifespan than secondary teachers. Perhaps not surprisingly, it was teachers who taught in schools, especially secondary schools, serving disadvantaged communities whose commitment was most at risk and who suffered relatively more personal health problems.

Professional life phases and experiences

Six professional life phases, relating to experience in teaching rather than age or responsibilities, were identified, and there were different challenges and concerns in each phase.

Early-career teachers: uncertain identities and engagement

Entry into teaching is generally recognized by researchers as a crucial phase in new teachers' professional lives. The first few years have been claimed to lay a foundation for their teaching beliefs, expectations and practices, and professional identity over the whole of their careers (Cherubini, 2009). As Lortie (1975:59) observed, 'one of the striking features of teaching is the abruptness with which full responsibility is assumed' by new teachers. They must learn quickly how to manage the motivation, expectations, needs, progress and achievement of each student, and master the curriculum whilst seeking to become a member of a school community which may itself be emotionally turbulent and dominated by the micro-politics of the staffroom.

> ... organisational influences were the major factors in teachers' decisions to stay, or leave. Most teachers enter the profession with an early commitment to teaching and to students, but find that factors in the structure and organisation of schools work against their sense of professionalism ...
>
> *(Certo and Engelbright Fox, 2002:69)*

For most of the day they may feel isolated from their colleagues. Induction and mentoring schemes, where they exist, may not be of sufficiently high quality to provide the support new teachers need. Faced with these challenges, it is perhaps not surprising that in this phase many teachers survive by 'coping' rather than 'managing' to overcome and thrive.

I. 0–3 YEARS—COMMITMENT: SUPPORT AND CHALLENGE[4]

Teachers' focus here was on developing a sense of efficacy in the classroom. Teachers in this professional life phase had either a developing sense of efficacy (60%) or a reducing sense of efficacy (40%). Poor pupil behaviour was seen as having a negative impact. A crucial factor in a successful negotiation of this period was the support of school/department/phase leaders.

II. 4–7 YEARS—IDENTITY AND EFFICACY IN THE CLASSROOM

The key characteristic in this second phase of early-career teachers' professional lives was the increased or decreased confidence in their ability to be effective in the classroom. The management of heavy workloads also had a negative impact on some teachers. Seventy-eight per cent of teachers in this phase had taken on additional responsibilities, which further complicated the construction of their emerging professional identities and capacities to teach to their best. Teachers in this professional life phase were grouped as either (a) sustaining a strong sense of identity, self-efficacy and effectiveness (49%); (b) sustaining identity, efficacy and effectiveness (31%); or (c) identity, efficacy and effectiveness at risk (20%).

There are few existing studies that portray the nuanced, longer-term, contextualized experiences of early-career and recently qualified teachers. For example, a group of researchers (e.g. Jugović *et al.*, 2012; Pop and Turner, 2009; Thomson and McIntrye, 2013; Thomson and Palermo, 2014; Thomson *et al.*, 2012) investigated pre-service teachers' teaching quality and preparedness in relation to their motivational typologies, professional goals, values, beliefs and levels of commitment. However, their work does not show how those typologies and orientations are enacted as teachers advance into full-time classroom teaching, or how they manage challenges to their initial motivation. There are studies, also, that have focused on early-career teachers' experiences in relation to the 'reality shock', challenges and struggles that many experience in many countries, in moving from predominantly university-based experiences as learners to school-based experiences as teachers (e.g. Flores and Day, 2006; Fantilli and McDougall, 2009; Farrell, 2003; Orland-Barak and Maskit, 2011; Shoffner, 2011). However, most of these studies have tended to aggregate rather than nuance teachers' experiences in the first few years of teaching (Ingersoll, 2011). It is necessary to investigate teachers' professional lives from a longer-term perspective if we are to understand better why some teachers remain committed and effective, why others do not, why some teachers stay, and why others leave (Johnson and Birkeland, 2003).

Mid-career teachers: reaching a plateau?

Previously, research into teachers' lives and careers has identified the possibilities for the plateauing of development: growing frustration because of lack of promotion, loss of self-confidence, and disenchantment among some teachers as a result of an increasingly alienating environment. Moore-Johnson (2015:119) has claimed that, 'Evidence is clear that teachers improve during their first few years of work … However, studies suggest that, on average, teachers' development levels off and they reach a 'plateau' of improvement relatively early in their career.' More recently, however, studies have called into question the inevitability of the 'plateau' (Ladd and Sorenson, 2014; Kraft and Papay, 2014). These studies suggest that teachers working in supportive professional environments improve their effectiveness more over time than those who work in less-supportive environments. Teachers in the seventy-fifth percentile of professional environment ratings increased their effectiveness, 38% more than a comparable teacher working in a school rated at the twenty-fifth percentile in the 10-year period studied (Kraft and Papay, 2014:476). Research has also shown that teachers who, for example, regularly change roles, work in a supportive culture, and are reflective and are able to participate in significant decision-making in school, maintain their motivation and satisfaction in the essential core of their work – classroom teaching (Huberman, 1993a, 1993b; Helsby and McCulloch, 1996). The VITAE research confirms these more nuanced findings.

I. 8–15 YEARS—MANAGING CHANGES IN ROLE AND IDENTITY: GROWING TENSIONS AND TRANSITIONS

This phase may be seen as a watershed in teachers' professional life phases. The majority of teachers were struggling with work–life tensions, and these were often associated with changes in the dynamics of personal and family lives. Moreover, most of these teachers (79%) had additional responsibilities at work and had to place more focus upon their management roles. Heavy workloads associated with these worked against their perceived effectiveness of their classroom teaching. Thus, for many it was a period during which they were making decisions about whether or not to focus on progression in their careers, whether to sustain a commitment to the intensive work rate in and out of school which is required for teaching well and to one's best.

II. 16–23 YEARS—WORK–LIFE TENSIONS: CHALLENGES TO MOTIVATION AND COMMITMENT

As well as managing heavy workloads, many teachers in this professional life phase faced additional demands outside school, making work–life management a key concern. The struggle for balance between work and lives was often reported as a negative. The risk during this phase was a feeling of career stagnation linked to a lack of support in school and negative perceptions of student behaviour. The three sub-groups of teachers identified in this professional life phase were experiencing (a) further career advancement and good results leading to increased motivation/commitment (52%); (b) sustained motivation, commitment, and effectiveness (34%); or (c) heavy workload/competing tensions/career stagnation leading to decreased motivation, commitment, and effectiveness (14%) and engagement.

Previous research has suggested that teachers aged 45+ find sustaining commitment to classroom teaching problematic partly for reasons of time, energy and health, and because they have become emotionally exhausted or 'disenchanted' (Raudenbush *et al.*, 1992; Vandenberghe and Huberman, 1999). However, in VITAE, combined support from leadership, staff collegiality, rapport with the pupils and PLD were key contributory factors to this group's positive sense of effectiveness. Of the teachers in this mid-career professional life phase, 76% had sustained their commitment, with 24% showing detachment/loss of motivation. However, around half of these teachers reported a lack of support from leadership (50%) and colleagues (60%), and were dealing with adverse personal or workplace events which created tensions between work and life.

Later-career (veteran) teachers

As teachers grow older, so do the challenges of maintaining energy for the complex and persistently challenging work of teaching children and young people whose attitudes, motivations and behaviour may differ widely from those with whom they began their careers. Moreover, their own professional agendas may have changed in response to their experiences of many diverse policy and social reforms, different school leaders and cohorts of students, as well as the ageing process and unanticipated personal circumstances. Throughout their professional lives, then, teachers will have been confronted by professional, workplace and personal pressures and tensions which at times, at the very least, are likely to have challenged their values, beliefs, practices, and for some, willingness to remain in the job. For others, these pressures and tensions are likely to have challenged the commitment and resilience of teachers which are so essential to their willingness and capacity to continue to strive to maintain effectiveness.

In their study on the sustainability of reform through the lens of teachers' nostalgia, Goodson *et al.* (2006) claimed that

> As teachers age, their responses to change are influenced not only by processes of degeneration (loss of commitment, energy, enthusiasm, etc.) but also by the agendas of the generation – historically situated missions formed decades ago that teachers have carried with them throughout their careers.
>
> *(Goodson* et al., *2006:42)*

Whilst this is likely to be the case generally, it assumes a world without the possibility of change for individuals whose responses may be affected by other, more contemporary interventions. Despite some later years' teachers' experiences of declining energy, 'embittered' experiences of the present (Lasch, 1991) and nostalgia for the past, many continue to demonstrate a strong sense of commitment to their work – particularly within a workplace where there is sympathetic and supportive management which provided opportunities, where appropriate, for re-invigoration of moral purpose and commitment by, for example, creating ways of sharing hard-won expertise and knowledge, providing advice, support and reinforcement.

I. 24–30 YEARS – CHALLENGES TO COMMITMENT, RESILIENCE AND EFFECTIVENESS

Teachers in this cohort were facing intensive challenges to sustaining their motivation. Key influences on the perceptions of their effectiveness were deteriorating pupil behaviour, the impact of personal life events, resentment at 'being forced to jump through hoops by a constant stream of new initiatives', taking stock of their careers (and lives) and length of service in the school, continuing tensions between fulfilling leadership or management roles outside the classroom and the energy required to fulfil the demands of classroom teaching.

Maintaining motivation in the face of external policies and initiatives, which were viewed negatively, and declining pupil behaviour were the core struggles for teachers in this phase. They were either sustaining a strong sense of motivation and commitment (54%) or holding on but losing motivation (46%). While 60% of primary teachers had retained a strong sense of motivation, over half the secondary teachers were losing motivation.

II. 31+ YEARS – SUSTAINING/DECLINING MOTIVATION, COPING WITH CHANGE, LOOKING TO RETIRE

Sixty-four per cent of teachers in this phase were maintaining high levels of motivation and commitment. Positive teacher–pupil relationships and pupil progress were the basis of this. Thirty-six per cent, however, were feeling 'tired and trapped'. Government policy, health issues and pupil behaviour were often perceived as the most negative factors by these teachers.

Later-career teachers are of particular interest in part because in many countries they form the largest group of teachers. In VITAE, key negative influences which were identified included national policies, excessively bureaucratic results-driven systems, disruptive pupil behaviour, poor health, heavy workloads and the consequent long working hours. The research found that for these teachers in the final phases of their professional lives, in-school support played a major part in their continued commitment to improving their knowledge within the classroom and professional identity so crucial to their sense of professionalism. Table 3.1 shows that relatively more of these, still with many years of teaching remaining, may be at risk of declining commitment and effectiveness.

However, in contrast to Huberman's observation (1993a) that there is a 'distinct phase of "disengagement" (serene or bitter)' towards the end of teachers' careers, a clear majority of the teachers in the later phase of their professional lives in the VITAE study had maintained a strong sense of purpose and agency (belief that they can make a difference in the lives and achievements of their pupils) to fulfil their enduring commitment to teaching – a meaningful profession which they believed shapes the lives of future generations. Pupils' progress and positive

TABLE 3.1 Professional commitment trajectories of teachers in later professional life phases

	24–30 years	31+ years
Maintaining commitment	54%	64%
Losing commitment	46%	36%

Source: Day and Gu, 2009:445.

teacher–pupil relationships were at the heart of these teachers' job satisfaction and sense of on-going commitment in the profession.

For most veteran teachers with over 24 years' experience, then, the immense value and self-worth that they derive from their pupils' growth serves to reinforce and fulfil their original call to teach, enhances their morale, and builds their psychological, intellectual, social and professional resources which served to charge them with the emotional strengths necessary to manage negative influences which they may experience.

Five challenges in building and sustaining career-long commitment and quality

1. Early-career teachers: unstable growth

In many countries, this period is one of high teacher attrition (e.g. Darling-Hammond, 2000; Ingersoll, 2003). Whilst there are little data on whether those who leave (and those who stay) are more, or less, effective in their teaching, there is considerable research evidence that teacher attrition in the early career years is due to particular combinations of factors, chief among which are conditions of work in the school, the effects of external policy on workload, relations with students and colleagues, and the quality of leadership (Day *et al.*, 2007, 2011a). It is important to recognize, therefore, that even in their early years of experience, development is likely to be nuanced. In an American study that investigated the development of teacher effectiveness (during their first five years) as judged by test score gains of the students that were either higher or lower than expected in maths and reading in elementary middle and high schools, the authors found that

1. On average, teachers substantially increase their effectiveness between their first and second years of teaching.
2. For teachers who remain in the profession for at least five years, returns to experience generally flatten after the third year of teaching.
3. Frequently, teachers who leave after their first year are less effective than those who continue teaching in their second or later years.
4. Teachers who leave after their third or fourth year are less effective in their final year of teaching, on average, than teachers who continue teaching into a fifth year.
5. The performance of teachers who leave after their third or fourth year of teaching often drops in the final year they teach.

(Henry et al., *2011:271–272)*

The research of Henry *et al.* (2011) concluded that early-career teachers have 'a tremendous capacity for on-the-job development' and that 'comprehensive induction programmes may increase early-career teacher retention and may benefit student achievement' (Henry *et al.*, 2011:278).

2. Mid-career teachers and work engagement

> Engaged employees are energetic, interested and enthusiastically engaged in their work (Leiter and Bakker, 2010) ... They approach their work with persistence, proactivity and often voluntarily expand their role when they feel that it will benefit the organisation.
>
> *(Macey* et al.*, 2009, cited in Kirkpatrick and Moore-Johnson, 2014:233)*

Evidence of well-being and job satisfaction among teachers is more likely to be found in their work engagement, defined as 'the feelings employees have about their work that influence how they choose to direct their effort and energy (Kirkpatrick and Moore-Johnson, 2014:233). Kirkpatrick and Moore-Johnson's (2014) findings in the USA elaborate those of the VITAE project in England. Teachers in the American study spoke of three patterns of engagement: (i) *modified engagement* as a result of the growth of responsibilities outside the classroom, e.g. families, additional managerial demands; (ii) *focused engagement* to improve their teaching through engaging in PLD; and (iii) *diversified engagement* as a result of increasing their professional work outside the classroom, e.g. mentoring new colleagues, after-school community events. They found, also, that most of the teachers in their study had received little active support, guidance or encouragement from school leaders or colleagues and that those who taught subjects which 'counted' for less in terms of test and examination results felt devalued. Not surprisingly, they highlighted the positive effects on teachers' work engagement of school contexts which were supportive of teachers' continuing PLD (Kraft and Papay, 2014; Day *et al.*, 2011a; Robinson *et al.*, 2009).

This relatively small-scale exploratory research found that 'second stage' teachers (with 4–10 years of experience, whose numbers have increased substantially over the last 20 years in America) are still 'quite vulnerable to attrition' and so need special attention (Kane *et al.*, 2008; Kirkpatrick and Moore-Johnson, 2014:234) and that whilst they are likely to be more effective than novice teachers, their effectiveness development as measured by student outcomes tends also to plateau (Kane *et al.*, 2008: Rivkin *et al.*, 2005; Rockoff, 2004). The authors pointed out that this group has received relatively less attention in terms of structured opportunities for PLD than either 'novice' or 'veteran' teachers. Which individual and groups of teachers are in receipt of more, or fewer, learning and development opportunities will likely depend upon the ways in which principals understand the influences upon teachers within, between and across their professional life phases, and the contributions that PLD can make in building and sustaining teachers' commitment and work engagement and, through this, student engagement and achievement.

3. Later-career teachers: maintaining the capacity for resilience[5]

According to the *Oxford English Dictionary* (2006), 'veteran' originates from the Latin word *veteranus*, meaning 'old'. A veteran is 'a person who has had long experience in a particular field' (2006:853). Based on this definition, veteran teachers are experienced teachers who have served in the teaching profession for a lengthy period of time. Much attention of research on teachers has focused upon those in beginning phases, because of the particularly pressing problem of attrition amongst these teachers (Ingersoll, 2003). In contrast, relatively less attention has been given to examining the nature of the tensions and challenges facing those who have had a substantial amount of experience in teaching (i.e. so-called 'veteran' teachers) and how and why they have managed (or not managed) to continue to fulfil their original call to teaching and sustain their effectiveness.

As Margolis (2008) reported in a study on teachers' career cycles, a veteran teacher is not necessarily a master teacher. His observation is in line with criticisms of traditional 'stage theory' which conceptualizes teachers' PLD as moving through a number of linear skills development stages – from being a 'novice' through to 'advanced beginner', 'competent', 'proficient' and 'expert' (see Benner, 1984; Dreyfus and Dreyfus, 1986; Day, 1999; Day and Gu, 2007).

> Whilst there can be little doubt that, 'from a developmental perspective, individual learning needs will be shaped by factors such as length of experience' (Bolam & McMahon, 2004, p. 49), the emphases on experience and linearity as defining features of teacher learning have been increasingly challenged by research which shows that whilst learning through experience of practice may lead to proficiency, it will not necessarily lead to expertise (Britzman, 1991; Bereiter & Scardamalia, 1993).
>
> *(Day and Gu, 2007:426)*

Thus, in relation to debates on experience and expertise, although veteran teachers may have experienced many years of teaching and become proficient in routines in their classrooms and schools, they will not necessarily have become expert teachers.

Yet many later-career teachers are likely to hold positions of responsibility within the school, receive greater remuneration and have experienced the impact of more policy and social change in their work than many of their less-experienced colleagues. More importantly, their resilience and effectiveness are likely to have been subject to more sustained challenges.

Some writers have claimed that, as a result of this, they may become disenchanted with their work (Huberman, 1993a). However, others suggest that supportive school leadership and culture which provides opportunities for continuing learning and collaboration contributes to their sustained commitment (Rosenholtz and Simpson, 1990). The literature in organizational psychology suggests growing recognition of the value to organizations of older workers, indicating that they perform as well as younger, less-experienced workers and that they demonstrate more positive work values (Rhodes, 1983, Warr, 1994, Griffiths, 2007a and 2007b). Griffiths (2007b) thus asserts that '*many common myths and stereotypes about older workers' decreased performance and availability for work are not accurate*' (p.124; see also Waldman and Avolio, 1986; Benjamin and Wilson, 2005). Capitalizing upon experience is, clearly then, a good investment strategy:

> On a more positive front, employers could focus on older workers' strengths; they could capitalise on their job knowledge, encourage them to take on mentoring and coaching roles, and encourage horizontal as well as vertical mobility. By exploring what older workers want from the latter stages of their working lives, it may be possible to maximise their job satisfaction and performance.
>
> *(Griffiths, 2007a:55)*

To ignore the specific commitment and resilience needs of veteran teachers is to fail to realize the long-term investment that they and their employers have made to teaching. It is this group which – at least in theory – should be at their peak of their expertise and teaching wisdom. It is this group which should be providing a model for their less-experienced colleagues. Rather than fighting off difficult challenges unaided, they should be beacons of hope and optimism for all.

4. Teacher attrition and the retention of quality

Researchers in Canada (Fantilli and McDougall, 2009), the USA (Ingersoll, 2004), Norway (Smith and Ulvik, 2014), Finland (Heikkinen *et al.*, 2012), England (Smithers and Robinson, 2000) and the Netherlands (Stokking *et al.*, 2003), among others, have identified continuing high rates of attrition among teachers in the first four years of their careers, and policymakers continue to express concerns nationally and internationally (OECD, 2005). Surveys of teacher morale suggest the causes are combinations of excessive workload, punitive government policies, relationship difficulties and poor leadership in schools. The focus of such research and policy concerns has been upon teacher 'attrition', the externally assessable result of loss of commitment, rather than upon the ways in which teachers may be retained. Yet, sustaining teachers' sense of commitment, effectiveness and resilience is not simply a matter of retention but of *quality retention*. It has profound implications for the standards agenda because the current teaching reality is that the population of teachers in most Western countries is ageing (OECD, 2004 and 2005). Thus, whilst it is necessary for governments to initiate interventions to recruit and retain capable and committed younger teachers, in the light of the now extensive corpus of research on variations in teachers' work and lives and the important associations between teacher identities, commitment, resilience and teacher effectiveness, it is equally necessary for them to take actions to promote mid and later teachers' willingness and capacity to give their best in the classroom and school, i.e. quality retention (Day *et al.*, 2007; Day and Gu, 2007). For example, in most OECD countries, the majority of primary and secondary school teachers are above 40; in the USA, two-thirds of its teaching force has to be renewed in the next decade (Guttman, 2001). In England, 40% of all teachers are aged 45–55 and those aged over 55 account for another 6% of the workforce (Chevalier and Dolton, 2004). So-called 'veteran teachers' may face at least another decade in the profession. Schools leaders and policymakers need to understand the factors which help or hinder teachers in mid and later professional life phases in the successful management of their work and lives if they are to support them in sustaining educational standards and fulfilling their moral responsibilities and obligations for the growth and quality of future generations.

5. In-school support

In the contexts of high attrition of teachers in their early-career phase, possibilities of plateauing or disengagement of those in mid-career when most would be unlikely to feel able to change career for financial and domestic reasons, and erosion or loss of energy experienced by teachers in their later-career phase which may have diminished their sense of commitment and thus their capacity to teach effectively, it is important to provide appropriate support.

For early-career teachers, in-school support plays a central role in helping them establish their professional identities within the classroom and the profession, whilst for mid-career teachers, such support will be crucial in enabling them to manage professional and personal tensions in the key watershed phase of their careers where, as the VITAE study has shown, teachers face the decisions about whether to continue as a committed full-time classroom teacher, climb the management ladder, reduce their levels of commitment or leave teaching. Many veteran teachers, who will have been recipients of generations of changes in educational policies and societal values over the past two or three decades, are likely to be challenged by the need to adjust. They will need particular in-school support in this process because reform is often synonymous with the need to change existing (and in the case of veteran teachers long-held) attitudes, values and practices. Reforms, however well intentioned and efficacious, may well be regarded, to a larger or lesser extent, as a challenge to or even denial of the values, status, experience and expertise which they have nurtured and honed throughout their professional lives. Teachers who are in different schools and experiencing different working conditions will also be likely to have different needs.

This may apply especially to those who work in schools in challenging socio-economic circumstances. The 'commitment and effectiveness' needs of these groups of teachers will be met best through on-going formal and informal dialogue with leaders in schools who have a close knowledge of staff, who engage in high levels of interaction, who nurture trust and respect and who themselves are committed to lifelong learning. Table 3.2. summarizes the key issues in the quality retention of teachers in their early, middle and later professional life phases. Whilst, according to research, these are more likely to apply to teachers in these phases, they may also influence individuals at any time of their teaching lives, depending on personal life, workplace and policy contexts.

The implications for those wishing to change how teachers construe, construct and conduct their work are clear: individuals' commitment to such change is essential. Changing operational definitions of professionalism and nurturing a stable, positive individual and collective sense of professional identity require working

TABLE 3.2 Key influences on teachers in different professional life phases

Professional life phases	Key influences
Early	Workload, reality shock, formation of teacher identity, resilience challenges, efficacy, stable/unstable growth
Middle	Work/life tensions, plateauing, work engagement, career stagnation, moral purpose and commitment doubts
Later	Resilience challenges, health/energy issues, coping with change, loss of moral purpose, agency

closely with teachers in environments and cultures which promote dialogue, shared values, informed trust, respect and achievement. Without these, reform is less likely to succeed in the longer term. Such supportive school cultures are of crucial importance to teachers' sense of effectiveness within and across all professional life phases.

Conclusions

> Good teachers possess a capacity for connectedness. They are able to weave a complex web of connections among themselves, their subjects and their students, so that their students can learn to weave a world for themselves. The connections made by good teachers are held not in their methods but in their hearts.
>
> *(Palmer, 2007:11)*

There is growing evidence that high levels of commitment by teachers in all professional life phases – expressed through high levels of emotional and intellectual engagement with their work – are likely to engage students more (Heller *et al.*, 2003; Hakonen *et al.*, 2006); increase teachers' sense of efficacy, well-being and job fulfilment; and result in relatively higher levels of student achievement (Day *et al.*, 2011a). Thus, variations in work engagement, like variations in commitment, are likely to have important positive or negative consequences for the quality of teaching and learning that teachers in all phases of their careers provide in the classroom and their broader commitment and loyalty to their school. Changes in policies, expectations of performance, pupils' attitudes to school learning, workplace cultures, career stagnation and adverse personal events are all important influences on teachers' sense of professionalism, professional identity, commitment and effectiveness. The individual and collective impact of these should not be under-estimated. Moreover, without appropriate support, many teachers are likely to struggle to maintain their sense of morale, moral purpose, commitment and resilience in the face of combinations of negative influences from outside and within the workplace and their professional and personal lives.

In-school support which focuses upon mediating the effects of external policy initiatives, and assisting teachers to adjust successfully to these, has a significant role to play in sustaining their motivation and commitment and enabling them to teach to their best and well (Day and Gu, 2007). The VITAE research identified teachers who were more, and less, effective in terms of their own perceptions and students' measured progress and attainment. The project concluded that

1. Teachers do not necessarily become more effective over time. Although the majority remain effective, teachers in later years are more at risk of being less effective.
2. Teachers' sense of positive, stable professional identity is associated with well-being, efficacy, agency and job fulfilment, and is a key contributory factor in their effectiveness.
3. The commitment and resilience of teachers in later professional life phases are more persistently challenged than others.
4. The commitment and capacities for resilience of teachers in schools serving more disadvantaged communities are more persistently challenged than those in other schools.
5. Attainments by pupils of teachers who are committed and resilient are likely to exceed those of teachers who are not.
6. Sustaining and enhancing commitment and resilience is a key issue for teacher quality and retention.

Conceptualizations of PLD as a linear continuum, though superficially attractive and plausible, are both over-simplistic and impractical since they are not based on a 'teacher-as-person' (occupational professionalism) perspective but on a system-defined managerial (organizational professionalism) perspective of 'teacher-as-employee'. An adherence to this might tend to over-simplify or skew provision towards meeting the 'functional' needs of the system whilst ignoring, at one's peril, the 'attitudinal' needs of the teachers within it. Policymakers, providers, system and school leaders need to recognize that some teachers may not have a 'staged', continuous sequence of life experiences … and that progress in learning is a process filled with plateaux, discontinuities, regression, spurts and dead ends' (Huberman, 1995b:196). Models of PLD which assume particular needs at particular linear career 'stages', whether these refer to roles and responsibilities or years of service, are likely to be limited in their contributions to teachers' learning and development needs. They need to take into account not only their career development but also 'landmark' phases of intellectual, experience, career, role or professional life phase development, and the historical and current organizational contexts and cultures in which teachers' work is located. Most important, built in to all PLD must be a focus on supporting and renewing teachers' individual and collective motivation and commitment and, as we have seen in Chapter 2, their abilities to form and sustain positive, stable professional identities in the challenging intellectual and emotional arenas in which they work.

National reform policies do not yet seem to consider associations between the success of external reform in enhancing teachers' quality and effectiveness and the support and renewal of teachers' professional identity and commitment. Nor does their management of the implementation of reforms seem to take account of relationships between these and the quality of their workplace environments. Consideration of teachers' willingness and ability to engage in change, with only a few notable exceptions, also continues to be absent. Moreover, as research on teachers' work and lives continues to demonstrate, sustaining their effectiveness over a career not only needs commitment, it also requires teachers who have an everyday capacity for resilience.

Notes

1   Pages 47–51 of this chapter are an adapted version of Day (1999:59–68) and are included with the permission of the author.
2   For a detailed consideration of this and other phases, see Huberman (1995b).
3   See 'Variations in teachers' work, lives and effectiveness' in Day *et al.*, 2007.
4   The boxed sections on pages 52–60 draw extensively and are adapted from Day and Gu (2009).
5   This section (pages 52–57) is adapted from Day and Gu, 2009.

4

A CAPACITY FOR RESILIENCE[1]

To teach to one's best and well each day over three or more decades requires teachers to have a resolute persistence and tenacious commitment to enhancing their students' learning, well-being, progress and achievements. To sustain such commitment requires an 'ability to maintain a stable equilibrium' (Bonanno, 2004:20), a positive stable sense of professionalism, a strong, stable sense of professional identity, and a capacity for resilience, 'a "frame of mind" that is characterized by the proactive enactment of "positive emotionality"' (Dewe and Cooper, 2012:124, citing Tugade and Fredrickson, 2004:320). Historically, the psychological literature has understood resilience as being the successful adaption to stressors or risk factors (Goldstein and Brooks, 2006; Patterson, 2002; Wright and Masten, 2006). Resilience as 'successful adaptation' often means restoring balance between the demands (stressors and strains) and capabilities (resources and coping behaviours) (Patterson, 2002). While these concepts of resilience in the discipline of psychology help clarify the personal characteristics of trait-resilient people (the ability to bounce back in adverse circumstances), they do not address how the relative strength of individual teachers' capacity for resilience may be enhanced or inhibited by the nature of the external and internal environments in which they work, the people with whom they work and the strength of their beliefs, values, aspirations and moral/ethical purposes. (Day and Gu, 2011). Thus, the 'resilience as a trait' literature has been challenged as presenting an unduly limited perspective. Positive psychology research has developed the notion of resilience not as a fixed attribute that is located in individuals' histories but as dynamic, subject to fluctuations in relation to environments and associated with notions of 'well-being' and 'flourishing' (Fredrickson, 2001; Keyes and Haidt, 2003), and socio-cultural research has further acknowledged the ways in which social conditions influence capacities for resilience (Luthar et al., 2000; Oswald et al., 2003).

Resilient teachers who teach to their best and well restore the balance between demands and capabilities not only by coping with the challenges, but also by managing the challenges actively and proactively, thus overcoming them and moving forward. Resilience is, therefore, better understood as 'a resource that goes beyond simply surviving to thriving, flourishing, improved performance, with a potential for increasing job satisfaction, and enhancing commitment, an attribute that among its range of qualities offers the capacity to reflect and grow from adversity (Luthans *et al.*, 2007:123, cited in Dewe and Cooper, 2012:127–128).

This implies that resilience in teachers – the willingness, ability and capacity to manage uncertainties successfully within a clearly understood and clearly articulated set of educational values and, in particular, school contexts – is latent, a dynamic capacity rather than a static or fixed trait. Teachers' capacities for resilience may fluctuate in relation to the nature of challenges, identities, personal resources (i.e. efficacy, agency, motivation and sense of vocation), relationship dynamics with students, parents, colleagues and school leaders, and personal and professional life circumstances, and their willingness and abilities to manage these factors (Day and Gu, 2014). Thus, whilst resilience has been defined traditionally as 'the process of, capacity for, or outcome of successful adaptation despite challenging or threatening circumstances' (Masten *et al.*, 1990:426), when applied to teachers' work in schools this definition has been adapted to become '*the capacity to maintain equilibrium and a sense of commitment and agency in the everyday worlds in which teachers work*' (Gu and Day, 2013:26). Maintaining equilibrium and sustaining a sense of commitment in challenging environments are likely to involve both the intellect and the emotions of teachers.

In sum, recent research on resilience in education has shown that

1. Teachers' capacity for resilience is not a static or fixed trait, but dynamic, subject to fluctuation in relation to the influences of internal and external challenges and strength of vocation, personal assets, relationships with students, parents, colleagues, school leaders, and personal or professional life circumstances (Day and Gu, 2014).
2. Resilience is not a quality that is innate. It is a product of the everyday interaction between personal and professional histories, exercised through professional dispositions and values, organizational cultures and personal factors. It is expressed through individuals' capacities to manage these in a range of anticipated and unanticipated scenarios.
3. Resilience does not only reside within individuals but also in their 'capacity for connection' (Jordan, 2012:73). This acknowledges the importance of supportive, reciprocal relationships in schools and, by implication, the key role of the head teacher in building social capital to 'enhance collective efficacy and shared beliefs of professional control, influence and responsibility' (Day and Gu, 2014:11).
4. There are associations between teachers' capacities for resilience and their perceived and relative effectiveness in terms of measurable student attainments (Day and Gu, 2014; Brunetti, 2006; Castro *et al.*, 2010).
5. Resilience is a latent capacity.

Everyday resilience

It is self-evident that teaching is emotional work (see Chapter 2 for a more detailed discussion), so understanding the influences on teachers' capacities for emotional resilience has become increasingly important as their roles, responsibilities and accountabilities have been extended and intensified by governments' quests to improve measurable student outcomes through policies that have demanded changes in teachers' practices. Parental expectations have also changed and students have become more discriminating about what they consider to be good teaching, and traditional forms of teaching have been challenged by developments in technology and social media (Day and Gu, 2014; Ebersohn *et al.*, 2015; and Chapter 1, this book). Over a career, at different times and for different reasons, teachers may also experience more acute challenges as a result of anticipated and unanticipated personal, workplace or policy changes.

Because teaching and learning in classrooms are not always predictable processes, to teach to one's best and well is inherently an 'everyday' challenge and, therefore, is likely to draw, to a greater or lesser extent depending upon circumstance, upon teachers' capacities for resilience (Day and Gu, 2014). The use of the term *'everyday resilience'* is premised upon two key research findings about the survival and well-being needs of teachers and the nature of teaching. In terms of the former, research in behavioural medicine has demonstrated a relationship between positive emotions and health (Davidson and McEwen, 2012), and it has been claimed that 'emotions are central to the function of the brain and to the life of the mind' (Davidson and Begley, 2012:ix). In terms of the latter, teaching studies reveal that a sense of vulnerability is not only an individual emotional state or experience which may trigger intense emotions in individual teachers but also a key 'structural characteristic' of teaching (Kelchtermans, 2009), since teachers are not fully in control of their working conditions or, indeed, able to predict a direct cause-and-effect relationship between their teaching and student outcomes (for a more detailed discussion, see Chapter 1).

Sustaining the capacity for resilience: emotionally resilient teachers

Research has found that there are four major influences which may affect teachers' capacity for resilience: the *personal* (related to their lives outside school); the *workplace* (related to their lives in school); the *professional* (related to their values and beliefs, and the interaction between these and external policy agendas); and the *emotional*. These are not static and change in one of these may affect teachers' abilities to manage the others. Within and between these, at any given time, teachers may experience fluctuations of different intensity (see Chapter 2 for a detailed discussion of the scenarios that teachers may experience). Patterson and Kelleher (2005:6) claimed that '... at any given time, the boundaries of your resilience capacity are determined by life's accumulated experiences ... resilience capacity is elastic over time. As you grow from adversity, you expand your resilience capacity through strengthened personal values, efficacy and energy'. However, more recent empirical research in England (Day and Gu, 2010) and Australia (Mansfield *et al.*, 2012) has identified resilience as a multi-dimensional phenomenon which is subject to fluctuation.

Figure 4.1 classifies the characteristics of the resilient teacher as falling within four interwoven dimensions: professional-related, emotional, motivational, and social. The work of Day and Hong (2016), and others reported later in this chapter, has also revealed the important role of a fifth, *personal dimension*, in influencing teachers' capacity for resilience.

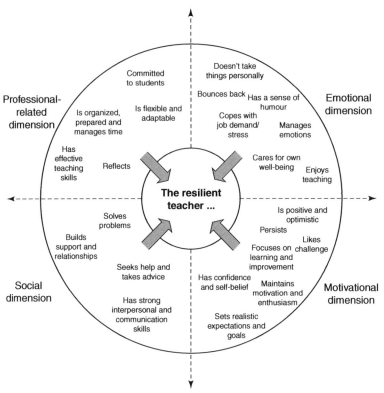

FIGURE 4.1 A four-dimensional framework of teacher resilience (Mansfield *et al.*, 2012:362)

The emotional as well as intellectual quality of relationships with their students is a key contributory factor to teachers' positive (or negative) sense of efficacy, agency, well-being, job fulfilment and, thus, their professional identities and continuing commitment. As a result, being able to call upon reserves of emotional energy needed to manage the interactions between the professional, the emotional, the motivational and the social dimensions of their work is key to teachers' abilities to grow and sustain their capacities for resilience as they manage the tensions of different internal and external challenges in order that their students receive their best teaching.

From declining self-efficacy to growing attachment

In her study on teachers' careers, Rippon (2005) observed teachers' strong desire to 'broaden horizons':

> Each new role marked a transition point when the teacher had become confident in their current role and needed to face a new challenge, taking on challenges in their current posts which took them beyond the direct responsibilities of their remit or finding new posts entirely. All are forms of proactively investing in the development of their career for altruistic, intrinsic or extrinsic motivations.
>
> *(Rippon, 2005:284)*

The following accounts of teachers in their early, middle and later careers illustrate the importance of a capacity for resilience, its relationship to teachers' continuing commitment and the different degrees of resilience needed in response to the differing challenges experienced during their careers and life journeys.

Harry: an early-career teacher[2]

Harry was a 27-year-old teacher of 9- to 10-year-old students in an urban primary school. He had worked there for five years, originally taking the job because of his ideological commitment to the school's poor socio-economic context. Initially, he had enjoyed teaching and the rewards that he gained from working with children. However, he often did not leave school until 7 pm and then did more work at home. He became increasingly aware that he did not have as much free time as his friends in other professions. Saturdays were spent catching up on jobs at home – shopping, washing, etc. – and then he spent Sundays working. He became unsure that he was prepared to continue to devote as much time and energy to the work:

> I don't know if I can take many more years of doing what I am doing. While I am young I'm fine. But as I get older, I don't know, as other commitments take over. I just want a bit of life really.

Further challenges to his continuing commitment and capacity for resilience were a lack of support from parents and the school leaders who did not always recognize or value the efforts which Harry made in his work: 'When I started this school I was expecting to be told I'd done something good or bad and I wasn't praised or told off for doing things, so I didn't really know where I was'.

Harry's capacity for resilience was able to be sustained by his positive interactions with other members of staff. These, together with the influence of a new deputy principal and career advancement, were major elements in the re-invigoration of his declining commitment and capacity for resilience and his reasons for staying at the school.

Andrea: a mid-career teacher

Andrea had taught English for nine years, the last four at this large 11–16 rural Community College. She had entered teaching with a strong sense of vocation, although she felt that over the years she had lost some of the 'rose-coloured ideas' that she had had when she first became a teacher. Her early years were character-ized by her efforts to settle in her current secondary school, her struggle with a lack of work–life balance and her deep resentment towards the national 'performativ-ity' agenda. These had begun to sap her commitment and capacity for resilience. As a result, she had considered leaving teaching, although she liked the working environment at her school and got on well with her colleagues. Always when she arrived home she still had more work to do and spent half a day at weekends doing school work. Her motivation had declined as she began to feel that she had 'less control over what I teach and how I teach it'. The pressures meant that she 'had less time to build relationships'. She spent a lot of time 'marking, reading, filling in results, feeling under pressure to teach something well and quickly'. This had led to a feeling of being 'overwhelmed' and 'overloaded' and resulted in her becoming 'more grumpy at work'. She had growing doubts about whether she would remain in teaching long term as she found it more and more 'emotionally draining' and 'mentally tiring'.

Sarah: a later-career teacher

Sarah, 47 years old, came from a teaching family and had always wanted to be a teacher. She had taught for 26 years, was a principal in a small, rural primary school and still enjoyed working with children. Although she suffered from 'relentless pressure' as a consequence of a combination of adverse personal events and heavy workload, she had, nevertheless, managed to sustain high levels of motivation, commitment and sense of effectiveness both as a teacher and as a leader.

During the week, Sarah often worked late in the office so that she could spend most of the weekends with her family.

> I think the teaching profession, if you're not careful it can totally destroy your home life – I think the hardest thing for people to do is to find the bal-ance – I've only realistically found the balance in the last five to six years …

Her high levels of self-efficacy and agency, together with the professional and per-sonal support from the staff and the governors, had been major factors in her sense of continuing commitment and resilience. Unanticipated personal events, how-ever, had recently had a detrimental effect on her work. Her husband was suffering from severe depression, which, coupled with an imminent Ofsted inspection at school, put her under tremendous pressure. Coming to work became a relief and remedy for her at the time, but she insisted that she had never felt out of control because she believed that she had the resilience to manage tensions in her personal and professional life.

The professional and personal experiences of these three teachers are reflected in their journeys of self-adjustment and professional growth within particular personal, workplace and policy contexts which mediated these. All were confronted by combinations of professional and personal pressures, tensions, and challenges to their values, beliefs and practices. What shone through were their capacities for resilience in building upon favourable influences and positive opportunities in their work and life contexts, and overcoming the challenges. In every case, these teachers' 'inner motivation to serve' (Hansen, 1995:6), sense of efficacy and ability to draw upon their capacities allowed them to varying degrees to manage negative work and life events and workplace environments. They had been able to draw upon their capacities to sustain their sense of moral purposes and commitment to teach to their best by managing the workplace environments.

Sustaining a sense of vocation

Hansen (1995) argues that, in contrast to professions which have an emphasis on public recognition and larger rewards, the language of vocation 'takes us "inward" into the core of the [teaching] practice itself', that is, 'what many teachers do, and why they do it' (Hansen, 1995:8). Both Andrea and Sarah had a strong calling to teach since childhood and continued to enjoy the pleasure of working with children in their current schools. Harry had deliberately joined his school to make a difference to students from socio-economically deprived backgrounds. Their response to the original call to teach had formed an important part of their professional identities, and had interacted with 'an inner incentive which prevents [the] person from treating his work as a routine job with limited objectives' (Emmet, 1958:254–255). This interaction had helped them sustain commitment in the profession.

These three teachers' 'moral values' (Nias, 1999:225) had, to a larger or lesser extent, functioned as internal psychological and emotional supports for them, encouraged them to be 'vocationally and professionally committed' (Nias, 1999:225), and helped them find the emotional energy to achieve 'personal autonomy and personal significance' (Hansen, 1995:6). Teachers' vocation is associated with a strong sense of professional goals and purposes, persistence, professional aspirations, achievement and motivation – the essential qualities that Benard (1995) has observed in resilience. Such vocation fuels teachers' personal resources with 'determination, courage, and flexibility, qualities that are in turn buoyed by the disposition to regard teaching as something more than a job, to which one has something significant to offer' (Hansen, 1995:12). However, what is clear from the examples of these three teachers is that their sense of vocation or 'calling' was not in itself sufficient for them to continue to teach to their best. Positive teaching and learning relationships in the classroom – where teachers spend most of their working lives – also served to mediate (Wertsch *et al.*, 1993) more negative social conditions in the school (e.g. poor leadership, unsupportive school culture, lack of adequate teaching and learning resources) and policy environments (e.g. changes in curriculum, forms of assessment, new professional standards, conditions of service). In addition, support from colleagues, supportive school cultures, family and friends contributed to their varying capacities for resilience and their retention in the profession.

Developing a sense of efficacy

In-school support had a significant impact upon Harry and Andrea's self-efficacy. For Harry, resilience was needed as he established his professional identity in the classroom as well as in the school. Internal promotion greatly improved his motivation and efficacy. Harry was no longer considering leaving teaching. Instead, he had a clearer vision of his work and was keen to prove himself. Andrea's self-efficacy grew as she prepared for transition to a new role in a different school.

In contrast with Harry and Andrea, Sarah, with 26 years of teaching experience, believed strongly in her problem-solving capabilities. She possessed a very high level of self-efficacy and remained strong and positive regardless of adverse influences either at work and/or in her personal life. She was particularly proud of her capabilities of leading her school in mediating the tide of government's target-driven initiatives and pursue the best broader education for the children.

Managing the workplace environment

Studies on resilience emphasize that both positive and negative external environmental factors 'create the resilience phenomenon' (Gordon *et al.*, 1999:2) in the process of resilience building. In their study on teacher turnover, wastage and movements between schools, Smithers and Robinson (2005:i) observed that

> Teachers are more likely to stay in schools where there is a clear sense of purpose, where the teachers are valued and supported, and where appropriate appointments have been made. The impact of good leadership could be outweighed, however, by factors largely outside a school's control such as location, cost of living, demographics and teachers' personal plans.

Nevertheless, the accounts of these three teachers provide powerful evidence of the complex interactions between the moderating and mediating influences of the workplace culture on teachers' commitment and resilience. Harry and Andrea's experiences, for example, illustrate that they would have been lost to the teaching profession if there had not been a positive change in leadership.

Resilience challenges for teachers in schools in challenging socio-economic communities[3]

There is a growing amount of research evidence that whilst there are generic qualities, strategies and skills which are common to all successful teachers in schools, teachers who work in schools that serve socio-economically disadvantaged communities face a greater range of more persistent, intensive cognitive and emotional challenges than others. Many of the students in these schools, along with their parents or carers, are likely, for example, to have had a history of failure and been alienated from school-based education, and it is likely that a significant number of students will live in highly unstable emotional environments. It has been argued that teachers in these schools not only need to possess these generic qualities, strategies and skills to a greater degree, but they also may need different qualities and skills which are specific to the social and emotional contexts of these schools and their communities (Chapman and Harris, 2004; Day and Johansson, 2008). In short, they are likely to need greater capacities for resilience. For those teachers for whom equity, care and social justice are central to their educational commitment, it is particularly important, therefore, to examine conditions which may work to improve this because many of these students are at greater risk of underachieving in their personal, social and academic lives.

The following extract from research on the challenges faced by teachers in one school in a highly disadvantaged urban community (Day and Hong, 2016) serves to draw together the tensions which all teachers face and demonstrates the particularities of sustaining the capacity for resilience in schools which serve socio-economically disadvantaged communities. The school was situated in a large public housing estate in a city in the Midlands region of England. The proportion of pupils eligible for free school meals (a proxy for socio-economic disadvantage) was more than twice the national average, and the proportion of students who had special educational needs was above the national average. Pupil attendance figures were also below average. Three resilience challenges, in particular, were noted: (i) challenges of students and parents, (ii) challenges of work–life management, and (iii) support of family and friends.

1. Challenges of students and parents

All the teachers were keenly aware of the social and emotional challenges that students brought. Lack of parental involvement in students' learning and social development and lack of home carers and support structures were often translated into *students' attitudinal and behavioural problems, lack of motivation and aspiration and school attendance problems.* Julie, a veteran teacher who had been teaching in this school for 27 years, commented

> We have high standards in behaviour at school and sometimes you feel that there aren't many behaviour expectations at home, so that can be a challenge.

> Sometimes you've got children coming in who have got quite sad home lives and it's how you deal with that and how you can support them. It's fairly consistent on a day-to-day basis.

Steven, who had been teaching the youngest children in this school for seven years, highlighted the *lack of parental support* and its impact on his work.

> Making sure that all the children are being looked after, better maybe at school than at home, and making sure the parents feel positive about school. I think that's a high challenge because the parents don't necessarily listen. They are very loud, very, very loud and the children are very much *on* you all the time.

Dorothy, a mature entrant to teaching, associated entrenched attitudes of parents with *students' lack of motivation and aspirations.*

> Their [students'] learning behaviour is different because they are not children in a suburb, with longer-term aspirations. We need to raise their standards, raise the game and give them something to fight for and let them see that you don't have to stay here. There is a much bigger world. Because they have got parents that come from here, grandparents that come from here who don't work, it just continues and it spirals.

Studies repeatedly note the social and emotional challenges faced by teachers who work with students living in deprived urban communities (Evans and English, 2002; Evans, 2004; Jensen, 2009). Researchers in different countries report that students' behavioural problems and lack of motivation are related to their home environment, especially family instability and lack of emotional nurturing (Ackerman *et al.*, 1999; Lichter *et al.*, 2002). Such family instability is often manifested in dysfunctional relationships, lack of trust, feelings of hopelessness, and stress. For example, parents or adult caregiver's unstable employment may result in high mobility and this may lead to unstable friendships and difficulties in building trusting relationships with teachers. Children in impoverished homes have also been reported to receive twice as many reprimands as positive comments from parents who tend to be less responsive to their children's needs (Risley and Hart, 2006). Studies by developmental psychologists have found that the lack of stable and caring family relationships have a negative impact on children's social competence and emotional regulation in the long term (Sroufe, 2005; Szewczyk-Sokolowski *et al.*, 2005). Such lack of emotional nurturing is likely to contribute to children's on-going behavioural problems, chronic stress and helplessness. When parents or carers do not provide the necessary support, teachers may be the only dependable and caring adult in their lives. *In effect, the scale and complexity of the social and emotional challenges faced by teachers in these contexts mean that the capacity for everyday emotional resilience is not an option but a necessity.*

2. Challenges of work–life management

For all teachers, managing and sustaining a work–life balance was not something that could be achieved easily, but was a continuing struggle. Work–life management was an on-going challenge for both inexperienced and experienced teachers in this school. Each managed these differently according to circumstance, but there was no doubt of the costs and consequences of professional commitment that most experienced. One teacher, for example, found that she had to take students' books home on a regular basis and so was 'not going out with my husband or the grand-children'. Even Julie, the most experienced teacher, still felt the workload pressures that being a good professional posed for her personal life.

> Saturday I spent all day doing reports because it's that time of year when there is no other way of doing it. That does impact on family and friends, because you know that you can't be arranging to do this, that and the other.

For another teacher, understanding and reminding herself of the importance of personal life helped her manage the demands of work.

> I think it just takes a lot of being really strong and making sure that you do get that balance because otherwise if you don't, then you suffer, your family suffers, your social life suffers … when you first start you're so enthusiastic to get everything done and to please everybody and do the best job that you can. I think as time wears on you realize I don't need to do that right now. I do this and this first, I will do that later and it's still going to be okay. I can still do my job.

Steven, in the later phase of his career, also realized the importance of guarding his personal life, but found that it was not always easy.

> It was work, work, work. The balance would come probably between 6 o'clock and 7:00 in the evening when you are so tired and you relax from work. It's all about having quality time. It's about maintaining that quality time in whatever you do and making it known to people that actually this is your life and you are going to have this time to yourself or your family, regardless of what comes up.

The continuing struggle to manage work–life balance, and thus the capacity for resilience, is applicable not only to teachers, but also school leaders. Christine, the principal, commented on the difficulty of separating work and life, and warned of the perils of allowing the commitment to work to overwhelm them.

> I think you have to be very careful and not let it overwhelm you. You need to carve out that time; that non-working time. No one can work 24/7.

> I think I'm fine if I know that I've done everything I can to sort out a situation before I go home. But if I know in my mind it's, I can't do anymore, then I'm kind of okay with that. But it's where I'll lose sleep. It is when I'm thinking, oh I have not been able to do that or a parent has threatened to talk to the [local] newspaper tomorrow … and that's hard.

Managing the allocation of time outside of school, spent working, with family and friends and in other personal activities, was the most dominant source of stress for teachers at the school. The heavy workload and its negative impact on personal life made teachers in this school, the principal observed, feel 'completely drained emotionally and physically because you put so much into the role as a teacher'. This continually posed challenges to their sense of well-being, capacities to teach to their best and their effectiveness in terms of the progress and achievement of students. The tension between work and family has been defined as 'a form of inter-role conflict in which the role pressure from the work and family domains are mutually incompatible in some respect' (Greenhaus and Buetell, 1985:77). While research is scarce on teachers' work–life management, existing studies consistently report negative outcomes of the conflict between work life and personal life such as burnout, low well-being, job dissatisfaction and early departure from the career (Cinamon and Rich, 2005; Palmer *et al.*, 2012; Panatik *et al.*, 2011). This work–life conflict can also create a work 'spillover' effect, resulting in stress and exhaustion, which negatively impacts both the quality of interaction with family members and the quality of work (Bolger *et al.*, 1989; Palmer *et al.*, 2012). The competing demands from work and personal life can, therefore, without active self-management and support from others, diminish teachers' physical, mental and emotional capacities for resilience.

3. Support of family and friends

Recent research has challenged the distinction between the 'personal' and the 'professional'. It draws attention to the differences that can be made by various types of support provided formally and informally, for example, the critical role played by family and friends and in-school task appreciation by school leaders and colleagues (Papatraianou and Le Cornu, 2014; Mansfield *et al.*, 2014). Clandinin *et al.* (2015:13) have claimed that 'often we do not consider teachers' lives beyond teaching, that is, that being a teacher is only part of a person, one piece of a larger unfolding life'. Among a growing number of researchers, Rosenfeld and Richman (1997) have drawn attention to the importance of emotional support from significant others, and Cefai and Cavioni (2014) have highlighted the roles played by a caring professional community. Besides school-level leadership and colleague support, personal support from outside the school (e.g. family, friends, community group members) was perceived by teachers to be an essential factor in sustaining their capacities for resilience. Elisabeth, for example, explained the importance of family support, especially in the beginning of her career and in times of professional stress.

It took an awful lot of understanding and support from my family … when I first started teaching, they understood that there was all of these extra pressures upon me and everything else that went with it: the fact that I was now responsible for thirty children, as well as having potentially thirty sets of parents who wouldn't necessarily speak to me or could be quite difficult, all those sorts of things. For a while it was challenging for my family to be able to understand, but then I was really open with them and then we talked about lots of things.

She emphasized the importance of protecting family time to maintain healthy dynamic and mutual support over the long term.

I always made sure that weekends were family time because I think we needed that time to just step away from all the reports and have our time so then come Monday morning we are all refreshed and ready to start again, and then we knew that for the weekend it would be family time again.

Dorothy mentioned how spending time with friends and having hobbies helped her release her stress.

I am lucky in that I've got a group of friends who do understand and do let me, in the times I do see them, just rant. I am lucky that I have a sort of hobby that distracts me. I have horses, so every evening I have to go and … you can't be worrying about school and have the horses trying to fill the hay. It's a complete shift away, a time when my mind just goes away from school.

These teachers' responses illustrate how supportive professional and personal relationships, as well as individual qualities, continually combined in different ways to support and sustain their capacities for resilience.

Coping for survival or managing for success?

Managing the self and others over longer periods requires additional energy from teachers and this may, sooner or later depending upon teachers' capacity for resilience, rob them of the energy they need to give to teaching to their best and well. In responding to everyday challenges, *coping* may be seen as enabling teachers to survive in the shorter or longer term without resolving the challenges, whereas *managing* may be seen as enabling them to resolve the challenges successfully. If teachers actively manage challenges, then the experiences of tension and disequilibrium may become a source for their learning and growth. However, not all teachers manage the tensions successfully and continuously, and not all school principals ensure that systems, cultures and people are in place to ensure that, where appropriate, teachers move from 'coping' to 'managing'. Early-career teachers' struggles, for example, have been well documented in the literature, and it has been suggested that a failure to manage these often leads to teachers' decisions to leave the profession (Borman and Dowling, 2008; Ingersoll, 2001; Johnson and Birkeland, 2003). The ways beginning teachers address and handle the various tensions and internal and external conflicts during the early years, transition phase vary – some may actively and proactively manage the challenges and others may barely cope with the challenges. However, as demonstrated in Chapter 2, it is not only early-career teachers who may struggle. *In other words, coping suggests a minimalist survival metaphor, whereas managing suggests a sense of commitment, academic optimism and resilience in overcoming challenges.*

Conclusions

Most teachers are faced each day with pupils, some, but by no means all of whom, will be eager to learn. Others will have quite challenging learning needs; some will not wish to learn; and not all will have stable, secure lives outside school. Thus, to teach to one's best each day, to be able to draw upon personal as well as professional resources, at different times and in persisting intellectually and emotionally challenging circumstances, requires that all teachers have an enduring and sustainable everyday capacity for emotional resilience. This is important for the maintenance of their moral purpose, commitment, positive sense of professionalism and professional identity and, ultimately, effectiveness. It requires the continuing investment of professional and personal resources: intrinsic motivation (Day *et al.*, 2011a; Chong and Low, 2009); vocational commitment and optimism (Day *et al.*, 2009; Gu and Li, 2013; Hansen, 1995); hope (Day, 2004; McCann and Johannessen, 2004); high self-efficacy (Brunetti; 2006, Kitching *et al.*, 2009); and agency (Castro *et al.*, 2010). However, as this chapter has demonstrated, whilst these personal attributes or assets are necessary, they are not sufficient. To be resilient every-day also requires combinations of individual and collective support and timely, sensitive intervention from colleagues and principals, friends and families if teachers are to build and sustain their capacities for emotional resilience.

Finally, it should be acknowledged that teachers' capacities to maintain resilience whilst managing the continuing daily mix of predictable and unpredictable behavioural and emotional challenges of students are likely to vary. Adapting to such on-going challenges requires psychological, social and emotional support and care (Day *et al.*, 2007; Barley and Beesley, 2007) as teachers seek to sustain a sense of competence, autonomy, well-being and achievement in their struggles to contribute to students' learning and achievement (Howard and Johnson, 2004; Ryan and Deci, 2002).

Committed teachers will strive to engage with all of their students and this requires not only a sense of positive, stable identity (Chapter 2) but also the willingness to call upon reserves of emotional resilience in managing tensions between their broader moral and ethical purposes and the more instrumental results-driven policy agendas. The more such emotional energy, and thus the capacity for resilience, is depleted – through adverse effects of personal, workplace or policy experiences –

the less it is likely that they will have the necessary willingness or abilities to teach to their best and well. This is why reformers from outside the school and those who seek to improve from within need to acknowledge the connection between attending to the well-being of the students and attending to the professionalism, professional identity, commitment, identity, resilience and well-being needs of the adults in the school.

Notes

1   Parts of this chapter are adapted from Day and Gu, 2011:15–31, cited in Schutz and Zembylas, 2011.
2   This section (pages 69–72) is adapted from Gu and Day, 2007:1302–1316.
3   This section (pages 73–77) is drawn from Day and Hong (2016).

5

PROFESSIONAL LEARNING AND DEVELOPMENT

Combining the functional and attitudinal

> Teachers of today and tomorrow need to do more learning on the job, or in parallel with it – where they constantly can test out, refine, and get feedback on the improvements they make. They need access to other colleagues in order to learn from them. Schools are poorly designed for integrating learning and teaching on the job. The teaching profession must become a better learning profession.
>
> *(Fullan, 2007:297)*

Changing demands upon schools and teachers made by government policy interventions, conditions of service, parents and students continue to challenge 'normative' (fixed) views of what 'being a professional' means in practice. Earlier chapters have pointed to professional identity, commitment, and the capacity for strong and enduring emotional and intellectual energy (resilience) as being key to teachers' positive, stable sense of professionalism and effectiveness. It is this energy that provides the fuel for teachers' work, that enables them to use what Hargreaves and Fullan (2012) term 'decisional capital' *wisely* in their teaching (see Chapter 1 for a more detailed discussion of this) and that contributes to their sense of well-being and job fulfilment. These are not 'soft' concepts. On the contrary, they are the bedrock of teachers' willingness and capacities to teach to their best and well. It is the lessening and loss of the energy to sustain moral purpose, a positive sense of professional identity, commitment and resilience, that is likely to reduce teachers' effectiveness. Given that teachers' work and lives are likely to be subject to a range of competing personal, professional and organizational challenges over a career, then, they are likely to benefit not only from supportive leaders, school cultures, colleagues, friends and family, but also from the regular provision of and participation in high-quality informal and formal PLD which they perceive as being timely, relevant and beneficial to their pupils, progress and achievement (Evans, 2008; Campbell, 2003; Kirkwood and Christie, 2006).

In the concluding chapter of *Visible Learning: A Synthesis of Over 800 Meta-Analyses Relating to Achievement*, Hattie (2009) offers six 'signposts' that highlight the complexities of teachers' work and provide a strong justification for the provision of an on-going range of high-quality 'fit-for-purpose' learning and development opportunities for teachers:

1. Teachers are among the most powerful influences on learning
2. Teachers need to be directive, influential, caring, and actively engaged in the passion of teaching and learning
3. Teachers need to be aware of what each and every student is thinking and knowing, to construct meaning and meaningful experiences in light of this knowledge, and have proficient knowledge and understanding of their content to provide meaningful and appropriate feedback such that each student moves progressively through curriculum levels
4. Teachers need to know the learning intentions and success criteria of their lessons, know how well they are attaining these criteria for all students, and know where to go next in light of the gap between students' current knowledge and understanding and the success criteria of: "Where are you going?", "How are you going?", and "Where to next?"
5. Teachers need to move from the single idea to multiple ideas, and to relate and then extend these ideas such that learners construct and reconstruct knowledge and ideas. It is not the knowledge or ideas, but the learners' construction of this knowledge and these ideas that is critical
6. School leaders and teachers need to create school, staff room, and classroom environments where error is welcomed as a learning opportunity, where discarding incorrect knowledge and understandings is welcomed, and where participants feel safe to learn, re-learn, and explore knowledge and understanding.
   (Hattie, 2009:238–239)

If we examine these signposts more closely, we can see why understanding the complexities of teachers' work and lives is an important pre-condition in building and sustaining quality teaching and learning. The first five of these 'signposts' to good, effective teaching pre-suppose that teachers are not only knowledgeable and skilful but also that they will have the cognitive and emotional energy and commitment necessary to engage each one of their pupils in learning on an everyday basis. They imply, also, that where developments have, for example, a direct (or directed) 'functional' focus on upgrading subject content knowledge or adopting new assessment, teaching and learning strategies for achieving success in tests and examinations, attention also will focus on the 'attitudinal'. Efficiency and compliance, in other words, do not imply effectiveness. Nurturing teachers' strong sense of positive stable professional identity, commitment, resilience, moral/ethical purposes, and willingness and ability to teach to their best and well is equally important.

Combining the functional and attitudinal

To focus solely upon analysis and fulfilment of the *functional* demands of the contexts in which teachers work and learn, whilst necessary, risks failing to draw attention to what Evans (2008) refers as '*attitudinal*' development. She argues that:

> ... as a factor influencing change it is much more potent than functional development since it reflects, to varying degrees, acceptance of and commitment to the change ... An ideally constituted professional development incorporates both attitudinal and functional development, since either without the other is unsatisfactory.
>
> *(Evans, 2008:33)*

Evans' connection between 'attitudinal' and 'functional' is important. Opportunities for PLD must be more than functional in their orientation if we wish them to enable teachers to review, renew and sustain their commitment as change agents to the broader ethical and moral purposes of teaching in contexts of national reform. If they are not, then it is likely that the dissonances between the demands of managerial professionalism and teachers' notions of occupational professionalism (see Chapter 1 for a discussion of these) will lead some to a growing sense of frustration, disempowerment, ennui and alienation, and risk a depletion of commitment, capacity for resilience and sense of stable, positive identity that underpin teachers' capacity for effectiveness (Bottery and Wright, 2000; Day *et al.*, 2007).

Sachs provides a commentary on contemporary aspects of teacher professionalism as they relate to policy and to individuals' PLD:

> Teacher professionalism is shaped by the external environment and ... during periods of increased accountability and regulation, different discourses of professionalism will circulate and gain legitimacy and impact on how professionalism is conceived and enacted ... in such a fluid environment teacher professional development will need to serve both a political purpose as well as a capability one ...
>
> *(Sachs, 2016:414)*

She is right to highlight the important role that PLD opportunities can play both in accentuating the legitimate, though largely short-term, instrumental agendas of government and complementing these with learning which focuses upon the underlying values, dispositions and qualities which all teachers need if they are to teach to their best and well in testing times.

In Figure 5.1, she provides a useful planning framework for individual teachers, but, perhaps more importantly, also for those responsible for the leadership and management of PLD in schools.

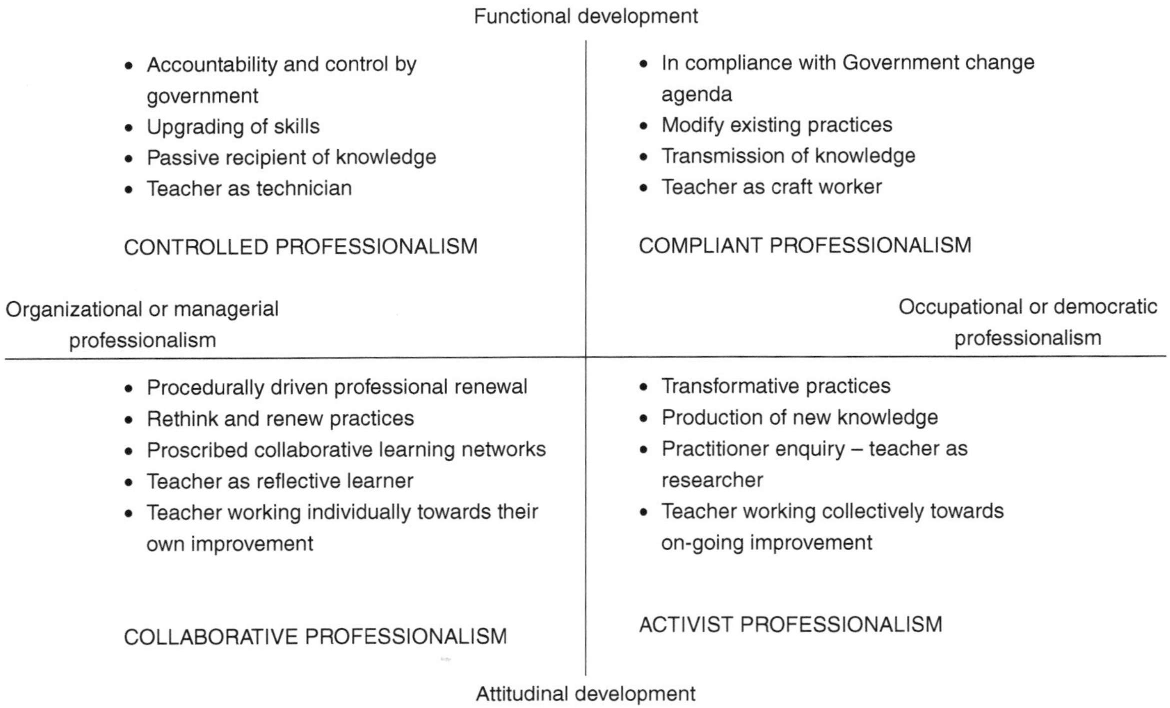

Functional development

- In compliance with Government change agenda
- Modify existing practices
- Transmission of knowledge
- Teacher as craft worker

COMPLIANT PROFESSIONALISM

Occupational or democratic professionalism

- Transformative practices
- Production of new knowledge
- Practitioner enquiry – teacher as researcher
- Teacher working collectively towards on-going improvement

ACTIVIST PROFESSIONALISM

- Accountability and control by government
- Upgrading of skills
- Passive recipient of knowledge
- Teacher as technician

CONTROLLED PROFESSIONALISM

Organizational or managerial professionalism

- Procedurally driven professional renewal
- Rethink and renew practices
- Proscribed collaborative learning networks
- Teacher as reflective learner
- Teacher working individually towards their own improvement

COLLABORATIVE PROFESSIONALISM

Attitudinal development

FIGURE 5.1 A PLD planning framework

Source: Sachs, 2016: 421

We have seen elsewhere in this book that governments worldwide are placing persistent emphasis upon the *functional* aspects of teachers' work. It is not surprising that school-led PLD activities also often reflect this, since principals are acutely aware that parents and politicians will judge their schools largely on that basis, and that teacher 'professionalism' is thus, at least in part, defined in relation to the extent to which they comply with this agenda. However, this need not necessarily be so. Sachs' framework offers other alternatives for planning PLD. It enables school leaders and teachers to be explicit about what values underpin and inform the range of informal and formal PLD opportunities available for teachers and acts as a means of judging whether the relative emphases that are reflected in the choices they make reflect their own values and views of:

- *teaching as an occupational or organizational profession;*
- *the breadth and depth of their commitment to the attitudinal and functional;*
- *their disposition to trust;*
- *their appreciation of the importance to teacher commitment and resilience of building and sustaining a sense in teachers of a positive, stable sense of individual and collective identity.*

It is not likely that teachers will be able to choose PLD that is located exclusively in any one of these quadrants. However, in the realities of education today and in the foreseeable future, without an enhanced understanding of the complexities of teachers' work and lives, and the ways in which the principles of professionalism enshrined in the activities' other three quadrants may enhance their commitment and the quality of their work and contributions to pupils' progress and achievements, it is likely that an undue orientation to so-called *'functional development'* will prevail. The issue for school leaders who are now charged with being primarily responsible for PLD is, then, to what extent they will also actively promote *'attitudinal* development'.

In a synthesis of 97 studies of teachers' PLD, Helen Timperley identified four evidence-based understandings of teachers and teaching (Timperley, 2008). I reproduce these below and add a further two as a reinforcement of what policymakers and principals often claim about the essence of teachers' work and the influence on student learning, but, as we have seen in previous chapters of this book, are not always taken into account in the design, content and processes of PLD programmes and activities:

1. Notwithstanding the influence of factors such as socio-economic status, home and community, student learning is strongly influenced by what and how teachers teach.
2. Teaching is a complex activity. Teachers' moment-by-moment decisions about lesson content and process are shaped by multiple factors, not just

the agendas of those looking for changes in practice. Such factors include teachers' knowledge and their beliefs about what is important to teach, how students learn, and how to manage student behaviour and meet external demands.

3. It is important to set up conditions that are responsive to the ways in which teachers learn. A recent overview of the research identified the following as important for encouraging learning: engaging learners' prior conceptions about how the world works; developing deep factual and conceptual knowledge, organised into frameworks that facilitate retrieval and application; and promoting metacognitive and self-regulatory processes that help learners define goals and then monitor their progress towards them.

4. Professional learning is strongly shaped by the context in which the teacher practices. This is usually the classroom, which, in turn, is strongly influenced by the wider school culture and the community and society in which the school is situated. Teachers' daily experiences in their practice context shape their understandings, and their understandings shape their practice.

(Timperley, 2008:6)

To these understandings of PLD may now be added

5. Teaching at its best is both an intellectual and emotional activity, which demands the engagement of the head and the heart, the personal and the professional.

6. Teachers' learning, development and expertise do not necessarily increase with experience. They are not linear.

Nevertheless, a range of research internationally suggests that governments worldwide are placing persistent emphasis upon the *functional* aspects of teachers' work in order to improve their performance in terms of productivity (Evans, 2008), with its implicit denial, minimizing or neglect of ensuring their on-going commitment, sense of positive, stable professional identity, care, and well-being and resilience which are also, arguably, at the heart of teachers' willingness and abilities to teach to their best (O'Connor, 2008).

Many teachers who work in unstable policy environments that challenge their sense of autonomy, arguably the core of their sense of professionalism, are likely to struggle to seek 'a sense of coherence, worth and belonging' in their work (Lumby and English, 2009:95). This is particularly so when one takes account of the workplace (i.e. challenges provided by students, relationships with colleagues), the quality (or lack of quality) of leadership, and personal influences. Since it has been widely acknowledged now that to teach to one's best and well requires the continuing – and sometimes substantial – personal investment of emotional as well as intellectual energy (see Chapters 2 and 3), it follows, then, that opportunities for

PLD should address both needs. To be successful, they – and their schools – need to be both task (functional) and person (attitudinal) centred.

Schools as person *and* task-centred communities

Fielding (2012), in writing about education and schooling as human flourishing, has provided a useful heuristic (see Table 5.1), a way of characterizing the different orientations of schools towards education as a means of reflecting upon the school culture which lies behind the design of PLD in schools. This provides a complement to the notion of combining the functional and the attitudinal but goes beyond this by placing the former at the service of the latter.

In schools as person and task-centred learning communities, PLD are likely to focus upon both the functional and attitudinal needs of individuals, with the former always having the latter at the centre of the planning, processes and evaluation. Take, for example, the importance of teacher commitment. As we have seen in Chapter 3, the VITAE research project in England on variations in teachers' work, lives and effectiveness (Day *et al.*, 2007) found not only that the 300 participating primary and secondary school teachers reported a qualitative association between their sense of commitment and their capacity to do a good job with their students but also that, over a consecutive three-year period, a *statistically significant association was found between teachers' levels of commitment and the measured progress and attainment of their students*. In other words, the more positive their sense of commitment (all teachers were judged to be at least competent in terms of knowledge and teaching), the more likely their students were to benefit from their teaching. It follows that a focus on building, revisiting and renewing teachers' commitment, positive sense of professional identity, and capacities for emotional resilience needs to form a core part of all PLD planning.

TABLE 5.1 Education and schooling for human flourishing

Schools as **impersonal organizations**	Schools as *affective* communities	Schools as **high-performance** *learning organizations*	Schools as **person-** *centred learning* communities	Schools as agents *of democratic* **fellowship**
The functional marginalizes the personal	The personal marginalizes the functional	The personal is used for the sake of the functional	The functional is used for the sake of the personal	The political expresses/ supports the personal
Mechanistic organization	Affective community	Learning organization	Learning community	Democratic fellowship
Efficient	Restorative	Effective	Humanly fulfilling/ instrumentally successful	Democratic living and learning

Source: Fielding, 2012:688.

In such person-and task-centred schools, policymakers and others from outside the school gates are, of course, an important as well as a necessary part of the discourse. However, the continuing health, well-being, commitment and effectiveness of those inside the school will be an equal priority. These will be supported not only through formal PLD opportunities but also through the school cultures, the 'way we do things around here' (Barth, 2002), as an expression of relationships which both act as the 'glue' and 'lubricant' of collegial cultures.

Webster-Wright (2009) has observed that the experience of continuing professional learning is still 'poorly understood' (p.704) and challenged the dichotomy often made between 'learning' (informal, often unrecorded, rarely monitored) and 'development' (formally constituted, programmed activities, often monitored and expected to result in change). Yet, even this observance, whilst helpful, does not fully explain nor is able fully to provide the support necessary for teachers as they pursue their core business of seeking to raise and maintain standards of teaching, learning and achievement in a range of classrooms, each of which has its own set of special challenges. To do this successfully over a career and in different contexts of change requires supportive workplace cultures.

To teach to one's best and well has been linked, also, with well-being: *'the higher the positive morale, the better the performance'* (Seligman, 2011:147). Seligman identified five elements associated with well-being: (i) positive emotion (derived from self-efficacy, optimism and job satisfaction), (ii) engagement (absorption in the task, what Csikszentmihalyi (1990) calls 'flow'), (iii) meaning (believing that one is contributing to something that is important and that is bigger than oneself), (iv) accomplishment (making a difference to the learning and achievement of students) and (v) positive relationships (with students and colleagues). Knowledge of their importance needs to inform the focus and forms of informal and formal PLD which are available to staff. From this perspective

> We do not see schools from an instrumental perspective but rather from a generative one. We do not believe that schools should serve externally determined goals and purposes ... [only] ... Instead they should be structured such that the central purpose is the learning of individuals who are engaged in the process of schooling.
>
> *(Mitchell and Sackney, 2000:xiii)*

Planning for PLD

In an increasing number of countries, individual teachers – and increasingly whole schools – are required to have co-ordinated PD plans. Yet, even today in many schools, these are

> often nothing more than a collection of teachers' individual activities over the course of a year, without a general design or specific focus that relates

particular activities to an overall strategy or goal … Professional development … is a collective good rather than a private or individual good. Its value is judged by what it contributes to the individual's capacity to improve the quality of instruction in the school and school system.

(Elmore, 2002:9–13)

Elmore is right to be critical of a lack of coherence in the opportunities and planning of PLD when he points to the purpose of PLD as being the 'collective good' of the system. However, when he separates this from the individual 'good', he fails to acknowledge the associations between individual motivations, well-being, identity and commitment, and teachers' willingness and capacities to teach to their best and well.

Cardno (2005) identified four 'add-on' PLD models: i) *the smorgasbord approach* – associated with free choice by teachers from a range of half- or full-day activities outside the school, ii) *the fill-the-day approach* – associated with external experts bought in as part of a full day of in-school activities, iii) *the do-it-all approach* – associated with a desire by the school to ensure that teachers are involved in responding to all external initiatives, and iv) *the weekly shot of PD approach* – associated with building PD time into a school's regular schedule of meetings. As others have, she also found these to be insufficient in meeting the development and improvement needs of individual teachers and schools. Darling-Hammond and Richardson found, similarly, that the kind of PLD that is *less* likely to support PD is that which

- Relies on the one-shot workshop model
- Focuses only on training teachers in new techniques and behaviours
- Is not related to teachers' specific contexts and curriculums
- Is episodic and fragmented
- Expects teachers to make changes in isolation and without support
- Does not provide sustained teacher learning opportunities over multiple days and weeks

(Darling-Hammond and Richardson, 2009:46)

Darling-Hammond and Richardson (2009) perhaps go too far in their condemnation of 'one-shot' activities which remain the predominant pattern of learning for many teachers in many schools. High-quality one-shot workshops and presentations, for example, can have a significant impact on teachers' thinking and practice, and teachers in different career phases have generic needs (e.g. renewing vision, managing stress, attending to well-being, preparation for new roles) that do not always relate to specific contexts and curricula. Nevertheless, their synthesis provides useful indicators of the relative effectiveness of different kinds of PLD.

Functional *and* attitudinal PLD opportunities in schools that are both task-*and* person-centred communities, then, are more likely to be effective when they are perceived by individual teachers as:

1. relevant to their intellectual, emotional and practical teaching needs and/or those of the school;
2. organized and led by those who understand and care how adult learners learn best;
3. integral to the dynamics of their school and departmental cultures;
4. timely;
5. provided in forms and at times that are convenient;
6. enhancing their sense of well-being, self-efficacy and agency;
7. likely to contribute towards improvements in their thinking and practice and that of their pupils;
8. enhancing their positive sense of professional identity;
9. valuing their commitment;
10. building their capacities for commitment and resilience.

In these schools, within any promotion of and planning for teacher learning and development there will be a consideration of their readiness, willingness and commitment to engage successfully with change, the extent to which the PLD opportunities are relevant to immediate, short-term (functional) and longer-term (attitudinal) needs in the prevailing external policy climate and internal school contexts in which they work, and their impact on teachers as well as students. Such planning needs to include active, differentiated consideration of the 'attitudinal','because teachers, like the students they teach, think and feel, are influenced also by their biographies, social histories and working contexts, peer groups, teaching preferences, identities, phase of development and broader socio-political cultures ...' (Day and Sachs, 2004:3).

Elmore highlighted the key tensions between learning and development needs defined by teachers and their schools and those defined by the need to meet external demands of accountability.

> There are two fundamental principles in tension here: the first suggests that professional development should be focused on system-wide improvement, which leads to limiting individual and school discretion; the other suggests that educators should play a major role in determining the focus of professional development, both for themselves and for their schools. These principles can be difficult to reconcile, especially in the context of an accountability system that emphasises measurable student performance.
>
> *(Elmore, 2002:8)*

Given the increasing devolution of responsibilities to schools themselves for the continuing PLD of their staff, it is perhaps not surprising that school-led PLD activities will often reflect these tensions and, in doing so, demonstrate how teacher 'professionalism' is defined in practice. In terms of PLD, this will be expressed through the relative emphasis placed on the 'functional' and 'attitudinal' learning

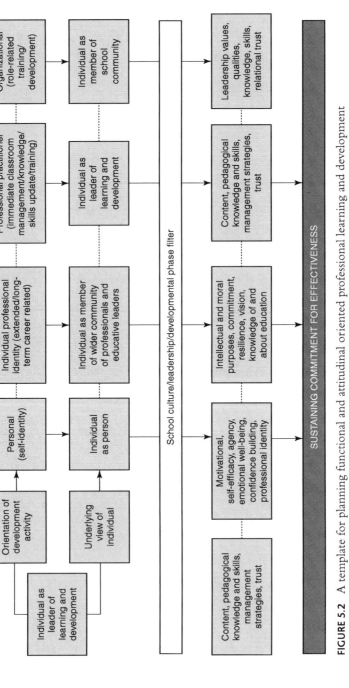

FIGURE 5.2 A template for planning functional and attitudinal oriented professional learning and development

needs of teachers, and this is likely to be associated with the view of the purposes of schools themselves held by the principal.

Figure 5.2 is a representation of the different 'learning for improvement' needs that all teachers are likely to experience to different degrees and during different phases of their teaching lives. It may be used as a basis for individual 'learning and development' profiles or a planning template for leaders of schools, faculties and departments.

This framework may be useful to PLD leaders who are concerned to balance the 'attitudinal' with the 'functional'. It enables them to frame provision not only in the results of more formal means of needs identification (e.g. annual performance management reviews, classroom observations) but also in the results of the teacher as a person, a member of a professional community of teachers, a classroom practitioner and, under a system of distributed leadership, an active contributor to the dynamic of school culture. There is a sense, also, in which this 'fits' with the aspirations and ideals embedded in schools' improvement journeys.

Evaluating the impact of PLD

> Currently, much evaluation of professional development (PD) by school leaders, practitioners and policy makers is still impressionistic, anecdotal and focused on simple measures. Its impact is rarely evaluated against intended aims or outcomes and there is still a focus on completing a post-event evaluation form (a 'happy sheet') or discussing performance during the appraisal process.
>
> *(Earley and Porritt, 2014:112)*

Goodall *et al.* (2005) evaluated the impact of PD in 1,000 schools in England, using Guskey's (2000) five-level framework: participant reaction, participant learning, organizational support and change, participant use of new knowledge and skills, and pupil learning outcomes. The research found that

1. teachers' experiences of PLD varied;
2. opportunities to participate in PLD were heavily dependent upon the support of their school;
3. the most effective kinds of PLD were perceived as being those which met both individual and organizational needs;
4. PLD leaders (usually senior members of staff) had limited knowledge and experience of evaluation approaches;
5. the most frequently evaluated factor was participant reaction and the least evaluated was pupil-learning outcomes.

Earley and Porritt argue that if 'impact' criteria are an integral part of planning, then it is more likely that PLD will become 'a powerful tool for making a difference to children's learning' (Earley and Porritt, 2014:113). They also cite Guskey's evaluation model (Guskey, 2000, 2002) which identifies five 'levels' of impact which might be evaluated and his suggestions of five questions that may be asked in associating the planning of PLD with its evaluation:

1. What impact do you want to have on pupils? How will you know that you have had this impact?
2. If that is what you want to accomplish, then what practices do you need to implement?
3. What does the organization need to do to support that, for example, what time/resources do people need?
4. What knowledge do people have to have and what skills do they have to develop?
5. What activities (e.g. training) do people need to gain those skills or knowledge?
(Cited in Earley and Porritt, 2014:114)

Goodall and her colleagues' (2005) project developed a comprehensive set of materials as a 'route map' for schools to use in auditing their existing states of readiness. Schools were classified as 'Emerging', 'Established' or 'Enhancing'. Here, I reproduce the table (Table 5.2) concerned with evaluation of the impact.

Evaluation of the impact of CPD

Table 5.2 enables the school to assess the current position or relative maturity of the PLD 'programme in terms of its impact'. Goodall and her colleagues provided a number of useful suggestions related to each category as a means of further development.

Most ticks in the 'Emerging' category

- Consider a simple system for filing and collating evaluation of CPD – is it possible to put the evaluation form online so that it is easy to access, fill in, store and retrieve?
- Consider a simple system for medium-term evaluation of impact.
- Send evaluation forms back to participants after a specific length of time has passed.
- Set up meetings with line manager/PM leader/critical friend, a specific time after the CPD event.
- Consider instituting some form of participant evaluation of new knowledge and skills:
  - Make clear links between before and after skills audits (beginning and end of academic year?) *NB – a simple form could be created.*
  - Encourage the keeping of reflective journals, learning logs, blogs, etc. among staff – set up examples in the staffroom, post links to online blogs.
  - Set up a board in the staffroom which allows staff to add sticky notes or bubbles to a 'what I've learned this year' brainstorm.

TABLE 5.2 Evaluation of the impact of professional learning and development

Evaluation	Evaluation of the impact of CPD not done Evaluation seen as quality control	Evaluation of the impact of CPD dependent on a few means (observation, scrutiny of work, etc.) Evaluation seen as quality control	Evaluation of impact of CPD done through a wide range of means Evaluation of CPD seen as quality control, dissemination and as involving evidence of impact
Level of evaluation	Immediate evaluation of events is used Participant reaction is only means of evaluation	Immediate and interim evaluation are used Participant-based evaluation (reaction, use of new knowledge and skills) is used Some events are evaluated by a return to the immediate participant reaction (after a lapse of a set period of time) No or little linkage of evaluation to future planning (perhaps only in terms of 'not using' a provider or course again due to adverse feedback)	Immediate, interim and long-term evaluation are used All levels of evaluation are used All events are evaluated by a return to the immediate participant reaction (after a lapse of a set period of time) Evaluation of impact clearly feeds into future planning of CPD Evaluation of impact of CPD feeds into planning in other areas: School Improvement Planning (SIP), etc.
Planning	Evaluation of impact not built into planning of CPD	Evaluation of impact built into planning of whole school CPD	Evaluation of impact built into all planning of CPD
Reporting	Report of evaluation of CPD is confined to the participant	Report of evaluation of CPD sometimes forms part of meeting structures	Report of evaluation XE "Evaluation" seen as part of team/department/school meeting structure
	Emerging	*Established*	*Enhancing*

Source: Goodall *et al.*, 2005.

Most ticks in the 'Established' category

Any of the 'Emerging' suggestions you feel might benefit your school plus

- Make a map of the means of evaluation you are presently using: what could be added?
- Consider how the means of evaluation you already use can be extended to cover the longer term.
- Consider how the results of evaluation can feed back into development planning – what would the mechanism for this be?
- Consider how the mechanisms used to evaluate the impact of whole school CPD might be extended to include other instances of CPD for individuals and teams.
- Consider how the means used now for dissemination (reports to teams, etc.) might be extended to include evaluation of *impact* as well as content, perhaps by delaying the report until impact can be seen?

Most ticks in the 'Enhancing' category

Any of the 'Established' suggestions you feel might benefit your school plus

- As Goodall *et al.* (2005:67–68) state, 'consider how you might involve pupils in the evaluation of the impact of CPD: through discussions, questionnaires, online forms, etc. Decide how to use this information (Would it be available only to the teacher involved? To the year group team?). Draw into this project any staff with experience of questionnaire design and analysis.'

Whilst these models are attractive in terms of achieving a balance between the '*functional*' and the '*attitudinal*', they are limited in their usefulness. First, they seem to assume that all PLD must be targeted directly at improving teachers' impact on pupils without apparently taking into account teachers' willingness, commitment, capabilities and capacities to do so and the difficulties in establishing direct 'cause-and-effect', 'means-ends' relationships (discussed in Chapter 1 of this book). Second, they seem to assume a linear relationship between one impact and another. Third, they seem to imply that teachers themselves are not involved in planning their own learning.

Learning through reflection: teachers as inquirers

With Stenhouse, I continue to believe that

> … long term improvement of education through the utilization of research and development hinges on the creation of different expectations in the system … The different expectations will be generated only as schools come to

see themselves as research and development institutions rather than clients of research and development agencies ... It is not enough that teachers' work should be studied; they need to study it for themselves.

(Stenhouse, 1975:143 and 222–223, cited in Grundy, 1994:35–36)

Teacher inquiry is not new. On the contrary, many teachers reflect upon their work in the classroom, both during the action itself and, later, as they analyse its effect and plan for the future. Whilst not all teachers will necessarily be lifelong learners with a passion for continuing improvement, it can be argued that at its most simple level, reflection is necessary if teachers are to be able to respond to the everyday teaching and learning needs of their students and the external demands for effectiveness. Schön (1983) coined the terms 'reflection *in* action' and 'reflection *on* action'. He was concerned then that most knowledge about teaching and learning was generated by university researchers from outside the classroom, many of whom had little experience of school teaching, and that this failed to acknowledge the role of teachers as knowledge holders and knowledge creators. The former, 'reflection *in* action', highlighted the need for teachers to think on their feet in order to respond to unanticipated questions or responses during their teaching processes.

This was later criticized by Eraut (1995), who observed that the depth of this kind of reflection would be limited by the time available to the teacher in the busyness of classroom life and the extent to which teachers would be able to formulate new thinking and actions rather than make decisions by selecting or re-configuring from within existing experience. 'Reflection *on* action', however, takes place outside the immediacy of classroom practice and so allows a more measured process of reflection – though, again, this is likely to be limited to memory and impression at a time when energy is likely to be depleted, unless part of a process of systematic inquiry and informed by data.

Neither the processes of reflection nor its outcomes are entirely rational. The capacity to reflect will be affected by workplace constraints (e.g. work overload, limited resources), personal limitations (e.g. phase of development, knowledge or skill level) and emotional well-being (e.g. self-confidence, esteem, response to negative criticism). In investigating impediments to reflective practice through analysis of the current conditions in schools, Cole (1997) has argued persuasively that 'the conditions under which teachers work have generated feelings and psychological states that militate against reflective practice and professional growth' (p. 7). By working conditions, she was referring to 'external structures imposed by schools and school systems, the profession, government and the public at large'. By psychological states, she was referring to perceptions which interfere with 'optimum productivity and practice' (p. 13).

There is a limit, also, to what can be learnt from examining one's own practice, whilst being simultaneously engaged in that practice. Reflection-in-action will usually be unsystematic with checks against realities constrained by the limitations of the single perspective available to teachers at the time. Even where teachers meet in order to share and analyse practice for assessment and planning purposes, to reflect *on* the action, often their reflections on action will be based upon talk about practice rather than the practice itself.

The nature and purposes of reflection

Distinctions between teachers as technicians and teachers as reflective practitioners are not always helpful. Good teachers will be technically competent and reflect upon broader issues of purpose, process, content and outcome. It is when technical competence ceases to involve reflection that the quality of teaching is likely to suffer. Such 'technicians' may identify a problem in the classroom as 'given' and plan strategies to solve the problem without questioning their own goals, values, moral purposes and accountabilities, or the broader assumptions which might, for example, contribute to the school setting, shape of the curriculum or the attitudes and behaviour of the students. Thus, simply to advocate reflection in, on and about action as a means of learning provides no indication of the depth, scope, purpose or challenges of engaging in the process. Unless a more critically reflective 'inquiry as stance' (Cochran-Smith and Lytle, 2009) is adopted, analysis and understanding are likely to be restricted to unarticulated values and assumptions. Pressures on teachers to meet externally determined achievement standards in a relatively limited number of (functional) areas of the curriculum are likely to reduce the potential for attitudinal teacher development through 'inquiry'.

> If teachers want to go beyond functional conceptions of their role then they must seek to maintain a broad vision about their work and not just look inwardly at their own practices:
>
> Teachers cannot restrict their attention to the classroom alone, leaving the larger setting and purposes of schooling to be determined by others. They must take active responsibility for the goals to which they are committed, and for the social setting in which these goals may prosper. If they are not to be mere agents of others, of the state, of the military, of the media, of the experts and bureaucrats, they need to determine their own agency through a critical and continual evaluation of the purposes, the consequences, and the social context of their calling.
>
> *(Scheffler, 1968:11, cited in Zeichner and Liston, 1996:19)*

Those who are responsible for policy may well view teacher inquiry as a technical means of improving the efficiency of, for example, curriculum delivery or classroom control rather than as a means of emancipation through knowledge. Thus it may be supported at the 'technical rational' (functional) rather than 'critical reflective' (functional and attitudinal) level.

In a review of teacher education in Scotland, Menter *et al.* (2010) identified four 'influential paradigms' of teacher professionalism which do much to inform school leaders and teachers about how they might identify the key functional and attitudinal dimensions in order to promote individual and collaborative PLD which extends rather than limits the growth of professional capital. I reproduce this below, with suggestions alongside each of the four as to how these paradigms may be related to the purposes and practices of 'functional' and 'attitudinal' PLD:

Restricted
professionalism

Extended
professionalism

1. the *effective* teacher: associated with a standards based approach to teaching which emphasises the measurable accomplishments of students in order to prepare them for work. This has been criticized as restricting teaching professionalism (*learning with functional purposes*)

2. the *reflective* teacher: associated with teachers as active participants in their own learning and improvement through collaboration and consultation with colleagues and students (*learning through inquiry with functional and attitudinal purposes*)

3. the *enquiring* teacher: closely associated with the 'reflective teacher' paradigm, but with an explicit emphasis on promoting improvements in teaching and learning through systematic inquiry in partnership with colleagues, other schools and universities (*learning as a social endeavour with functional and attitudinal purposes*)

4. the *transformational* teacher: associated with the promotion, equity and social change in and beyond the classroom (*learning through action research with functional and attitudinal purposes*)
(Menter et al., 2010:21)

These paradigms suggest strongly that effective PLD models are those which emphasize teacher ownership, participation and agency and a range of reflective practices as essential to interrogating and improving teachers' work. The review associates these paradigms with 'restricted' and 'extended' professionality' (Hoyle, 1975), terms used many years ago to distinguish between teachers whose perspectives on their work were based on learning primarily from their own experience and are, therefore, ultimately restricted and those whose perspectives are not only informed by their own experience but also extended by experiences of collaboration with colleagues, observations of others teaching and engagement with the interface between theories and practice.

It may be argued that changes in the school accountability context in many countries (for example, annual school improvement plans, individual performance appraisals, and more transparency in classroom teaching and learning) have caused these terms to be less applicable in this century. Nevertheless, there remain schools and teachers in many countries who do not yet embrace all parts of the continuum of PLD which are represented in the review by Menter and his colleagues. Two examples representing the extremes of these paradigms are discussed briefly here. Action research represents what Menter and his colleagues call 'the transformational teacher' who is, in their terms, an 'extended professional'. The example of 'evidence-based' practice represents the 'effective teacher' whose agenda, paradoxically, is clearly focused on the functional and who represents the 'restricted professional'. Those between these two extremes will be discussed in more detail in Chapter 6.

Action research

Action research is a form of reflective teacher inquiry in which exponents place change through understanding explicitly at the centre of its purposes. This has been defined as 'the study of a social situation, involving the participants themselves as researchers, with a view to improving the quality of action within it' (Somekh, 1988:164). It is, then, not about only understanding practice through, for example, 'self study' or limiting reflection on practice to improve it without a parallel concern with the social and power structures in which teaching and learning take place. Critical theorists have referred to it as 'reflection *about* action' (Zeichner, 1993) in order to ensure that the broader contextual and policy influences on contexts of teaching are considered and, where necessary, challenged, where they are seen not to serve the best interests of students. It is characterized by systematic inquiry that is primarily qualitative, collaborative, self-reflective and critical. Successful action research relies, however, both on the desire of teachers to engage in reflection as a means of development, to be willing to change existing beliefs and practices where appropriate to better teaching and learning, and the on-going support of the school in which they work to provide appropriate support.

Participation in collaborative action research requires a quite different 'mindset' by those who engage in it from that required in most other research endeavours. In summary, it requires

1. equitable relationships between participants;
2. the assistance of critical friends with an ability to engage in collaboration which is not always comfortable;
3. an understanding of change processes as both rational and non-rational;
4. a willingness to reflect upon and move from single to double loop learning;
5. a belief that authentic settings are best researched by those practitioners experiencing them direct, but that outsider viewpoints may enrich these through challenge and support;
6. an acceptance that those affected by planned changes have the primary responsibility for deciding on courses of action which seem likely to lead to improvement, and for evaluating the results of strategies tried out in practice; and
7. a supportive organizational culture.

Engeström's (2006) model of expansive learning provides for a sequence of actions that is not dissimilar to those in 'practitioner research'. It requires participants to move systematically through cycles of questioning (existing beliefs and practices) through analysing classroom practice with the help of others, receiving and acting upon feedback by implementation, and, finally, reflecting on the process and consolidating the new practice for confirming the results of the systematic review of effective PD, which showed that sustained, collaborative PD resulted in (i) increased teacher repertoire of classroom strategies; (ii) increased their commitment to further learning; and (iii) the improved learning of their students. The model relates well, also, to research on the processes which characterize PLCs. These are discussed in Chapter 6 and described by Engeström (1987) as 'shared transformative agency' (Engeström and Sannino, 2010:7).

Evidence-based teaching

In the current era of results-driven curricula, 'evidence-based teaching' has become associated with primarily quantitative measures to accelerate students' progress in learning to achieve pre-determined and measurable outcomes related to achieving success in external tests and examinations. Pre- and post-testing, for example, can now be found in most, if not all, school classrooms as teachers seek to determine what their students have learnt and collect, process, document and report formative assessments of students' progress. Such reports are used not only for quality control and assurance purposes in schools but also as evidence available to students themselves, parents and external school inspectors. What is common in these is that they are conducted in contexts of use, over time and by teachers who are able to combine the 'hard' data with their own professional judgments. These and other evidence-based practices that seek to establish short-term cause-and-effect relationships are also closely associated with experimental or quasi-experimental designs.

The notion of 'evidence-based' practices is seductive, particularly to schools in which some or many students are disadvantaged in terms of literacy and numeracy and so 'fall behind' others in their performance in national tests and examinations. There are an increasing number, also, of so-called 'randomized control trials' (RCTs) in which one group or class of students (the experimental or treatment group) receives particular 'interventions' in the form of particular teaching strategies, for example, over an agreed time period designed to result in accelerated improvements in performance, whilst students in another group (the control group) judged to have similar characteristics, continues with their normal work. It is assumed that there will be no change in the behaviour of the control group over time. Lemon *et al.* (2014) provide analyses of findings from five RCT experiments in education. Although in the short term these appeared to show improvements in, for example, literacy levels, over the longer term the control group's results had become similar to those of the experimental 'treatment' groups, thus decreasing the relative benefits. In reality, then, it seems that contexts of learning change in unpredictable ways for the individual student (since learning is not continuous, incremental or linear).

This is not to reject the use of such quasi-experimental, evidence-based research by schools and teachers, nor intended to suggest that there is no value in its use. There may well be an argument for learning how certain kinds of interventions may result in more efficient teaching of certain content or the use of more impactful learning processes. However, its limitations should also be noted.

Six challenges of teacher inquiry

Many years ago (Day, 1999), I identified a number of challenges of engaging in teacher inquiry. They remain true today for teachers whose working lives have become more rather, than less, complex and demanding.

Challenge 1: engaging with the possibilities of change

Important though these forms of reflective practice are, understanding ourselves in order to understand others, being able to be as questioning of the bias in our own views as we are of those held by others, does not necessarily lead to change for improvement. It is one thing to understand, for example, more about the curriculum, pupil learning, one's own teaching and the influences upon it, it is quite another to engage in change processes which may be difficult to sustain. In order to develop and sustain their critical thinking through reflection, teachers will need to engage in processes of metacognition and systematic collection, description, synthesis, interpretation and evaluation of data. The quality and authenticity of the data will depend upon their abilities to engage in reflective analytical conversations with themselves and others as well as their capacities to do so. Teachers who are reflective inquirers need to recognize that inquiry is likely to raise issues of change and that this will involve a confrontation of inconsistencies within and between existing core values and practices. If teachers are to engage in critical forms of teaching, they will need not only to be concerned with describing what they do and informing themselves and others of the meaning of that description. They will need also to confront their practice by asking questions such as

- Why do I do what I do?
- Does what I do reflect my educational ideals?
- How am I able to express my educational ideals whilst taking into account the legitimate needs of policy, school and student needs?
- Are there discrepancies between what I think I do when I am teaching and what I do?
- How is this received by the students?
- How do I find out more about this?
- How did I come to be like this?
- Do I want to continue to do this in this way?
- Do I want to reconstruct my ideals and/or practices so that I might do things differently?

In short, they will need to be prepared to engage with possibilities of change. Processes of reflection may not in themselves lead to confrontation of thinking and practices nor take account of broad institutional and social contexts necessary as precursors to decisions about change when carried out by the teacher alone. Relatively little attention has been given also (outside the action-research movement) to what engaging in reflective processes which are both rational and non-rational will mean for the teacher. It is clear that there are parts of ourselves that we might prefer to remain private. Alone these are rather easier to hide, but as part of a group much more difficult – unless there is a tacit agreement concerning 'boundaries' and, thus, a kind of collaboration by collusion.

Challenge 2: managing the self in change

Inquiry is likely to involve a confrontation of inconsistencies within and between existing core values and habitual practices. Argyris and Schön (1974) called this a 'theory of action'. Within this are our 'espoused theories' (what we intend to do and think we do when we teach) and 'theories in use' (what we do). In order to become more effective, they suggest, we need to examine discrepancies within and between each in order to 'narrow the gap'. Yet while change involves cognition, it is not only a cognitive process. It involves emotion. Jersild's (1995) seminal work in exploring the effects of anxiety, fear, loneliness, helplessness, meaning and mean-inglessness, and hostility in relation to understanding self is also relevant here. He argues that these emotions are prevalent in teachers' lives in schools and classrooms and must, therefore, be addressed as part of teachers' professional education. In short, reflection is a necessary but insufficient condition for change.

Challenge 3: exploring the continuum

The third challenge is for teachers to take a broader view of the ways in which they can learn through inquiry into their practices and the contexts which influence these over a career. Reflective and non-reflective practitioners are not two funda-mentally irreconcilable groups. Rather, they are teacher inquirers who are at differ-ent points on a continuum. The continuum spans unsystematic, intuitive inquiry to inquiry through systematic research, defined by Stenhouse (1975) as 'systematic inquiry, made public', and manifested particularly through action research. It may be that teachers will be working in different modes during different phases of their careers, in different school contexts and for different purposes (see Day et al., 2007 for a detailed discussion). Ebbutt's (1985) developmental classification of a range of insider research-related activity was based upon the observed reality of teachers' working lives and continues to provide an important frame of reference for those engaged in inquiry. He identified the teacher as an inquirer within a continuum of practice: (i) 'Usual Teaching Mode' where isolated learning predominates and conscious, systematic reflection is sporadic; (ii) 'Teacher Self-Monitoring' where data on classroom practice are regularly if informally collected, sometimes with the help of a critical friend colleague, and reflections are incorporated into practice; and (iii) more rigorous 'Teacher-Researcher' modes of inquiry in which data from a number of sources (e.g. students, self, observer, documents) are collected and triangulated, analysed and used to inform decisions about change at individual and school levels.

Challenge 4: time to think

It has been argued that the mind works at three different speeds:

1. Rapid thought – this 'unconscious' level of working is the most common in the classroom, where teachers must often react instantaneously to a multitude of demands. It involves reflection in action.
2. Deliberate thought – this involves 'figuring matters out, weighing up the pros and cons, constructing arguments and solving problems' (Claxton, 1997:2). This is similar to reflection in action.
3. Contemplative thought – this 'is often less purposeful and clear-cut, more playful … In this mode we are ruminating or mulling things over … What is going on in the mind may be quite fragmentary' (Claxton, 1997:2).

Many years later, Kahneman (2011) in a much-celebrated book, *Thinking, Fast and Slow*, elaborated on the way the mind works in making wise or unwise decisions. Although not aimed at educationalists, his work can be related to teachers' work. In the everyday busyness of their classrooms, on-the-spot decisions are often required. In these contexts, there is little room for deliberate or contemplative thought. Yet to make wise decisions, to build 'decisional capital', such an important part of 'professional capital' (Hargreaves and Fullan, 2012), requires more than teachers' intuition and experience. Kahneman's most important contribution was to add to existing knowledge on 'implicit' knowledge (Polanyi, 1967) and reflection in and on action (Schön, 1983) in applying it to decision-making. He identified Systems 1 and 2 thinking:

> System 1 corresponds to thinking fast, and System 2 to thinking slow. Kahneman describes System 1 in many evocative ways: it is intuitive, automatic, unconscious, and effortless, it answers questions quickly through associations and resemblances, it is non-statistical, gullible, and heuristic. System 2 in contrast … is conscious, slow, controlled, deliberate, effortful, statistical, suspicious … System 1 is automatic and reactive, not optimizing. As a consequence, when we make a judgment or choice, we do that on the basis of incomplete and selected data assembled via a System 1-like mechanism. Even if the decisions are optimal at this point given what we have in mind, they might not be optimal given the information potentially available to us both from the outside world and from memory.
>
> *(Shleifer, 2012:17)*

It is deliberative System 2 ways of thinking that are in danger of being lost in the intensification of teachers' working lives through the rise of 'technopoly' (Postman, 1992) in which contemplation is regarded as a luxury. Technopoly is based upon

… the beliefs that the primary, if not the only goal of human labour and thought is efficiency; that technical calculation is in all respects superior to human judgment; that in fact human judgement cannot be trusted, because it is plagued by laxity, ambiguity, and unnecessary complexity; that subjectivity is an obstacle to clear thinking; that what cannot be measured either does not exist or is of no value; and that the affairs of citizens are best guided and conducted by 'experts'.

(Postman, 1992, cited in Claxton, 1997:2)

Because historically teachers' work has been regarded as 'contact time' with students, they have had few built-in opportunities or expectations placed upon them, for example, to collect data, share practice with colleagues, or collectively reflect in depth 'on' and 'about' their teaching and its contexts. Hargreaves (1994) identified three dimensions of time in teaching: the *micro-political*, relating to the distribution of time in relation to status; the *phenomenological*, relating to the way the use of time is constructed in schools; and the *socio-political*, relating to the claims on teachers' 'discretionary' time made by administrators.

Whilst time is always at a premium where conditions of service effectively define teaching only as contact time, this is not the case universally. In Chinese schools, for example, time is built into the working day which could be used for deliberative thought, perhaps in recognition that making sense of complex, ill-defined and ambiguous situations is a key determinant of quality teaching and that providing time for reflection which is more contemplative is an essential part of teacher development.

Challenge 5: sustaining engagement

Establishing, nurturing and developing collaborative work over time requires 'sustained interactivity' (Huberman, 1993b), and this requires that teachers engage in discussions in their schools about the use of each of the three dimensions of time identified by Hargreaves for their learning. *Talk* is the means by which teachers deconstruct, test out and reconstruct their beliefs and 'espoused theories' of education (Argyris and Schön, 1974). Most 'co-construction', whether it takes place through anecdote, ideas, information and material swapping, or the sharing of problems, issues and opinions will need to challenge teachers to move beyond exchange to critique. Success in this depends upon the level of individual trust and institutional challenges and support. In schools which value more expansive and critical teacher learning, it is likely, for example, that there will be opportunities for the development of reflexive practitioner inquiry (Cochran-Smith and Lytle, 2009; Mockler and Sachs, 2011), action research groups (Somekh, 2006; Townsend, 2013) and network learning communities (Stoll and Seashore-Louis, 2007). Critique involves both disclosure and feedback from 'critical friends' whose integrity is trusted and whose considered feedback is respected.

Challenge 6: critical friendship

Teacher inquiry of different kinds offers teachers extended opportunities to engage in the systematic investigation of self, practice and practice contexts, either over extended periods or through an intensive, relatively short timespan. They can be a successful mechanism for helping teachers translate their PLD experiences into their practice and to explore the impact on student achievement (Bell *et al.*, 2010; Timperley, 2008; Crippen *et al.*, 2010). However, if reflection in, on and about practice is to probe current realities in challenging ways, there will also need to be practical and moral support from within and without the school in terms of that most valuable of all commodities, time. Because it is often difficult to be dispassionate in reflecting upon one's own work, perhaps the most important aid will be the commitment of a '*critical friend*'.

Teachers do not always learn best only through examining their own experience of teaching. Such learning, whilst useful, is likely to be unnecessarily limiting to the growth of expertise since it may only be the re-configuration and recycling of personal experience without external critical friendship support, even learning through collaborative activities with colleagues is likely to be limited. In short, examining existing practice does not necessarily result in improvement. Teachers need both the internal support of colleagues and the external support of trusted *critical friends* in building their skills in collecting evidence, for example, about student progress or aspects of their own 'presentation of self' in the classroom and staffroom (Parr and Timperley, 2010; Bell *et al.*, 2010), and applying this to their practices and ways of thinking.

Recently, Wennergren (2016) has provided a useful definition of critical friendship which highlights its key elements and links this to the challenges of teacher learning and development in social settings.

> A characteristic of a critical friend is the unexpected combination of, on the one hand, friendship built on trust, support and affirmation and, on the other, criticism based on analysis, assessment, evaluation and quality … Challenging a teaching colleague … means dealing with a situation involving relationships and emotions … strong professional communities depend on teachers' capacity to blend commitment with doubt, along with healthy disagreements about teaching.
>
> *(Wennergren, 2016:263)*

Critical friendships are based upon practical partnerships entered into voluntarily, pre-suppose a relationship between equals and are rooted in a common task of shared concern and mutual respect and trust. The role of a critical friend is to provide support and challenge within a trusting relationship. It is different from the 'mentor' relationship in which one person (the mentor) holds a superior position by virtue of his/her experience, knowledge and skills. The critical friend is recognized as having knowledge, experience and skills that are complementary.

Although, ideally, teacher inquiry enables teachers to develop the ownership of PLD through the choice of its focus and direction of travel, there is a temptation in schools that are concerned with complying with the regulatory and measurement demands of government (See Chapter 1 for a discussion of these) to use inquiry as a vehicle to improve the efficiency and effectiveness of existing curricula for the achievement of externally defined purposes only (Kemmis, 2006). Where this is the case, both the early ideals of action research as a vehicle for transformation and, where appropriate, educational critique and the development of teachers as inquirers envisioned by Schön (1983), and others, will become lost.

'Effective' PLD

A persuasive set of evidence in support of combining the functional and attitudinal in a range of formal PD activities is to be found in the OECD's 'Comparison of Impact and Participation by Types of Development Activity' (2007–08), in which teachers from its member countries reported on the moderate or high impact of the formal professional development in which they participated (OECD, 2009:75). Figure 5.3 illustrates this. What is shown clearly is that within a relatively wide range of PLD opportunities, those which are perceived to have the highest impact relative to their provision are individual and collaborative research, qualification programmes, professional development networks, mentoring and peer observation, observation visits to other schools, and education conferences and seminars.

Five observations may be made from this:

1. All the activities may encompass both the functional and the attitudinal.
2. They involve social learning.
3. They all involve extended periods of reflection on and reflect notions of occupational professionalism, the building and reinforcement of positive professional identities, efficacy and agency.
4. They all involve extended periods of reflection on action.
5. They all focus on possibilities for improvements in thinking and practices.

In their synthesis of a review of American research, Darling-Hammond and Richardson (2009) provided a useful reminder of the kinds of effective PLD opportunities which are *likely to benefit* teachers. These are those which

- Deepen teachers' knowledge of content and how to teach it to students
- Help teachers understand how students learn specific content
- Provide opportunities for active, hands-on learning
- Enable teachers to acquire new knowledge, apply it to practice and reflect on the results with colleagues
- Are part of a school reform effort that links curriculum, assessment and standards to professional learning

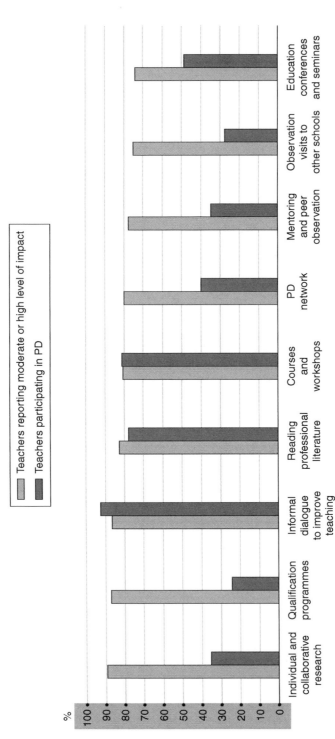

FIGURE 5.3 Comparison of impact and participation by types of development activity (2007–2008)

Activities are ranked in descending order of the percentage of teachers reporting a moderate or high impact of the professional development they took

Source: OECD, Tables 3.2 and 3.8

- Are collaborative and collegial
- Are intensive and sustained over time

(Darling-Hammond and Richardson, 2009:46)

Another study in the USA found that long-term 'investment' produces a very good 'return' and that an average of 49 hours spent on staff CPD over a year boosted student achievement by 21 percentile points. Teachers who received 80 or more hours of PD were significantly more likely to put the given teaching strategies into practice than teachers who had participated for fewer hours (Darling-Hammond *et al.*, 2007). In contrast, more limited time (5–14 hours) showed no statistically significant effect on student learning.

Research internationally has acknowledged, also, that leadership is a key influencing factor in the efficacy, commitment and effectiveness of all teachers (Day and Leithwood, 2007) and a key mediating factor in building and supporting teachers' capacity for effectiveness. This has important positive or significant negative effects upon their motivation and commitment. In the research on teachers' commitment and effectiveness across different phases of their careers reported in Chapter 3 (Day *et al.*, 2007), two broad groups of teachers were identified:

1. teachers who had sustained commitment (74%);
2. teachers whose commitment was declining (26%).

Table 5.3 provides a synthesis of the factors that influenced the 300 teachers who participated in that research. It illustrates how, in the various phases of teachers' professional lives, for a significant proportion, pupil behaviour, unsupportive leadership and workload contributed to a decline in commitment, and shows the importance of the quality of leadership, relationships with peers and personal support to those whose commitment was sustained.

Other empirical research internationally also demonstrates the strong positive (or negative) direct and indirect influence of the school principal on pupil learning and attainment (Leithwood *et al.*, 2006; Robinson *et al.*, 2009; Day and Gurr, 2014). It is the primary responsibility of school and system leaders to create the conditions necessary to enable teachers, who are at the heart of the business of educating pupils, to teach to their best and to make a tangible difference to the learning and achievement lives of the pupils they teach, especially those who are drawn from high-need communities (James *et al.*, 2006).

Conclusions

Not all teachers at all times have the same boundless energy required to engage in sustained periods of professional learning, even with colleagues' support. Learning needs will differ for a variety of reasons, e.g. teachers are managing a particularly challenging group of students and this may take all their emotional, intellectual and practical energy; they have unanticipated personal challenges; they may learn

TABLE 5.3 Teachers with sustained commitment and declining commitment comment on the factors affecting them

Group a: sustained commitment	Group b: declining commitment
The combination of factors mentioned most frequently by teachers as contributing to their sustained commitment were	A total of 26% teachers were in this group. Those who were considering leaving the teaching profession for a new career were either looking for promotion out of the classroom (e.g. to advisory roles) or, having suffered health problems connected to the stress of teaching, were seeking different kinds of work
• Leadership (76%) 'It's good to know that we have strong leadership with a clear vision for the school'	The combination of pressures identified most frequently as challenging their sustained commitment in the comments over three years were
• Colleagues (63%) 'We have such a supportive team here. Everyone works together and we have a common goal to work towards'	• Workload (68%) 'It never stops, there's always something more to do and it eats away at your life until you have no social life and no time for anything but work'
• Personal support (95%) 'It helps having a supportive family which doesn't get frustrated when I'm sat working on a Sunday afternoon and they want to go to the park' Teachers in this group were enthusiastic about their work and confident in their ability to make a positive difference in the learning and achievement of their pupils	• Pupil behaviour (64%) 'Over the years, pupils have got worse. They have no respect for themselves or the teachers' 'Pupil behaviour is one of the biggest problems in schools today. They know their rights and there's nothing you can do'
	• Leadership (58%) 'Unless the leadership supports the staff, you're on your own. They need to be visible and need to appreciate what teachers are doing'

Source: Day *et al.*, 2007:125–126.

better alone or from a 'one-shot' workshop at particular times. In addition, since learning needs are rarely singular (in that to address them almost always means locating them in the personal, professional and workplace contexts which give rise to and influence them), it is likely that any learning experience, whether functional or attitudinal in its orientation, will have cumulative elements and result in incremental rather than transformational change effects on teachers and/or their teaching practices.

It is likely, also, that where teachers cease to believe that they can make a positive difference to their students' lives (a loss of self-efficacy, commitment and moral purpose), their willingness to teach to their best and well and, thus, their capacity for effectiveness will diminish. As we have seen in earlier chapters, such loss of belief in the ability to 'make a difference' may be influenced by both anticipated and unanticipated personal events, e.g. illness, the conditions of their work caused by policy changes which affect their sense of autonomy, and the everyday culture of the schools in which they work. It is the latter which will have the strongest positive or negative influence.

Key to successful planning, its translation into practice and its potential for impact, is the school culture, and key to this is the role of the principal and senior leadership team. The 'staff development outcomes study' (SDOS) in England, led by Bubb and Earley, found that 'school ethos was fundamental to staff development and in those schools where it was strong, leaders fostered – and all staff felt – a sense of both entitlement and responsibility for their own development and learning, closely linked to benefits for the pupils. Staff turnover was low and morale was high at these schools' (Earley, 2010:474). The study also found 'a positive association between school outcomes and staff development' (Earley, 2010:474). Whilst school leaders' influence on student learning and achievement is second only to that of teachers, such influence is, however, likely to be indirect. Thus, school leaders improve teaching and learning most effectively through the influence of their strong sense of moral purpose and social justice and the combination and accumulation of timely, context-specific improvement strategies on staff motivation, commitment and resilience, and working conditions. Chapter 7 discusses in more detail the key role played by school leaders in promoting opportunities for PLD.

How schools combine the functional *and the* attitudinal *in their planning and provision of PLD is likely to be an important factor in teachers' commitment to learning.* Equally important will be the ways they learn together. Chapter 6 explores these factors in more detail.

6

LEARNING AS A SCHOOL-LED SOCIAL ENDEAVOUR

> During the past two decades, empirical research has demonstrated that
> effective PL [professional learning] … continues over the long term and is
> best situated within a community that supports learning (Darling-Hammond,
> 1997; Garet et al., 2001; Stoll, Bolam, McMahon, Wallace and Thomas,
> 2006; Wenger, 1998; Lieberman and Miller, 2001; Oakes and Rogers,
> 2007)…Effective PD … [professional development] … is based on a notion
> of PL as continuing, active, social, and related to practice.
>
> *(Webster-Wright, 2009:703)*

Inter-connectedness and close social ties with others are important because schools
are, as Bryk and Schneider note, an 'intrinsically social enterprise' (2002:19).
Moore-Johnson (2015:119) also found that 'the more robust the teachers' instructional repertoire and the more opportunities they have to exchange and integrate
promising ideas and techniques into their own teaching, the more likely it will be
that all students … will experience the benefits of expert teaching … [and] … successful school wide improvement increases norms of shared responsibility among
teachers and creates structures and opportunities for learning that promote inter-
dependence – rather than independence – among them'. She suggested, also, that
incoming teachers in schools can be supported in their development by interactions with others and that through these processes (e.g. PLD) 'the school organisation becomes greater than the sum of its parts … [and that this] … increases the
school's overall instructional capacity and, arguably, its success' (Moore-Johnson,
2015:119).

In an international review of the literature, Villegas-Reimers (2003) provides
a useful classification of PLD 'models' (Table 6.1), distinguishing between those
which 'imply certain organisational or inter-institutional partnerships in order to be
effective' and those that 'can be implemented on a smaller scale' (p. 69).

TABLE 6.1 Models and types of professional development

Organizational partnership models	Small group or individual models
PD schools (promoting PLD at pre- and in-service levels)	Supervision: traditional and clinical
Other university–school partnerships	Students' performance assessment
Other inter-institutional collaborations	Workshops, seminars, courses etc.
Schools' networks	Case-based study
Teachers' networks	Self-directed development
Distance education	Co-operative or collegial development
	Observation of excellent practice
	Teachers' participation in new roles
	Skills-development model
	Reflective models
	Project-based models
	Portfolios
	Action research
	Use of teachers' narratives
	Generational or cascade model
	Coaching/mentoring

Source: Villegas-Reimers, 2003:70.

This represents a useful and useable range of possibilities for consideration by those who are responsible at the school level for planning and selecting 'fit-for-purpose', 'time-sensitive' PLD opportunities. Often, it will be the diagnosis of system needs that will influence the focus of PLD. More than these, however, will be the willingness of teachers themselves, in the energy-sapping busyness of their professional lives, to recognize the potential benefits of participation, and this will depend upon their own internal commitment to career-long learning and the part played by their departments and schools in establishing cultures of learning.

Systematic reviews (e.g. Cordingley *et al.*, 2005) have compared collaborative PLD (where teachers provide and receive support from other teachers from either their own schools or other schools) with individually oriented PLD opportunities (which do not use collaboration as a learning strategy). The studies of individually oriented CPD showed only some evidence of changes in teachers' practices and beliefs, and a modest impact on behaviours and attitudes of pupils rather than on learning outcomes, whereas

1. all the studies of collaborative PLD found links between the PLD and positive changes in teachers' practice, attitudes or beliefs;
2. almost all of the collaborative studies that collected data about student impact reported evidence of improvements in pupils' learning and most also found that there were positive changes in either their behaviour, attitudes or both; and

3. around half the collaborative studies provided evidence that changes in teachers' classroom behaviours were accompanied by positive changes in attitude to their professional development.

(GTC, 2005:3)

Clarke and Hollingsworth (2002:963) provide a useful illustration in Figure 6.1 of the powerful influence of the school context:

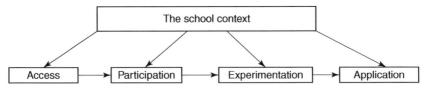

FIGURE 6.1 Influence of the school context

All teachers have the capability to generate change for improvement in student motivation, learning behaviours, progress and achievement and, potentially, even the social and organization structures in the school. However, the application of such ability is conditional on the strength of their own moral purpose, their commitment, their positive professional identity, their professional competence, their resilience and their willingness and capacity to reflect and evaluate.

In working towards establishing, developing, sustaining and, where appropriate, refreshing and renewing schools as PLCs in which teachers add value to pupils' learning and achievement lives, school leaders need to provide the conditions (space, resources, time) and strategies (progressively engaging teachers in department and whole school decision-making processes, building professional capital) that regularly enable teachers to interact in collegial environments which are perceived by them to be psychologically and emotionally 'safe', but which also challenge them to interrogate existing beliefs, values and practices: in short, environments in which there is trust.

> For better or worse, principals set conditions for teacher community by the ways in which they manage school resources, relate to teachers and students, support or inhibit social interaction and leadership in the faculty, respond to the broader policy context, and bring resources into the school.
>
> *(McLaughlin and Talbert, 2001:98)*

Structural reforms, which have created opportunities for collaboration and inquiry, by themselves are insufficient means of realizing the potential of effective PLD. Unless PLD is seen and enacted as a joint responsibility – between the employer (in the interests of the organizational purposes) and the employee (in the interests in being the best they can be) – it is likely that the employee will struggle to continue to learn and develop their own and their 'organization's' satisfaction. Where schools promote the development of shared vision, self-efficacy, strong interpersonal relationships, the deprivatization of classroom practice, data-rich classrooms, individual, relational and organizational trust, and continuing PLD, it is likely that teachers' commitment, capacity for resilience and sense of agency will be strong. Table 6.2 shows three major orientations of PLD. They are not always mutually exclusive, nor exhaustive. Each is derived from different views of the primary purposes of PLD and each is likely to be more – or less – effective in terms of influencing teachers' beliefs, commitment and practices:

Six examples of collaborative PLD which have been found to be effective

1. Lesson study

Lesson study originated in Japan in pre-service education programmes and focused on teachers in elementary schools initially. It 'is based on the principle that change/ improvement in teaching and learning in classrooms is best achieved by teachers themselves, empowered to make their own decisions through collaborative research-informed practice' (Williams *et al.*, 2014:156).

> Through live research lessons, written reports, videos and sharing of experiences with colleagues, lesson study spreads thoughtfully – designed lessons on a wide-range of topics, creating a system that learns. […] lesson study can help educators notice gaps in their own understanding and provide a meaningful, motivating context to remedy them.
>
> *(Lewis, 2002:11,31)*

The process usually consists of a cycle of i) questioning and planning, in which teachers will jointly plan the lesson to be studied; ii) action and observation in which one teacher will present the lesson to a class of students whilst being observed; iii) reflecting and revising in which the group will meet to discuss and analyse the lesson as 'critical friends'; and v) critiquing future lesson plans in which there will be further joint planning, implementation and observation, and critique phases.

The central feature is the 'observation of live classroom lessons by a group of teachers who collect data on teaching and learning and collaboratively analyse it' (Lewis *et al.*, 2006:3). The lessons themselves are known as 'research lessons' which are not seen as ends in themselves but as 'a window on the larger vision of education shared by the group of teachers, one of whom agrees to teach the lesson while all the others make detailed records of the learning and teaching as it unfolds. These data are shared during a post lesson colloquium, where they are used to reflect on the lesson and the learning more broadly' (Lewis *et al.*, 2006:3).

The aim is to improve practice in the local school context rather than to produce generalized knowledge that can be disseminated more widely; and, although lesson observation is central to the process of improvement, its effects may stretch beyond

TABLE 6.2 Three major orientations of PLD

Awareness raising (de-contextual)	Classroom efficiency/effectiveness	Situated learning/learning as a social practice/schools as learning communities
'One-shot' workshops aimed at raising teachers' awareness, new subject developments, new knowledge of teaching and learning – these have often been criticized but, within limitations of time and space, may have transformational effects for some teachers. However, they rely heavily on the quality of the PLD leader, whether from within or outside the school 'One-shot' workshops aimed at increasing teacher skills – these have been widely criticized as a 'deficit' model of PLD	*Series of meetings/workshops* aimed at developing, applying and evaluating new approaches to teaching and learning – these rely upon a series of inputs, each followed by classroom-based tasks. Here teachers have the choice of task opportunities for reflection and dialogue over time – these emphasize teacher agency, but require more time and energy commitment on the part of the teacher *Series of meetings/workshops* aimed at implementing change policies initiated at school and/or system level – these also rely on a series of inputs, each followed by classroom tasks. This is based on a deficit model where teachers are regarded primarily as those who are obliged to implement rather than choose whether or not to implement *School 'closure' days* are aimed at system-level maintenance and/or development *Mentoring* (for new and newly appointed staff) aimed at providing regular 'in-time' supports – these serve two essential needs: those of the school in inducting staff into the culture (norms of behaviour, expectations, values, practices) and those of the individual in forming a workplace identity. However, success depends upon the commitment and quality of the mentor *Coaching* aimed more often than not at supporting particular needs of individuals for improvements in all aspects of teaching – this is based on a deficit model of teachers who are deemed to be 'below standard'. As with mentoring, success depends upon the commitment and quality of the coach	*Collaborative development* aimed at improving classroom efficiency and effectiveness, e.g. lesson study, peer observation – these 'deprivatize' classroom teaching and learning by ensuring a sharing of planning, teaching and assessment *Collaborative research* aimed at promoting professional growth through teacher engagement in cycles of need identification: designing tools for systematically investigating classroom and school-wide cultures and practices with a view to developing these further through experimentation – these are often associated with 'action research' projects, involve teachers as active agents of change and require additional time and energy. They may be undertaken within and across schools and networks and may involve school–university partnerships *Networked learning experiences* aimed at broadening teachers' knowledge and skills through opportunities to work with a broader group of colleagues from outside their particular school context – these are a more expansive version of collaborative research and development at single-school level

the walls of the classroom itself. Matoba *et al.* (2007), for example, investigated the process of successful change over three years in one Japanese school which engaged in a school–university project designed 'to help teachers change their assumptions about school leadership, their roles, leadership for learning, educating students and to apply "jugyon kenkyuu" (lesson study) as a shared professional culture for acquiring professional knowledge' (2007:55–56).

Whilst lesson study is attractive since it places ownership, relevance and coherence of the learning with the teachers themselves, this pre-supposes that the participants are likely to share the same educational values and beliefs, that the broader departmental and school values and culture in which they work is supportive and that its norms, like those of lesson study itself, are based upon relational trust. Without such trust and the dedication of the time necessary to engage in the sustained cycle of planning, inquiry, observation, feedback, discussion and future planning, its aims are unlikely to be realized. Lewis *et al.* (2006) developed a USA 'improvement' version of the original as a means of focusing more directly upon the improvement of 'instructional' quality. However, this changed the original broader focus of lesson study upon both functional and attitudinal needs of teachers towards a primary focus on the functional.

2. One-to-one PLD: mentoring and coaching

i. Mentoring

Broadly conceptualized, mentoring is about *non-judgemental support* provided in the workplace by one (more-experienced) person to another (less-experienced) person that enables the less-experienced person to identify, understand and examine their roles (as teachers, as leaders) and what qualities and competences they need in order to fulfil them successfully in the contexts in which they work. School-based systems of mentoring have been incorporated widely for early-career teachers, middle leaders and new principals, and less widely for experienced teachers who are new to the school (Hobson *et al.*, 2009). Pre-service school–university education and training partnership models often also implicitly include the 'mentoring' of school-based mentors themselves through on-going training and support programmes, some of which may be accredited. Wasik and Hindman (2011) have emphasized the importance of using evidence-based group work techniques to structure reflective dialogue and found mentoring and coaching to be key components of effective CPD.

Whilst such forms of support have been present in some schools for many years, more recently they have become almost universally part of their quality assurance systems as concerns to raise standards of teaching, learning and leadership at all levels within growing national climates of performance management have mounted. Mentoring training manuals, programmes, research, journals and books devoted to disseminating knowledge of and about mentoring have grown on an industrial scale. For example, in England, the government has produced a comprehensive national framework for mentoring and coaching (CUREE, 2005).

Strengths and weaknesses of mentoring systems

In a comprehensive review of over 300 research-based articles across three disciplines (education, medicine and business), Ehrich *et al.* (2004:523–524) identified a number of positive and negative outcomes of mentoring that remain applicable today. Across all studies, the four most positive benefits for mentees centred upon the quality of the relationship: support, empathy, encouragement, counselling and friendship (42.1%); help with teaching strategies, subject knowledge and resources (35.8%); discussion, sharing ideas, problems and advice from peers (32.1%); and feedback, positive reinforcement and constructive criticism (27.7%) (see also 'critical friendship' in Chapter 5). For mentors, key benefits were collegiality, collaboration, networking, sharing ideas and knowledge (20.8%); reflection (19.5%); PD (17.6%); and personal satisfaction, reward and growth (16.4%).

On the other hand, the authors found that the most cited negatives by mentees were lack of mentor time (15.1%); lack of professional expertise and personality mismatch (12.6%); mentors who were critical, out of touch, defensive, staffing and untrusting (10.7%); and difficulty in meeting, observing and being observed teaching (9.4%). For the mentors, the negatives were lack of time (27.7%); professional expertise (lack of) and personality mismatch (17.0%); lack of training, lack of understanding of programme goals and expectations (15.1%); and the extra work burden and responsibility (15.1%).

Problems of available time, mentor expertise, poor role modelling and mismatch of interpersonal relationships have also been identified as impediments to success, as well as issues of the unequal distribution of power (and so the possibility of the presence of distrust in a relationship that needs to be built upon trust in order to succeed), managing 'constructive friction' (Vermunt and Verloop, 1999) and emotional literacy (the ability to understand and express feelings). We may conclude, then, that in terms of the opportunities provided for PLD, *simply having a structure for mentoring is a necessary but not sufficient condition for success.* Whilst there are potential benefits for both mentees and mentors, in order for these to be realized in practice, close attention needs to be paid to

- provision of time for mentors and mentees to engage in extended interaction;
- mentor training that focuses upon developing intra- and interpersonal qualities and skills;
- matching the professional expertise, values, beliefs and personal qualities of mentors to those of the mentee;
- creating an inclusive, school-wide culture for PLD;
- acknowledging that mentoring and being mentored involve the emotions as well as the intellect.

Space does not allow the further detailed exploration of mentoring as a form of PLD. I have highlighted here the core elements – which would apply equally to the more co-equal relationships established more informally through 'critical friendships'. Both are necessary in order to establish the unique one-to-one learning opportunities provided by mentoring in and between schools and other agencies and to ensure that mentors are selected not only because of their experience or the quality of their own teaching – though both are important criteria – but also for their high levels of emotional literacy in bridging the social and the academic.

ii. Coaching

Coaching is sometimes used interchangeably with mentoring, yet it is very different, and more oriented to skill development and is often used as one development tool within a mentoring relationship. It can promote high fidelity of evidence-based practices from training settings to real classroom settings, emphasizing the importance of using observations – including teachers learning to learn from observing the practice of others – plus a combination of instructive training and individualized follow-up coaching. The process is often intensive and over a relatively short period. Once improvement is achieved, the 'coaching' relationship is unlikely to continue.

3. Communities of practice

One of the dimensions of Hargreaves and Fullan's (2012) notion of 'professional capital' needed by teachers in order to be able to teach to their best is 'social capital', though this is likely also to enhance 'human' capital (see Chapter 1 for a more detailed discussion). As Coleman (1988) has argued, '*human capital ... is transformed for the benefit of the organisation by social capital, which [is] inherent in the structure of relation between actors and among actors*' (p. S98).

Figure 6.2 is an adaptation of Lesser and Storck's (2001) 'business-oriented' representation to educational contexts. This provides a useful map of the connections between communities of practice, social capital and organizational performance.

Like their original business model, it shows how collaboration over time not only stimulates individual growth but also contributes to raised expectations, an increased collective sense of trust, a sense of individual and collective identity and well-being, and raised standards of teaching and learning across the school. As Wenger and Snyder assert:

> The strength of communities of practice is self-perpetuating. As they generate knowledge, they reinforce and renew themselves. That's why communities of practice give you not only the golden eggs but also the goose that lays them. The farmer killed the goose to get all the gold and ended up losing both; the challenge for organisations is to appreciate the goose and to understand how to keep it alive and productive ... Although communities of practice are fundamentally informal and self-organising, they benefit from cultivation.
>
> *(Wenger and Snyder, 2000:143)*

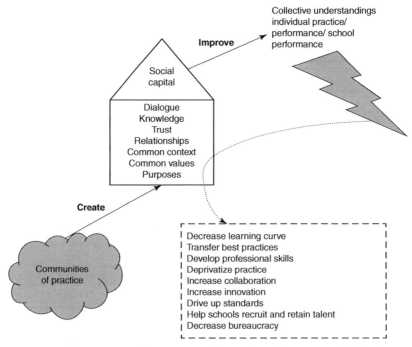

FIGURE 6.2 Communities of practice, social capital and classroom and school improvement

Source: Adapted from Lesser and Storck, 2001:833

4. PLC: ideal or reality?

> By using the term *professional learning community* we signify our interest not only in discrete acts of teacher sharing, but in the establishment of a school-wide culture that makes collaboration expected, inclusive, genuine, on-going, and focussed on critically examining practice to improve student outcomes … The hypothesis is that what teachers do together outside of the classroom can be as important as what they do inside in affecting school restructuring, teachers' professional development, and student learning.
>
> *(Seashore-Louis* et al., *2003:3)*

PLCs have been defined by Hord (1997) as being present when 'teachers in a school and its administrators continuously seek and share learning and then act on what they learn. The goal of their actions is to enhance their effectiveness as professionals so that students benefit' (Hord, 1997:2). Because the reality of the working conditions for most teachers is that they continue to spend most of their time working in isolation and are able to observe colleagues and discuss in any depth problems of practice only rarely, there can be no doubt that learning in collegial and collaborative ways can have advantages. However, although Stoll *et al.* (2006) have claimed that in terms of globalization and 'rapid change', learning 'can no longer be left to individuals' and that 'whole school communities need to learn together and take charge of change' (Stoll *et al.*, 2006:222), this is, perhaps, an over-simplification since much informal learning is conducted by individuals and there is a plethora of evidence that individuals, whether children or adults, can and do learn alone as well as with others. Yet to improve their teaching and understand better the complexities of student learning and the influences of contexts on this, they need to do both. Furthermore, if teachers are to use their 'decisional capital' wisely, then they themselves need to participate in the design of their own learning opportunities with others. PLCs enable them to do this. In fact, at least in theory, they create opportunities for teachers to engage in the full range of PLD activities reported in this and Chapter 5. In PLCs, most teachers are likely to find satisfaction and benefits from the high levels of ownership of and engagement with activities concerned with furthering both their understandings of their classrooms and the means of improving these, and, given the norms of working for the most part alone, from collaborating with colleagues.

Characteristics of PLCs

Lieberman and Miller defined learning communities as 'on-going groups ... who meet regularly for the purposes of increasing their own learning and that of their students' (2008:2) and much attention has been given over recent years to their benefits. Although such groups might be different in form and context, they 'share some fundamental core beliefs and values' (Lieberman and Miller, 2011:16), for example, nurturing a collaborative environment, honesty between participants and 'a commitment to the growth and development of individual members and to the group as a whole' (Lieberman and Miller, 2011:16). Their list of practices, which characterize successful learning communities derived from the authors' own extensive experiences, is useful:

- They must meet regularly and take the time to build collegial relationships based on trust and openness
- They work hard to develop a clear purpose and a collective focus on problems of practice
- They create routines and rituals that support honest talk and disclosure
- They engage in observation, problem-solving, mutual support, advice giving, and peer teaching and learning
- They purposefully organise and focus on activities that will enhance learning for both the adults and students in the schools
- They use collaborative inquiry to stimulate evidence-informed conversations
- They develop a theory of action
- They develop a set of core strategies for connecting their learning to student learning

(Lieberman and Miller, 2011:19)

In reporting the findings of the *Effective Practices in Continuing Professional Development* project, Earley and Porritt (2009) found four key factors which underpinned success, 'irrespective of the activity' (p. 119):

- Participants' ownership of PD activity
- Engagement with a variety of PD opportunities
- Time for reflection and feedback
- Collaborative approaches to PD

(Cited in Earley and Porritt, 2014:117)

This is at the heart of the rationale for establishing 'learning communities', rather than continuing to rely only or predominantly upon externally provided PD which 'is often perceived by teachers as fragmented, disconnected, and irrelevant to the real problems of classroom practice' (Lieberman and Mace, 2008:226–234). Stoll *et al.* (2006) identify and discuss five key characteristics of PLCs: i) shared values and vision, ii) collective responsibility, iii) reflective professional inquiry (deprivatization of practice), iv) collaboration and v) group learning (op cit. p.226–227). They acknowledge that these require time to become established. Relational trust – an essential part of these – is paramount. It underpins, for example, successful leadership distribution and collaboration. In later research, Wong (2010) also provides a useful idealized model (Figure 6.3) that summarizes the key elements:

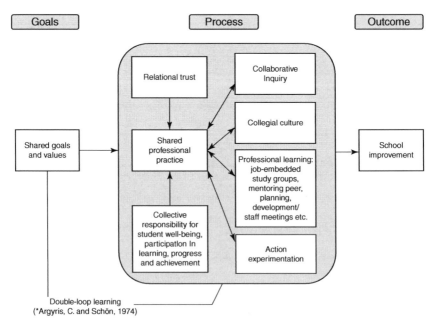

* In researching how professionals think in action, Argyris and Schön (1974) distinguished between *single-loop* and *double-loop* learning. In the former, practitioners search for solutions to immediate problems without consideration of the underlying principles, values and contexts. In the latter, more reflective mode, they address these.

FIGURE 6.3   Elements of a professional learning community
Source: Adapted from Wong, 2010:625

Establishing PLCs

Whilst much has been written about the desirability and positive effects of membership of PLCs on teachers' learning and well-being, for many schools they will be an end in view, rather than a present reality, since there will always be some teachers, however small a minority, who will not engage fully. Nurturing, establishing and sustaining PLCs, then, will be an aspiration of school leaders and teachers with particular sets of values. It will require particular values, practices and relationships. Becoming and remaining a PLC is conditional upon the establishment across the school of principles and practices of collaboration, trust, a willingness to engage in reflection, and change, where appropriate, as a result. Kruse and Louis (2007) identified five factors in achieving success in establishing and sustaining successful PLCs:

- *Extended time*: 'helping teachers beyond comfortable positions in "fragmented communities" is a long-term proposition' (p. 115);
- *Keep all eyes on teaching and learning*: 'not just on raising test scores, but on increasing teachers' ability to think about how their collective work affected student learning' (p. 115);
- *The need for top-down initiatives*: '… there is an important place for top-down initiatives to create PLCs' (p. 116);
- *Resilience*: the sustained commitment of change leaders and their capacity to manage and overcome obstacles is key to success;
- *The district as initiator of PLC initiatives*: in the English 'self-improving' school system, local authorities (school districts) play a less-prominent role. However, TSAs, 'chains' of schools and MATs may be said to have the primary responsibilities for PLD functions in the interests of school improvement and so, as part of this, provide opportunities for the development of the *individual, social and decisional capital* of their staff.

PLCs require the discipline of learning to start with dialogue 'while traditional organizations require management systems that control people's behavior, learning organizations invest in improving the quality of thinking, the capacity for reflection and team learning, and the ability to develop shared visions and shared understandings …' (Senge, 1990:287). To achieve this requires leaders with particular vision, values, qualities and abilities and teachers with a strong commitment to their own learning and that of others.

Capacity-building

Nurturing and sustaining human and social capital among teachers as a means of extending their individual and collective motivations and capacities to influence student learning and achievement takes time and is not always a smooth journey. Hipp and her colleagues documented the on-going journeys of two schools which aspired to become PLCs (Hipp *et al.*, 2008). They did so on the basis that

Definitions, descriptors, and images of what schools should look like are abundant in the literature … What is missing is documentation as to how these visions become a reality and detail about what people do … the complexity of their journeys; and the investment of effort, time and determination needed to build and system those cultures.

(Hipp et al.*, 2008:174)*

They provide an analytical framework through which schools – especially principals – might find useful in identifying, charting and judging their progress (see Table 6.3).

Like Stoll and her colleagues (Stoll *et al.*, 2006), they found a direct association between the nature of the school cultures in general – 'the shared assumptions, beliefs, values, and habits that constitute the norms for the school that shape how professionals think, feel and act'– and their relative opportunities and capacities to build a PLC (Hipp *et al.*, 2008:176). Like Stoll and her colleagues, also, they do not regard a school's culture as static or stable. Key indicators of success in both

TABLE 6.3 PLC dimensions and descriptions

Dimensions	Description
Shared and supportive leadership	Administrators share power, authority and decision-making, while promoting and nurturing leadership
Shared values and vision	The staff share visions that have an undeviating focus on student learning and support norms of behaviour that guide decisions about teaching and learning
Collective learning and application	The staff share information and work collaboratively to plan, solve problems and improve learning opportunities
Shared personal practice	Peers meet and observe one another to provide feedback on instructional practices, to assist in student learning and to increase human capacity
Supportive conditions – relationships	Peers meet and observe one another to provide feedback on instructional practices, to assist in student learning and to increase human capacity
Supportive conditions – structures	…include respect, trust, norms of critical inquiry and improvement and positive, caring relationships among the entire school community
External factors	…include parents, community and central office

Source: Hipp *et al.*, 2008:175.

schools were, perhaps not surprising in view of the existing research intentionally that focuses upon successful school principalship,

- a strong moral purpose, evidenced by an emphasis upon student learning or the drive for improvement decisions;
- shared vision, purpose and direction for the school;
- leadership which was focused on and pro-actively engaged in building and supporting social capital among teachers through the establishment of collaborative learning and team building, broadening the base for informed decision-making;
- cultures of inclusion and relational trust;
- high expectations of themselves and students;
- deprivatization of classroom life;
- communities of instructional practice in which classroom teaching and learning were the focus of regular, sustained observation and discussion.

Phases of development

Stoll *et al.* (2006) suggest a direct association between the progress of educational reforms and individual teacher and organizational capacity as 'a complex blend of motivation, skill, positive learning, organisational conditions and culture, and infrastructure of support' (Stoll *et al.*, 2006:221) and raise important issues for all who wish to lead and participate in PLCs. We know, for example, that

1. It is unlikely that all teachers will necessarily always be able to maintain a consistently high level of motivation throughout their careers. They are likely to experience fluctuations and these are likely to be associated with the quality of relationships and leadership in their work environments as well as the nature of new policy demands, changes in *societal* expectations and unanticipated changes in personal circumstances. For example, energy levels for many teachers erode over time (Day *et al.* 2007).
2. The nature of organizational culture, conditions and support infrastructure will, by and large, depend upon the presence, quality and continuity of school leadership.
3. Such quality is likely to vary both within and between schools.
4. PLCs take time to grow.

Tables 6.4 through 6.7 identify three phases in the formation and development of the norms of group identity, the navigation of 'fault lines' and the tensions that are necessary parts of the process of moving towards communal responsibility for the growth of individuals that is an essential feature of PLCs.

These tables should not be taken to represent a prescriptive checklist. In fact, it is likely that PLCs will develop as a result of the combination of accumulation of these dimensions over time. The realities of schools as living, dynamic organ-

TABLE 6.4 Formation of group identity and norms of interaction

Beginning	Evolving	Mature
Identification with sub-groups Sense of individualism overrides responsibility to group norms Undercurrent incivility	Pseudo-community Recognition of unique contributions of individual members Open discussion of interactional norms Recognition of need to regulate group behaviour	Identification with whole group Recognition that group is enriched by multiple perspectives Developing new interactional norms Communal responsibility for and regulation of behaviour

Source: Grossman *et al.*, 2001, cited in Lieberman and Miller, 2008:14.

TABLE 6.5 Navigating fault lines

Beginning	Evolving	Mature
Denial of difference Conflict goes backstage	Appropriation of difference by dominant position Conflict erupts onto main stage and is feared	Understanding and productive use of difference Conflict is expected feature of group life and dealt with openly and honestly

Source: Grossman *et al.*, 2001, cited in Lieberman and Miller, 2008:14.

TABLE 6.6 Navigating the essential tensions

Beginning	Evolving	Mature
Lack of agreement over purposes of professional community	Begrudging willingness to let different people pursue different activities	Recognition that teacher learning and student learning are fundamentally intertwined

Source: Grossman *et al.*, 2001, cited in Lieberman and Miller, 2008:14.

isms which are subject to a complex mix of external and internal influences and interventions in which leaders, teachers, students and parents interact are reflected in an extract from private correspondence by Margaret Wheatley (an advocate of complexity theory as a means of understanding organizations), cited by Hipp and her colleagues:

> There is no objective reality out there waiting to reveal its secrets. There are no recipes or formulae, no checklists or advice that describes 'reality'. There

TABLE 6.7 Communal responsibility for individual growth

Beginning	Evolving	Mature
Belief that teachers' responsibility to students' intellectual growth is an individual responsibility Contributions to group are acts of individual volition	Recognition that colleagues can be resources for one's learning Recognition that participation is expected	Commitment to colleagues' growth Acceptance of rights of individuals and group obligations

Source: Grossman *et al.*, 2001, cited in Lieberman and Miller, 2008:14.

is only what we create through our engagement with others and with events. Nothing really transfers; everything is always new and different and unique to each of us.

(Wheatley, 2001, cited in Hipp et al., 2008:192)

Challenges to the successful establishment of PLCs: the influence of workplace culture

Elmore (2002:26) argues persuasively that regardless of the quality of PD activities, they are likely to have only a 'modest to negative' effect if the culture and conditions of the classroom to which the teacher returns are exactly the same: '… to use professional development as an instrument of instructional improvement, schools and school systems will have to re-organise themselves in order to make substantial changes in the conditions of work for teachers and students.'

In effect, without the presence of such associated, more general, school improvement, it is likely that the growth of PLCs will be limited. Lieberman and Miller (2011:20) highlight five important change challenges that learning communities may face:

1. the norms of behaviour (e.g. openness to new ideas and practices) that may be in conflict with those prevalent in the department, faculty or school as a whole;
2. the press from inside and outside the school for 'quick-fix' solutions to problems of practice without trying first to understand and address the root;
3. finding time to engage in sustained conversations that enable complexities of practice to be unpacked and taking collective decisions about how to move forward;
4. finding time to develop mutual trust through honest talk about differences as well as similarities between participant's beliefs, values and practices;
5. sustaining a commitment to the learning community in the face of 'routine pressures' of school life and, often, 'rapidly changing demands' by policymakers on teachers, teaching and learning.

The more a school culture is characterized by high levels of individual teacher and/ or department isolation (Lortie, 1975), the more difficult it will be to change to one which provides the optimum conditions for establishing a PLC. Perhaps this is why there are still so few empirical studies of 'successful' PLCs (Joyce, 2004; McLaughlin and Talbert, 2001, 2006; Cowan *et al.*, 2004; Bolam *et al.*, 2005; Marzano *et al.*, 2005; Stoll *et al.*, 2006, Stoll and Seashore, 2007; Harris and Jones, 2010). So, whilst collaborative developments among staff are likely to develop greater motivation, self-efficacy, collegiality, trust, sense of agency and teacher commitment and effectiveness (Day *et al.*, 2007), without the leadership-led development of cultures of collegiality, they are less likely to be achieved.

5. School-to-school support: networked learning

As Little and Veugelers (2005: 278, 290) have asserted '… a school's or group's capacity to exploit the resources of external (network) participation seemed clearly contingent on internal leadership and professional community … Networks cannot be proclaimed, they have to be built through formal and informal processes …'

Although participation in school-to-school networks in theory enables teachers and others to experience a broader range of practices and ways of thinking about practices, their success is likely to depend upon two key factors: i) who determines the focus of their work and ii) support from inside their own school. For example, in the 1990s the Dutch government stimulated the formation of networks between universities and schools as part of a strategy for re-structuring secondary education. However, as Veugelers (2005:286) reports,'school participants in the 'network' had no feeling of ownership and empowerment … collegial and horizontal learning … They had no feeling that it was their network. They were just passive consumers.'

The result was that most stopped functioning after a short time. In the first decade of this century, the newly established National College for School Leadership (NCSL) launched a 'Network Learning Communities' initiative to encourage schools to form 'inquiry' networks. Half of the funding for these was provided by the NCSL and half (in kind) by the schools. Some networks formed working relationships with universities, but it was their choice whether to do so. Although most of the schools in England who participated reported positive learning gains for their teachers, when the government funding ended four years later, many gradually fell away. Although there had been a strong sense of ownership, this had been mixed with some resentment caused by the monitoring, bureaucratic reporting and accountability measures that had been conditions for receiving the funding. As noted in earlier chapters, more recently governments in England have encouraged a 'self-improving school system' through the formation of TSAs, again using financial incentives. These are groups of schools (primary, secondary or a mix) which, under the leadership of 'Teaching Schools' (judged to be 'outstanding' by Ofsted), engage in a prescribed range of entrepreneurial (income-generating) and improvement activities consistent with the government's commitment to raising pre-service and in-service standards of education: initial teacher preparation programmes, leadership training, school-to-school support, continuing PD programmes, curriculum development through specialist and local leaders of education and research and development. At the time of writing, it is too early to judge whether this version of networked learning communities as embedded within system-based structures of groups of schools will succeed as an improvement, standards-raising model. Certainly, its success or otherwise will be based upon the willingness, ability and capacity of 'Teaching Schools' to be entrepreneurial. Once again, the initial financial incentives from government are time limited and the sustainability of the business model itself is unproved.

6. The challenges of establishing and sustaining school–university partnerships: a third space

> Oftentimes what university faculty bring to schools through partnerships are deemed to be unusable by classroom teachers. Teachers are often looking for quick practical applications of techniques or resources they can use in their classrooms rather than exploring the deeper theoretical underpinnings. In contrast, the other side of the coin, university faculty are looking to make connections with theory and practice that may not be apparent in teachers' classroom decisions …
>
> *(Yamagata-Lynch* et al.*, 2007:365)*

School–university partnerships are not new by any means. Historically, they have related to initial or pre-service training relationships, primarily embedded in the 'practicum' or teaching practice element. Some of the most imaginative were in the form of 'PD schools' in which universities worked with school mentors to enhance the learning of students, and such learning 'spilled over' into in-service work. In the USA, Lieberman has pioneered school-centred partnerships, again with universities in a support role (Lieberman and Wood, 2003: Lieberman and Miller, 2004). In England, also, colleagues from Cambridge launched the IQEA (Improving the Quality of Education for All), in which schools 'bought in' to an improvement programme which was, though highly participative, school-centred and school-led, essentially a sustained programme of support by university staff.

> The old paradigm of university-based teacher education where academic knowledge is viewed as the authoritative source of knowledge about teaching needs to change to one where there is a non-hierarchical interplay between academic, practitioner, and community expertise.
>
> *(Zeichner, 2010:89)*

When Zeichner wrote of the problem of 'disconnect' between universities and schools in the context of pre-service teacher preparation, he was acknowledging the wider problems of academia. In many countries, government policies of self-sufficiency and entrepreneurship have caused universities to become more business oriented, with the rise of metrics to assess the worthiness of academic publications. 'Grant capture' has become a familiar challenge as universities seek to establish their positions in national and global league tables. Alongside demands to increase 'impact' and 'engagement' of 'user communities', the pressure to publish increases year by year – and the fact is that involvement by academics in school–university partnerships provides little hope of sustained academic outputs of these kinds.

Although there are exceptions, this statement of division is still largely true. This is despite policy changes in many countries that have acknowledged school- and classroom-generated practical knowledge as being fundamental to high-quality teacher education. In some countries, for example England, practical knowledge and 'evidence-based practice' is embedded in pre-service teacher education, much of which takes place in and is run by schools, and in the advocacy of recent governments for a 'self-improving system' of schools in which collaboration within and between schools has become the norm and in which universities are firmly placed at the periphery, becoming 'service' agents. In these partnerships, the traditional authority of the knowledge held by academics is diminished.

Zeichner, in what might be regarded by some as a voice in the wilderness and by others as a reasonable idea now overtaken by time and circumstance, uses the concept of a 'third space' (p. 92) that would enable school- and university-based teacher educators to work together in less hierarchical ways. Such a third space, defined as 'a transformative space where the potential for an expanded form of learning and the development of new knowledge are heightened' (Gutiérrez, 2008:152), is precisely what successful partnerships already demonstrate through, for example, the location where meetings occur, the on-going dialogue in which neither academic nor practitioner dominates, the initial engagement and joint decision-making, the clear but adaptive differentiation of roles and responsibilities, and the building of trust and the commitment of all partners. These partnerships represent a commitment to 'mutuality', a change from the traditional transactional relationships to the transformational where trust, knowledge sharing, collaboration and inter-dependence are central in achieving their success through their

1. structures: change from university-centred to school-centred;
2. relationships: change from one-way to reciprocal;
3. co-construction of knowledge: from learning as independently constructed, dependent upon either only experience or only theoretical to learning as co-constructed, self-regulated but drawn from multiple knowledge sources;
4. mutuality: engagement in recursive cycles of collaborative inquiry focused on understanding and resolving problems of practice which they identify
5. quality, in-time support in decisions to change: effective school partnerships focus on constructive ways to produce collaboratively beneficial change by affirming members and stakeholders (Calabrese, 2006:173).
6. social capital: key for the development of school–university partnerships. The attributes of social capital are bonding, bridging and linking. Bonding

represents the strength of the relationship that members have with one another, the relationship is based on similarity of beliefs and values and the informality associated with close relationships. Bridging represents the relationship of group members based on shared interests and can occur within and across communities. Linking refers to associations that are formed between or among communities, individuals and groups with the goal of gaining access to needed resources for social and economic development (Healy, 2003, cited in Calabrese, 2006:174);

7. trust building: closely linked to social capital;
8. appreciative inquiry: this process is in contrast to the monitoring and assessment culture that pervades many schools and classrooms, and arguably it results in greater gains. It fits well with the values that lie behind emphases in i) to vii) since it represents a collaborative rigorous process of seeking to ask positive questions of teachers and their schools, which both affirm existing strengths, success and potential, and identify new possibilities for action which build on these. So dialogues about teaching and learning are perceived to be appreciated rather than threatening to professional identify and through which 'problems of practice' become 'challenges of expanding practice';
9. practitioner inquiry/action research: these modes of operation have been widely documented and are closely associated with social capital, trust and appreciative inquiry.

Until the recent past, school–university partnerships have been led by university staff. With system change in many countries, however, the nature and scope of these relationships have changed. Nevertheless, there continue to be several potential problems that need to be resolved:

1. power (Who decides on the focus, process and intended outcomes? How can parity be assured?);
2. roles, responsibilities, relationships (Who is responsible for what, and how are resources gained and distributed?);
3. time (How may work, once begun, be sustained? How is time financed? By whom?);
4. reciprocity (How can trust and trustworthiness be built?);
5. credibility (How may university staff show that their knowledge and skills add value?);
6. from co-operation to collaboration (How may the process move from contrived collaboration to authentic collaboration?);
7. outcomes/reward (How can both/all parties benefit in ways which will enhance their own moral purposes and fulfil organizational requirements?);
8. boundary management and boundary crossing as languages, norms of thinking/habits of mind implicit in the different academic and practitioner communities need to be understood and learned (between roles and responsibilities within the partnership);

9. sustainability (How can parties plan for the ending of the partnership?);
10. knowledge (How can academic and practical knowledge be equally respected and used?).

Conclusions

There is increasing evidence internationally that school learning cultures and teaching and learning practices are likely to improve as a result of teachers' participation in social learning through, for example, lesson study, mentoring and coaching, communities of practice, PLCs, networks and school–university partnerships. It must be acknowledged, however, that the level of their commitment will be enhanced or constrained by the extent to which the purposes and processes of, and intended outcomes of, participation match teachers' own values and pre-dispositions and are embedded in school culture (Stoll *et al.*, 2006).

Teachers will be influenced by their past experiences of the benefits (or otherwise) of collaborative work, current relationships, the quality and disposition of the principal, and whether they believe that their work will benefit through placing group interest either alongside or over their own self-interests. Ning *et al.* (2015) analysed the effects of individual teacher values and dispositions towards collegiality and collaboration on the effectiveness of their professional learning in teams – arguably a key component of PLCs – in 96 Singapore schools. They found, for example, that 'collectivism' was both directly and indirectly associated with the quality and effects of collaboration for teams working in 'low power distance' cultures in which hierarchical power distance relationships are less in evidence (for example, in schools in which leadership roles are widely distributed and where open discussion and shared decision-making are the norm); and that authentic, as distinct from contrived, team collegiality is a 'crucial determinant of team collaboration' (Ning *et al.*, 2015:350). They found also that in 'high' collectivist cultures, knowledge sharing is likely to be more prevalent than in 'low' collectivist cultures.

> In low collectivist cultures, knowledge sharing can be more difficult as individuals view knowledge as a source of power, and knowledge hoarding [as] a tool which can produce advantages and success for oneself. But in high collectivism cultures, knowledge sharing is much more common if it is seen to be beneficial to the group.
>
> *(Ning* et al., *2015:340)*

Although it is important to acknowledge the particular country-culture influence in which higher power distance (acceptance of hierarchy) and collectivism prevail (group well-being is more important than individual reward), their findings have relevance to the development of PLCs in schools in other countries.

It seems, then, that success in learning and development activities as social endeavours is likely to be achieved and sustained when:

1. Each teacher is able to feel that the investment of time – often additional to what is required by their formal conditions of work – is beneficial in that what they do and what and how they learn, whether directly or indirectly, is relevant to their personal and professional needs (e.g. revisiting vision, sense of agency and autonomy, emotional commitment, job satisfaction, well-being), as well as those of their schools and students.
2. There is evidence that the functional and attitudinal purposes and needs of teachers are met.
3. There is a growth of teachers' autonomy through, for example, distributed leadership and decisional capital (Hargreaves and Fullan, 2012).
4. Within school social learning, school-to-school and school–university partnership learning are particularly valuable when learning is then able to be fed back into each single school and single classroom in which all teachers spend most of their working lives and through which they can provide the most impact on student learning and achievement.
5. School leaders promote teacher learning actively in their own schools through building cultures of collegiality and trust. An important means of achieving these is by providing conditions of work which minimize stress (Leithwood *et al.*, 1999; Ware and Kitsantas, 2007) by, for example, ensuring that changes demanded by external initiatives are managed internally in ways which support teacher autonomy, nurture their professional capital, build trust, minimize disruptions to teachers' sense of positive, stable professional identity and build their capacities for commitment and resilience.

Implicit in what is reported in research on the kinds of learning as social endeavour discussed in this chapter is that effective PLD requires (i) the provision of space and time for teachers to reflect on their existing beliefs and practices with colleagues – *not all schools provide these*; (ii) emotional support in environments of individual, relational and organizational trust – *not all schools invest in the care of teachers as learners*; (iii) teachers who are lifelong learners – *not all teachers are*; and (iv) school leaders who are able to create cultures of sustained commitment by teachers to both individual and collective learning that is both functional and attitudinal in its orientation, ensuring that high levels of teacher commitment and resilience are nurtured, developed and sustained throughout their careers – *not all leaders do this*.

7

THE IMPORTANCE OF
HIGH-QUALITY LEADERSHIP

It is not surprising that ensuring the quality of school leadership has become a priority in education policy agendas in governments across the world. It plays a 'key role in improving classroom practice, school policies and connections between schools and the outside world' (OECD, 2008:19). This chapter focuses upon what research tells us about the nature and practices of successful school principals' work as it applies to teachers' worlds and work. It draws upon a range of empirical research in examining how successful principals, as leaders of learning, influence teachers and build their capacities to teach to their best through their values, qualities, strategies and actions and how they do so during different phases of school development. Whilst it does not necessarily follow that teacher and teaching effectiveness will depend directly upon the quality of the principal, a range of research internationally (e.g. Day *et al.*, 2000, 2011; Leithwood and Hallinger, 2012; Robinson *et al.*, 2009; McKinsey, 2010) has shown that he or she has the power to influence these indirectly through vision, values, structures, cultures and relationships. Additionally, support by principals has been found to be the most significant factor in teachers' decisions to stay or leave teaching (Boyd, 2010). This connection between teacher commitment, resilience, retention, the quality of teaching and learning and the work of the school principal supports the findings of a raft of empirical research that:

1. The influence of principals on pupil outcomes is second only to that of teachers (Leithwood *et al.*, 2006).
2. Of the five key dimensions of effective leadership, it is the promotion and participation in professional learning and development by principals which has the greatest effect (Robinson *et al.*, 2009).

These claims provide strong, research-informed recognition of the important role played by school principals in creating and sustaining 'can do' cultures of high expectations, care and achievement and, as a key part of these, promoting a range of professional learning and development opportunities as a means of supporting, extending and, where appropriate, challenging the functional and attitudinal development of staff. In a school that values learning for all, it would be reasonable to find leaders who themselves are learners through, for example, the promotion and participation of inquiry-oriented activities, for example, of the kind discussed in Chapters 5 and 6, which are designed to interrogate existing thinking and practices, and ways of being and behaving and, where appropriate, challenge these to find ways of improving them.

Although it has been claimed that, 'The quality of a school cannot exceed the quality of its teachers' (Southworth, 2011:73), as we have seen in Chapter 1 of this book, there are other influences on students that most teachers will be able to manage but not always be able to counter or build upon fully, regardless of their on-going commitment to teach to their best and well.

Essentially, there are two sources of support on which teachers will need to call if they are to be persistent in their efforts to provide all students with continuing knowledgeable, differentiated, time-sensitive, skilfully constructed and emotionally responsive opportunities for deep learning and achievement. The first source is their inner sense of moral purpose, professionalism, professional identity, motivation, commitment and resilience. The second source that provides professional nourishment is the quality of the workplace environment. It is the school principal who has major responsibility for this. The increasingly complex and diverse, sometimes conflicting, social, emotional and performance-oriented demands on schools not only create pressures upon teachers but also require their principals to be more overtly successful in demonstrating a greater range of value-added achievements among all their students, especially those which relate to measurable outcomes and those (attitudinal outcomes) which relate to well-being, social harmony, equity and democracy (defined differently in different countries). This has caused the work of principals to become more demanding internally in the school, and externally as they work with an increasing number of diverse and sometimes conflicting communities of interest. The combinations of demands are not all new but they are certainly more intensively driven through government policy agendas in this century than in the last (Day, 2014:638).

Models of successful leadership: a brief appreciation and critique[1]

In the recent past, it has been claimed that four conceptual models dominate research that seeks to identify those principals who are likely to meet with success: 'transformational', 'instructional', 'distributed' and 'contingency' (Day *et al.*, 2016). The following features are central to each of these models:

1 Transformational

This involves raising levels of intrinsic motivation among staff and students through a combination of building a shared vision, setting directions, re-designing the organization, developing people, providing support for teaching and learning and connecting with the school's external community (Leithwood, 2010). The work of these principals has been characterized as, 'a pursuit of common goals, empowerment of people, development and maintenance of a collaborative culture as well as promoting processes of teacher development' (Hargreaves and Fink, 2006:99). This model is often presented as a counter to the rewards and punishment (exchange of goods) model of behaviour implicit in the 'transactional exchange' model of leadership.

2 Instructional

This has been offered as a more effective alternative through a particular focus upon the core business of classroom teaching and learning. It has been claimed that the more leaders do this, 'the greater their influence on student outcomes' (Robinson, 2010:12), and that transformational leadership which focuses upon improving the quality of relationships between leaders and staff 'is not predictive of student outcomes' (Robinson *et al.*, 2008:665). This model has been criticized for its failure to identify the overlap with similar categories concerning teaching and learning, which are contained within the four original core components of the transformational leadership model – *setting directions, developing people, redesigning the school organization and improving the instructional program* (Leithwood and Sun, 2012).

3 Distributed

This is based on the undeniable truth that a single leader is highly unlikely to be able to improve a school without entrusting other multiple individuals with leadership responsibilities. Thus, successful leadership for school improvement in this conceptualisation, becomes the 'product of the interactions among leaders, followers and aspects of their situation' (Spillane and Healy, 2010:256). The key to the success of distributed leadership is claimed to lie in 'enhancing the skills and knowledge of people in the organisation, creating a common culture of expectations around the use of those skills and knowledge … and holding individuals accountable for their contributions to the collective result' (Elmore, 2000:15). 'Distribution', however, is not the same as 'delegation'. Whilst both approaches may be pragmatic, the latter (delegation) implies less trust in sharing power in decision-making than the former, which implies a more democratized view of leadership. Moreover, there is increasing empirical research which reveals that successful leaders do not distribute leadership in the absence of informed trust (Day *et al.*, 2011).

4 Contingency

Essentially, this model suggests that decisions made by successful leaders are made solely in response to the interaction between environmental uncertainties, organisational structures and aspects of performance (Pennings, 1975). Whilst this calls for 'responsiveness', 'adaptivity' and 'flexibility', characteristics which are associated with successful leadership, it does not take account of the mediating influence and effect of leadership values, for example, moral and/or ethical educational purposes which have been found to be fundamental to successful leadership.

5 Values-led integrated leadership

Recent empirical research has found, however, that a fifth model, 'values-led integrated leadership', best represents the work of principals of successful schools. This model exposes the narrowness of the conception of 'instructional leadership', which focuses upon leaders' responses to policy demands for raising standards of classroom teaching, learning and student achievement. In the United States, Marks and Printy (2003) found that 'responding to these demands with an outmoded conception of "instructional" leadership was senseless, but engaging teachers in a collaborative dialogue about these issues and their implications for teaching and learning was essential' (Marks and Printy, 2003:392). These researchers and more recent large-scale mixed methods empirical research have shown that successful principals are those who draw from each of these through what has been described as *integrated* leadership:

> When transformational and shared instructional leadership coexist in an integrated form of leadership, the influence on school performance, measured by the quality of its pedagogy and the achievement of its pupils, is substantiated.
> *(Marks and Printy, 2003:370)*

National mixed methods research on the impact of leadership on pupil outcomes in effective and improving primary and secondary schools in England (Day *et al.*, 2011; Day, Gu and Sammons, 2016) has nuanced this further by finding clear evidence of the presence of *values-led integrated leadership*, which combines the essence of 'transformational', 'instructional' and 'distributed'. *This research found that what successful principals say and do and how they respond to the performance-related mandates of results-driven government reform agendas is contingent upon broader sets of educational values, that building success means that principals' work on a number of different personal, interpersonal and organizational levels simultaneously, and that building values-led integrated leadership takes time.*

Five key actions for success

1 Building organisational capacity takes time

> Developing school capacity is central to the principal leadership work of fostering school conditions that support effective teaching and learning.
> *(Lai, 2014:165–166)*

In reporting the findings of a series of analyses of quantitative studies on the effects of collaborative leadership on school improvement capacity and student learning in US primary schools over a four-year period, Hallinger and Heck (2010) concluded that:

> Empirical research finds that successful school leadership creates conditions that support effective teaching and learning and builds capacity for professional learning and change ... focuses on strategic school-wide actions that are ... shared among the principal, administrators and others ... [and entail] ... the use of governance structures and organisational processes that empower(ed) staff and students, encourage(d) broad participation in decision-making, and foster(ed) shared accountability for student learning.
>
> *(Hallinger and Heck, 2010:97)*

School principals can play a fundamental and continuing role in promoting change for improvement by virtue of their position and power and individual and collective influence. It is equally clear that their values and their expression of these, through the management and leadership systems which they establish and the cultures which they nurture, play a key part in their success or otherwise.

Writing in the context of continuing externally initiated school reform, Elmore defined capacity as 'the fund of skill and knowledge that the organization can bring to bear in responding to external pressure' (Elmore, 2008:43). In the context of building schools as learning communities for adults as well as pupils, Mitchell and Sackney (2000) identified the need for a 'direct, sustained, focused attention on building capacity' (p. 12) in three areas – the *personal* (on the basis that caring, commitment and creative energy are essential qualities in effective teachers), the *interpersonal* (on the basis that relationships of trust, respect and collective purpose count in identifying and solving problems) and the *organisational* (on the basis that school structures and cultures that work best are flexible, able to adapt to changes from the outside within a clearly held and articulated set of values, and open to new ideas from inside the school. Frost and Durrant (2003) later added a fourth capacity, *classroom practice* (on the basis that teachers need to be effective leaders of learning in their classrooms). Arguably, building individual capacity, interpersonal capacity as well as organizational capacity is at the heart of the improvement agendas of all principals and teachers themselves.

2 School improvement phases

Building capacity is a complex process, takes time and depends upon principals' abilities to diagnose both organizational and individual needs and to find ways of addressing these.

A national research project with principals of effective and improving schools in England, for example, revealed four 'generic' school improvement phases:

1. Foundational
2. Developmental
3. Enrichment
4. Renewal

(Day et al., 2011)

Each of these phases contain within them combinations of fit-for-purpose context and time-sensitive improvement strategies, which received more, or less, emphasis within and across phases according to their purposes and levels of impact. Figure 7.1 provides an example of one such school's improvement journey.

Research findings about the importance of building relational trust, shared professional practice, individual and collective efficacy and agency, professional learning, collective responsibility for student and staff well-being, participation in learning, progress and achievement, collaborative inquiry and collegiality, during processes of school improvement, reveal the mix of complex factors which underpin success in and across each of these phases. It is important, also, to note that the time spent in each phase will differ between schools, for it is the combined and accumulated effects of these that enable them to progress. Strategies in each phase do not always end, but may continue through each phase (though the relative effort and energy many be different); and effective, successful principals do not move from one phase to another until they judge the school to be in a state of readiness to do so. Witness the words of one teacher who attests to the importance of the support of school leaders.

> The support of the senior management sustained my efforts. It is an external recognition and affirmation – which means you could keep trying, particularly in selected areas. This is not the same as trying in every area as before but to have more in-depth experiment with several areas ... Also, the principal was like a mentor. He demonstrated excellent strategic leadership and helped us make good decisions.
>
> *(Choi and Tang, 2009:774)*

This quotation from a mid-career teacher in a Chinese school supports the evidence from teachers in the VITAE project (see Chapter 3 for a detailed discussion) and is replicated by others across the world who work in schools that are led by effective, successful leaders.

3 Nurturing collective values

Since principals have considerable influence over workplace structures, cultures and conditions, the presence and extent of teachers' commitment, sense of professional identity and capacity for resilience and emotional energy – as well as sense of job fulfilment, efficacy and well-being – will in part be dependent upon the leaders' values, qualities and actions and the way they articulate these through what they do and who they are. As we have seen elsewhere in this book, the development of trusting, productive relationships is likely to lead to increased social, human and decisional capital. The observation that relationships 'can have positive effects because they constitute a form of social capital that is of value to children's academic success' (Goddard, 2003:59) might equally apply to the effects on teachers of strong relationships with colleagues and school and departmental leaders.

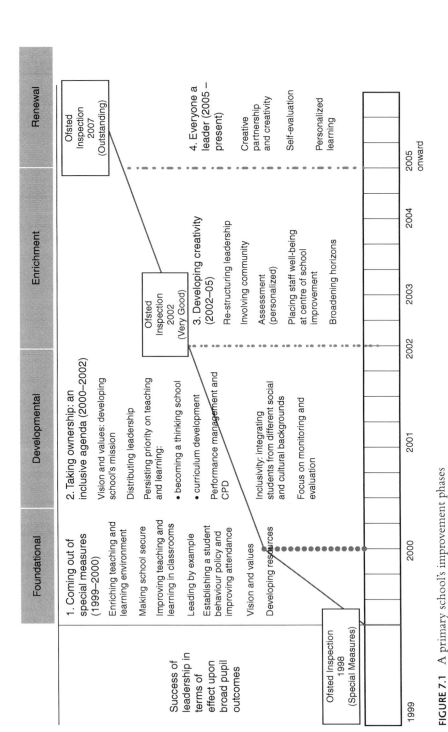

FIGURE 7.1 A primary school's improvement phases

Source: Day *et al.,* 2010:13

Productive, caring, trusting relationships contribute as much to the motivations and commitments of adults in the school as they do to those of students in the classroom. Leaders who strive for the emotional well-being and professional success of *teachers as well as students*, who see these as connected, will ensure that staff are provided with learning and development opportunities which are designed to contribute to their continuing intrinsic motivation, job satisfaction and emotional well-being, commitment, capacity for resilience and sense of positive professional identity (*attitudinal*) as well as those which focus upon curriculum and classroom teaching (*functional*). When teachers feel positive about themselves and their school, it is more likely that they will have a positive effect on both the learning climate in the classroom, the interest and motivation of students and, indirectly, student outcomes (Blasé, 2001; Robinson *et al.*, 2008; Day *et al.*, 2011).

In a study of Hong Kong secondary school principals' work, Lai (2014) created a typology of principal leadership practices in capacity-building, which provides a useful heuristic for reflection, since it is able to connect to the different purposes, substance and forms of professional learning and development which principals with different sets of values promote and which teachers in their schools may experience (See Table 7.1).

4 Distributing leadership

A fourth key action for success is the sharing of decision-making through the distribution of leadership. However, to be effective, the extent of the distribution will depend upon the level of trust and trustworthiness that the principal is able to grow and establish. There are many ways in which researchers have conceptualized the different patterns of distributed leadership: additive and holistic (Gronn, 2008); autocratic and ad hoc (Harris, 2008); leader-plus and parallel performance (Spillane, Camburn and Pajero, 2009); planned alignment and spontaneous alignment (Leithwood *et al.*, 2008); as well as pragmatic and opportunistic (MacBeath, 2008). In each, it is easy to see (a) differences in the range of organizational members to whom leadership in distributed, (b) the degree to which distributed forms of leadership are coordinated, (c) the extent of interdependence among those to whom leadership is distributed (d) the extent to which power and authority accompany the distribution of leadership responsibilities; and (e) the stimulus for leadership distribution.

Whilst much is now known about different forms of distributed leadership – from those which offer more to those which offer less participation in and, therefore, ownership of, decision-making processes – much less is known about 'when' and 'to what extent' heads distribute leadership during the school improvement journey and to what effect. Mascall, Leithwood, Strauss and Sacks (2008) found a significant relationship between a co-ordinated form of leadership distribution, which they label *planned alignment*, and a teacher variable labelled *academic optimism* (Woolfolk Hoy, Hoy, and Kurz, 2008). Planned alignment entails members of a leadership group planning their actions together, periodically reviewing their impact and revising accordingly. Academic optimism was measured as a compos-

TABLE 7.1 A typology of principal leadership practices in teacher capacity-building

Teacher capacity-building approaches	Teacher capacity-building practices	Teacher learning activities	Contextual conditions
Deficit approach	Favour an individualistic mode of teacher development and external sources of expertise to support teacher learning	Attend external PD courses. Pursue further studies at local universities	Emphasize the school's teacher resource constraints. Strive to accommodate reform requirements within existing structures
Interactive growth approach	Recognize the collective power of teacher learning and acting in communities of practice for school improvement	Enquire around curricular and pedagogical problems in professional/communities within and beyond school	Change organizational norms and structures (people, time and space) to attain effectiveness
Participatory-growth approach	Empower teachers to make decisions and initiate activities for school improvement	Enquire around curricular and pedagogical problems in professional communities within and beyond schools. Participate in making curricular and pedagogical decisions and initiating activities	Change organizational norms and structures (authority, people, time and space) to attain effectiveness

Source: Lai, 2014:170.

This table originally appeared in A. Maj (Ed.), *Post-privacy culture: Gaining social power in cyber-democracy* (pp. 223–239), first published by the Inter-Disciplinary Press.

ite of teacher trust, teacher efficacy and organisational citizenship behaviour, each of which has been significantly associated with student achievement. However, few educational researchers have, at the time of writing, established associations between the timing and forms of leadership distribution and the development of relational and organizational trust.

In the IMPACT project (Day *et al.*, 2011), the distribution of leadership responsibilities was associated with the growth of *informed* trust. It was progressive, beginning with the involvement of a few trusted senior colleagues and becoming more inclusive as informal trust was built through collaboration. Over time trust building and the distribution of leadership roles and responsibilities grew and were key to the success of successful leadership in all instances. Trust building acted both as a 'glue' to the growth of productive collaboration and as a 'lubricant' to its processes. Both trust, the distribution of leadership, and the growth of the organization capacity, were developed through the application of combinations and accumulations of context-sensitive, fit-for-purpose leadership strategies, relationships and actions. It was through these that success grew and was sustained. (See Day *et al.*, 2011, for a detailed discussion.) The extent to which leadership was distributed depended upon the principals' judgements about:

- The extent of staff members' expertise
- Forms of external pressure that prompt efforts to distribute leadership more broadly, for example, pressure to improve disappointing school performance
- The leadership functions(s) in relation to the scope of the goals to be accomplished
- The principals' experience and self-efficacy
- The principals' dispositions towards collaborative organizational cultures
- The quality of personal and interpersonal relationships.

In these successful schools, distributing leadership:

- Took time.
- Was associated with a strong belief by heads in the professionalism of their staff
- Depended upon existing levels of trust and trustworthiness
- Was nurtured strategically through on-going development of opportunities for consultation, participation, engagement and the exercise of agency in individual and collective decision-making processes
- Was associated with increases in job fulfilment, efficiency, effectiveness and a sense of the work of teaching and learning as a collective endeavour which encompassed shared instrumental and moral purposes
- Was associated with trust.

5 Leadership and organizational trust

> As well as the ethical imperative, there is a powerful business case for paying careful attention to trust. Trust underlies effective working relationships, and compelling research evidence points to the positive impact of trust on employee attitudes and behaviours, group functioning and levels of organizational performance.
>
> *(Dietz and Gillespie, 2011:7)*

Trust in others relies not only on the values and attributes of individuals or groups, but also is influenced by their predispositions and reactions and interactions in particular contexts and at particular times. Trust cannot, therefore, be viewed as simply a psychological pre-disposition or individually pre-determined characteristic or trait. Although personal dispositions contribute towards the creation and growth of trust, they will interact constantly with other variables to create an environment for improvement, making trust 'a necessary ingredient for cooperative action' (Seashore-Louis 2007:3). There is a clearly identifiable interplay, then, between heads' qualities or attributes, the interactive individual and social settings in which they conduct much of their leadership work and the development of individual, relational, organizational and community trust.

Why trust is important in schools

Molina-Morales *et al.* (2011:120) defines trust as:

> [T]he mutual confidence between parties to an exchange that none of them will engage in opportunistic behaviour that would exploit any others' vulnerabilities, and thereby violate the values, principles and standards of behaviour they have internalised as part of the exchange.

There is little doubt that the presence of trust can serve to diminish interpersonal boundaries at an informal level and assist in pursuing common interests within and between departments, schools and groups of schools. Trust and its companion, fairness, have been identified as important aspects of 'social exchange theory'. Social exchange theory has been defined as 'the voluntary actions of individuals that are motivated by the returns they are expected to bring and typically do in fact bring from others' (Blau, 1964:91). The theory has been described as 'one of the most important paradigms for comprehending employees' attitudes to others in the workplace (DeCorninck, 2010:1349). DeCorninck (2010) identifies three core elements which he regards as the bedrock of social exchange theory: *interactional, distributive* and *procedural*. Each of these elements can be seen in the everyday processes of school life. However, in schools, teachers are driven by ethical, altruistic principles, which cause them to go beyond the expectations of their work and which will primarily result in benefits to them. Much of the way in which success in schools is or is not achieved is likely to be influenced by the quality of the interactional, distributive and procedural elements of social exchange theory as applied not only to the teachers themselves, through the quality of relationships between teacher–student, teaching–learning, teacher–teacher and teacher–school leader(s), but also the attitudes towards learning, the academic attainments and the personal and social growth of their students, because teaching is essentially an altruistic endeavour, concerned with the functional and attitudinal.

Trust can facilitate knowledge sharing, the development of teaching (through, for example, peer tutoring, mentoring, lesson study and appraisal processes), and has been claimed to be a key factor in successful capacity-building, teamwork and in the growth of professional learning communities (see Chapters 5 and 6). Seminal empirical research by Bryk and Schneider (2003) on reasons for elementary schools' improved results in student attainment found that the 'relational trust' between teachers was a central factor. Research on elementary school principal effectiveness by Tschannen-Moran (2004) has also pointed to relationships of trust between teachers, parents and principals as key to improvement across a number of areas of school performance.

Trust and empowerment

[T]rust cannot be easily separated from expanded teacher empowerment and influence. Teachers are not passive actors in the school, but co-constructors of trust. As active professionals, teachers who feel left out of important decisions will react by withdrawing trust, which then undermines change.

(Seashore-Louis 2007:18)

Seldon (2009, Preface) argues that, 'a presumption of trust rather than a presumption of mistrust helps individuals and organisations to flourish' and that:

Trust builds better communities ... It facilitates people working together for common purposes, rests upon bonds rooted down at local level – in schools, clubs and professional organisations – and can only be built up over time.

(Seldon, 2009:10)

Leaders' attitudes towards trust and towards people significantly affects the way that relational trust develops. The actions of leaders, whose trust in staff is ethically driven, aim at individuals' *attitudinal* development, their motivation and commitment to their work and to the organization. Leaders whose trust is pragmatically or functionally driven, aiming to get tasks completed on a specific timescale, regardless of the cost or benefit to the individual, are likely to give staff very different messages about power and authority.

Fullan (2003: 64) captures the complexity of trust in organizations:

Only when participants demonstrate their commitment to engage in such work and see others doing the same can a genuine professional community grounded in relational trust emerge. Principals must take the lead and extend themselves by reaching out to others. On occasion, the principal may be called on to demonstrate trust in colleagues who may not fully reciprocate, at least initially. But they must also be prepared to use coercive power to reform a dysfunctional school community around professional norms. Interestingly, such authority may rarely need to be invoked thereafter once these new norms are firmly established.

The benefits of trust

Tschannen-Moran's research with principals of elementary schools found that

Trust functions as a lubricant of organizational functioning; without it, the school is likely to experience the overheated friction of conflict as well as a lack of progress toward its admirable goals.

(Tschannen-Moran, 2004:xi)

Handford (2011) went further by suggesting that trust in leaders,

1.   Affects students' test scores, citing the findings of Bryk and Schneider (2002:111) that elementary schools with a high-trust factor are three times as likely to increase test scores in reading (+8%) and mathematics (+20%) over a five-year period as those that do not have high-trust ratios.
2.   That teacher morale is strongly associated with higher student achievement, citing the findings of Hoy *et al.* (1991:183) that morale, defined as 'the sense of trust, confidence, enthusiasm and friendliness among teachers', is one of the seven features of a 'healthy' school.
3.   That the presence of trust between people facilitates change (Handford, 2011:3). Drawing on Bryk and Schneider (2002), Robinson (2007) also suggested associations between 'determinants', conditions for establishing relational trust, high-trust organizations and student achievement. See Figure 7.2.

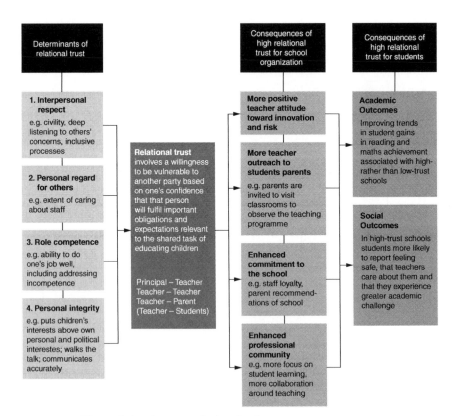

FIGURE 7.2   How relational trust works in schools
Source: Robinson, 2007: 20

Trust and trustworthiness: a reciprocal relationship

When teachers make trust discernments based on their own willingness to be vulnerable to another role group, they interpret the other parties' actions in terms of benevolence, reliability, competence, openness, and honesty.

(Hoy and Tschannen-Moran, 1999, cited in Van Maele
and Van Houtte, 2014: 173)

Trust which works best is that which is reciprocal. In other words, unless teachers trust the principal, it is unlikely that they will enter fully into different ways of teaching (a risk, especially for those experienced teachers who have established ways of working with students that they regard as 'successful'), behaving towards one another, parents and students in new ways, or even engaging in professional learning and development designed to encourage new ways of thinking about their work, unless they trust the principal. Individual and organizational development, as expressed, for example, through high individual and collective efficacy and teacher leadership, are therefore likely to be influenced by the extent to which staff are persuaded that the principal's leadership (vision, direction setting, initiatives) can be trusted to result in progress and improvement or further improvement in the conditions in which they work, their sense of professionalism and well-being, and the students' education. In other words, trust and trustworthiness are in a reciprocal relationship. Research suggests, also, that not only do principals need to be able to identify whom to trust but also how much and when to extend the trust. Additionally, leadership qualities of positivity and transparency, as expressed through, 'hope, resiliency, optimism and efficacy' are related to trust in principal leadership (Norman, Avolio and Luthans, 2010:351).

Active trust is exercised 'where our critical faculties are engaged when deciding who to trust or not to trust ... (that) ... we must make reasoned calculations on the trustworthiness of other individuals and organizations' (Seldon, 2009:6). It is 'the opposite of blind trust ... Trust has to be earned' (Seldon, 2009:26). Teachers' trust in the principal will be based upon the close knowledge and experience of the extent to which their experience change as progress and relationships as trusting and trustworthy. Accountability for the successful development and outcomes of organizational trust, like organizational learning and development, is a shared responsibility. Thus, the principal's trustworthiness is a mediating factor in successfully gaining and sustaining teacher trust. The relationship between trust and trustworthiness is therefore, reciprocal. Both are of equal importance in contributing to building teacher quality.

Emergent trust

Schools are

fundamentally social institutions that depend daily on the quality of the interpersonal relations with which they are imbued.

(Goddard, Salloum, Berebitsky, 2009, p. 293)

Trust and trustworthiness in schools can be built quickly or slowly. They are likely to be built with some staff (who share similar educational and relationship values with the principal) sooner than with others (who do not). They will be influenced by the quality of interactions as well as the keeping of promises (e.g. the meeting of deadlines or the provision of time to reflect) and may be developed or damaged by particular, sometimes unpredictable, interactions. Tschannen-Moran (2004), for example, outlined key leadership behaviours and specific actions that engender trust. For example, 'competence' is demonstrated when principals engage in 'problem solving, setting standards, buffering teachers, pressing for results' (p. 34). Growth is likely to be uneven across all staff, and likely to be experienced at different levels of intensity across an organization at any given time. Growth or lack of growth will be influenced by individual dispositions, the nature of the policy, school culture, 'the collective set of norms, values, and beliefs' (Collins and Smith, 2006:547), and relationship contexts. For both the principal and staff, then, trust and trustworthiness are 'emergent states'. They are founded in part upon the disposition of each party to trust others, for trust involves disclosure and feedback and, therefore, vulnerability. Pre-dispositions of teachers to trust may be based upon positive or negative experiences of other leaders. Trust building, therefore, involves both the cognitive and the affective.

Levels of trust

> Trust is a condition underlying co-operation and risk taking ... resulting in employee extra role behaviour ... trust moderates workplace performance and affects positive attitudes to work.
>
> *(Dirks and Ferrin, 2001)*

Although existing research points to close associations between the exercise of principal trust and higher teacher job satisfaction, well-being and commitment, it has not examined levels of trust, whether these fluctuate individually and collectively, why or how organizational trust is built, and the relationship between this and students' achievements. There has been very little research, which closely analyses how, when, and to what extent trust is built and enhanced by principals. An exception to this is a large-scale empirical national research project that focused upon unpicking the values, qualities, strategies and skills of successful principals over time (Day *et al.*, 2011). This found associations between the levels of trust in their colleagues and the timing and extent to which these principals distributed leadership (Day *et al.*, 2011). Perhaps not surprisingly, principals reported that they distributed leadership to just a few when they began their tenure; and it was only after some years of building trust and trustworthiness that they distributed leadership more widely. This kind of trust was not 'blind', purely 'principled' or 'ideological', but based upon close knowledge and the experience of working with and observing individuals in a variety of settings over time.

Three limitations of trust in organizations

Low trust

> Low trust between teachers presents a significant barrier to the establishment
> of these new norms of professionalism and collaboration. When teachers do
> not trust their colleagues, whether due to perceptions of a lack of compe-
> tence, benevolence, reliability or other factors, they are not likely to feel
> comfortable putting their own professional practice at risk through shared
> instructional planning, peer observations, or reflective dialogue.
>
> *(Tschannen-Moran, 2014:61)*

Levels of trust and fairness are likely to have important negative and positive influences on teachers' individual and collective professional identities, efficacy and agency
and well-being, and, arguably, their willingness and capacities to teach to their best
and well. For example, there may be a 'low trust' culture in the school. This may be
the product of leadership, which is perceived by teachers to fail to provide conditions that are perceived by teachers as below the standard required to enable them to
teach to their best and well; or where educational values of teachers and leaders are
in conflict; or where leaders make but do not keep promises. The increased monitoring and surveillance of teachers and whole schools that is a feature of results-driven
agendas may communicate low trust in the professional qualifications and professionalism of teachers to be effective. Schools may, for example, mimic Ofsted inspection
processes internally, creating their own internal surveillance cultures.

> [I]t is not formal controls per se (bureaucratic formalization and centraliza-
> tion) that are destructive of trust, flexibility, and cooperation … it is the
> perceptions and feelings of those in the organization toward the particular
> bureaucratic structures under which they work that can threaten trust.
>
> *(Forsyth and Adams, 2014:86)*

Principals may present inspection processes not as deficit, judgemental processes
but as improvement opportunities. Thus, 'surveillance' may become 'sharing practices' and 'monitoring' may become 'peer support'. The choices made by principals
will indicate different attitudes to teachers' professionalism and different levels of
trust. For successful principals, trust levels will vary and the variation will likely
depend on how they resolve the tensions between their own values, those embedded in reform initiatives from outside the school and knowledge of the teachers.

Distrust

Because trust requires a level of vulnerability between those who wish to develop it,
when distrust is felt, it is likely to develop quickly. In their study of teacher leadership, efficacy and trust, drawing particularly upon the work of Brewster and Railsback (2003) and Tschannen-Moran and Hoy (2000), Angelle and her colleagues

(2011) noted that principals who violate trust may have difficulty regaining it. If not challenged immediately it may become a dysfunctional part of the school culture.

> Once distrust becomes a part of the organization, it perpetuates. Examples of ways in which principals may violate trust include "public criticism, incorrect or unfair accusations, blaming of employees for personal mistakes, and insults" (Tshannen-Moran and Hoy, 2000, p. 576). This is true of the principal-teacher relationship as well as the teacher-student relationship. Obstacles to trust in a school also include frequent leadership turnover, personnel lay-offs, poor communication, top down decision making, and failure to remove ineffective teachers (Brewster and Railsback, 2003).
>
> *(Angelle et al., 2011:11)*

The comfort of togetherness

Molina-Morales *et al.* (2011), writing in the context of the capacity of business organizations to continue to develop and engage in innovation, argue that whilst the presence of trust is clearly beneficial for organizational development, it may also have a 'dark side'.

> Some level of trust is beneficial because it enables transfer of tacit knowledge and risk taking, but firms that over invest in trust, trust too much, or invest in trusting relationships that have little value for the firm, may be misallocating precious resources and/or taking unnecessary risks that could have substantial negative effects on their innovation performance.
>
> *(Molina-Morales et al., 2011:118)*

Too much trust among the same group of people or organizations for too long, may, they suggest, result in diminishing returns, as 'remaining with familiar patterns ... Is likely to lead to a cognitive "lock-in" that will tend to isolate them from the outside world' (Molina-Morales *et al.*, 2011:119). They suggest a mix of relationships. Although applied to businesses, there may be parallels in their findings with what Hargreaves (1995) characterized as 'comfortable collaboration' in schools, where tried and tested relationships had become so personally affable that initiatives targeted at growth and innovation, both of which involve degrees of risk, interact unhelpfully with the felt need to maintain existing harmonious relationships and may be subservient to that.

Leadership approaches

> Trust requires a balance of individual and collective needs ... a sensitive balance between the freedom of expression of the individual ... and the claims of the collective.
>
> *(Seldon, 2009:26–27)*

No single leadership approach can be regarded as relevant to promoting trust in all situations, but rather successful leaders use approaches which are appropriate to the needs and circumstances of varying situations and values led. They engage with others over time in:

- **Acts of individual, relational, organizational and community trust**: the increasing distribution of internal and external leadership influence and broadening of stakeholder participation
- **Building, broadening and deepening trustworthiness**: through repeated trustful interactions, structures and strategies which show consistency with agreed values and vision.

The principals in the IMPACT project (Day *et al.*, 2011) provide testimony of this as they spoke of growing success by:

1. Modelling care in their relationships with staff, pupils and parents, and the wider local community;
2. Enhancing teachers' professionalism through CPD (internal and external) and enabling and encouraging collaboration between teachers so that responsibilities and professional ethics were shared;
3. Demonstrating that whilst care was not used as a means to improve student performance, its presence did, nevertheless, have an indirect effect through the associated increases in pupil attendance, engagement with learning, self-efficacy, sense of agency and commitment.

Research in elementary and high schools in the USA (Bryk and Schneider, 2002; Seashore Louis, 2007) has identified 'social cohesion' as an important indicator of organizational trust and organisation trust as a predictor of student achievement. Heads, staff, students and parents in the IMPACT project spoke of the collective sense of purpose and participation, application of common behaviour protocols, co-operation and data-informed (rather than data-led) decision-making as the norms of their schools.

> Trust is established through a commitment period during which each partner has the opportunity to signal to the other a willingness to accept personal risk and not to exploit the vulnerability of the other for personal gain ... As participants begin to feel more comfortable with one another, there may be a tacit testing of the limits of trust and influence and attempts to arrive at a mutual set of expectations ...
>
> *(Tschannen Moran, 2004:42)*

Building trust is a constant process and the head must continually assess his or her 'trustworthy reputation' (Seashore-Louis 2007:18). A secondary head in the IMPACT project spoke of the ways in which his autocratic approach to leadership at the beginning of his tenure changed over time.

> For the first 5 years of headship here I was more autocratic because I needed things to be done. I kept people in the loop but didn't involve colleagues. The next 5 years, I started to delegate leadership across SLT and middle managers. I'm the king pin – I have high expectations of myself and of others. Devolving sometimes means you get high standards back, but I have to watch people make mistakes – people have to try new things. I've put systems in place throughout the school.
>
> *(Secondary Head)*

Twelve years on he had now established a high-trust environment:

> If a member of staff needs a day off, it's not a problem. The head trusts the staff and he likes to stand back and let the SLT do the role he used to do and he adjudicates, giving neutral feedback. Any staff can have training, they just have to sign up and go and the head trusts that it will be good for the school.
>
> *(Secondary Assistant Head)*

Successful heads recognize that building successful leadership takes time and depends upon the establishment and maintenance of individual and collective vision, hope and optimism, high expectations and repeated acts of leadership integrity in order to nurture, broaden and deepen individual, relational and organizational trust. The extent and depth of initial or provisional trust will depend upon a number of past as well as present factors, including the organization's current culture and past history of improvement.

Figure 7.3 illustrates the need for each growth point of trust to be followed by further actions which earn trust and reduce distrust. It is this interplay of trust and trustworthiness that creates reciprocal trust and the development of a culture of trust within the school.

Diagnosis of trust history
⬇
Initial/provisional trust
⬇
→ Actions which earn trust and reduce distrust
⬇
Growth of personal and relational trust
⬇
School members experience success
⬇
Growth of organizational trust
⬇
Consequence of trust: a learning and achieving community for all

FIGURE 7.3 The progressive distribution of trust

Source: Day, 2009: 728

Clearly, then, the progressive distribution of trust is an active process, which must be led and managed and become embedded in the culture of schools. Success in this will require more than actions. It will require that leaders possess qualities of wisdom, discernment, strategic acumen and a disposition to trust.

Building organizational capacity: an example of whole school improvement

Writing from a secondary school principal's perspective, Jackson (2000) tells the story of how he led improvements in his school's *capacity for sustained improvement* over an eight-year period:

> [W]e have attempted to grapple with the complexities of organisational learning and the internal restructuring which is required fundamentally to change the *metabolism* of school in order to encourage the various levels of learning required for sustained improvement. I would identify these levels as being: teacher learning through enquiry into practice; collaborative learning through the shared struggle to gain knowledge from our practice; organisational learning (about how we need to restructure organisationally to become more adaptive); and learning about leadership ...
>
> *(Jackson, 2000:62)*

An important word here is *metabolism*, defined by the Oxford English dictionary, in relation to architecture, as a movement 'which viewed the city [school] as a single entity and emphasised the need for an integrated approach to urban [school] life, with buildings survey both public and private functions and being adaptable to changes in the city [school] as whole'; and in relation to biochemistry as 'processes that occur within a living organism [school] in order to maintain life; the interconnected sequences ... in which a cell, tissue, organ, etc., sustains energy production ...' (OD, 2006). Both of these definitions are pertinent, since both are based upon a view of schools as living organisms in which both maintenance and development occur in parallel and in which there is ongoing struggle not only to survive but also to grow. Social organizations, such as schools, need, as we have seen throughout the chapters of this book, both intellectual and emotional energy if they are to have the capacity to adapt – an essential quality in the face of uncertainty and change – and grow. They need values-led integrated leadership.

Improvements to Jackson's school were led by Jackson himself, but supported through a partnership with the Improving the Quality of Education for All (IQEA) project, itself led by university personnel (Hopkins and Stern, 1996; Ainscow *et al.*, 1994). In this project, the school established a school improvement group (cadre), which included teachers (and support staff) from a variety of departments, with a range of ages and experience. This leadership structure created and expanded the school's improvement capacity, and ran in parallel and with reciprocal membership also drawn from the school's senior management team. See Figure 7.4.

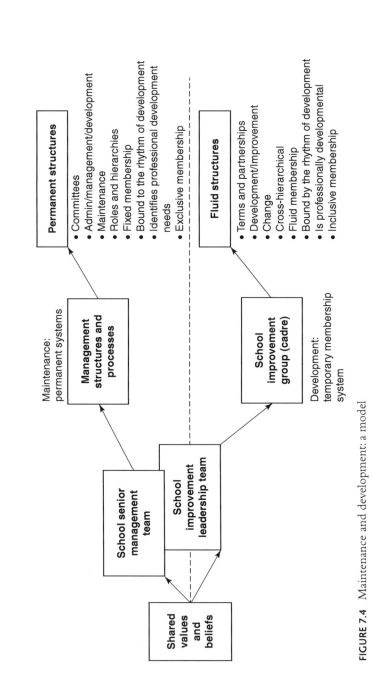

FIGURE 7.4 Maintenance and development: a model

Source: Jackson, 2000:64

Although, as Jackson acknowledges, even this is an oversimplification of the complexity of the improvement processes, it does provide an illustration of *intent* (to maintain and develop), *consensus values* (in distributing the leadership of change), *practices* (in promoting collaborative inquiry) and *vision* (in working closely with external university partners who were committed to contributing to school-led improvement with a focus on professional learning and development); and capacity-building over time and with different communities of practice. The importance of the role of school leaders in establishing and promoting this work is emphasized by Jackson:

> Here, leaders are stimulators (who get things started); they are storytellers (to encourage dialogue and add understanding); they are networkers and copers; problem scavengers too ... They tend to have wider social repertoires than has been customary in hierarchical educational settings, so as to encourage openness and to perpetuate relationships whilst wrestling with ambiguity. They will be improvisational and comfortable with spontaneity ... They will care, deeply, about teachers, about students and about education. They will be less personally ambitious, perhaps a long time in post, and instead will be remorseless about improvement. In such settings leadership provides a context for adult learning focusing on "helping staff to confront, make sense of and interpret the emerging circumstances" of the school (Louis *et al.*, 1994).
>
> *(Jackson, 2000:71)*

Relationships matter with adults in schools as much as they matter with students in classrooms. In a multilayer, qualitative study in the USA, Youngs' and King's research reinforced associations between the kinds and quality of principals' leadership, professional learning and development, school organizational conditions and the quality of teaching and learning.

> [E]ffective principals can sustain high levels of capacity by establishing trust, creating structures that promote teacher learning, and either connecting their faculties to external expertise or helping teachers generate reforms internally.
>
> *(Youngs and King, 2002:643)*

Their work provides further support for the emphasis placed by Jackson in England, in pursuing an ambitious, values-led, collaborative improvement agenda, and Lai's typology of principal leadership in which the 'interactive-growth' and 'participatory-growth' approaches to teacher capacity-building were associated also with leadership distribution and teacher empowerment. The findings from all three – and many other studies – provide powerful evidence for the development of trust as an essential element in successful capacity-building and school effectiveness.

Conclusions

There's still another crucial truth about leadership. It's something that we've known for a long time, but we've come to prize even more today. In talking

> to leaders and reading their cases, there was a very clear message that wove itself throughout every situation and action. The message was: leadership is a relationship ... It's the quality of this relationship that matters most when we're engaged in getting extraordinary things done.
>
> *(Kouzes and Posner, 2007:24)*

During the last three decades, there have been increasing concerns expressed by successive governments about the quality of schooling. Emphasis on competition and individualism have increased and it can be argued that these are now valued over co-operation and interdependence. We continue to witness a development towards a stronger focus on educational quality defined in terms of student measurable attainments. The external policy focus has shifted to more closely defined expectations of what has to be achieved by whom, and only those outcomes, which meet their predefined criteria, seem to denote success (Hopmann 2007). Yet, *research on successful school principals* continues to provide strong evidence of how sustaining their moral and ethical values and purposes, particularly those concerned with promoting equity and social justice, contributes to the success of their schools.

Trust and distributed leadership are bound up closely with what Halpern (2009) has termed 'the economy of regard':

> The economy of regard, and the fabric of social capital in which it is embedded, is worth more than the real economy in monetary terms (consider, for example, the value of social care) and, perhaps more importantly, matters far more to most of us in our everyday lives than the focus of conventional economics.
>
> *(Halpern, 2009:16)*

David Halpern's argument is that social capital – 'the extent to which individuals and communities trust each other, reciprocate helpfully and are connected to other people' (Halpern, 2009:10) – applies to matters concerned with national wealth. However, he also identifies other benefits to individuals and societies from higher investment in social capital. He suggests that there are powerful physical and mental health benefits to individuals and that social capital affects the educational attainment of pupils. Investment in social capital may account, for example, for the high levels of self-efficacy, low levels of staff (and student) absenteeism and high staff retention rates commonly associated with schools which are judged to be successful (Day et al., 2011:221–222).

International research in 14 countries over the last 15 years through the 20-country strong International Successful School Principalship Project (ISSPP) has shown again and again that successful principals are those who challenge the boundaries of teaching and learning for the intrinsic and extrinsic moral good of the learners, rather than compliance with the relatively narrow attainment targets of governments (Day and Leithwood, 2007; Day et al., 2011). Such principals engage not in policy 'implementation, but in policy enactment' (Ball et al., 2011). In doing so, they interpret policy so that it may be absorbed into their own existing successful practices, adapting these within a broad set of educational values and practices.

If such policy enactment, as defined here, is to be successful, however, it is likely to depend upon the extent to which school leaders understand the complexities of work and lives of teachers, the extent to which such understandings translate into collegial cultures of evidence-based trust, their willingness and ability to enact change at classroom level and the support they provide for this through the values, qualities, strategies and relationships they have and are able to nurture, build and sustain.

Note

1   This section is drawn from Day *et al.*, 2016.

8

UNDERSTANDING COMPLEXITY, BUILDING QUALITY

It is self-evident that all school students have an entitlement to the best opportunities to learn, thrive and achieve. Yet, for this entitlement to be fully realized requires them to be taught by teachers who are all willing and able to teach to their best and well over the whole course of their careers in what are likely to be contexts of changing expectations and demands. To do so requires them to have a positive sense of professionalism and professional identity that fuels, builds and sustains their motivation. These play an important role in enabling them to manage the emotional uncertainties and vulnerabilities that are an inherent part of their work. The previous chapters have discussed the nature of professionalism, identity, commitment, resilience, PLD and leadership, and their influence on teachers' worlds and work. Although each is important, it is the connections between them that best illustrate the complex nature of the challenges faced by all teachers who strive to provide the best learning and achievement opportunities for all pupils. Acknowledging these connections and the interactions between them, and appreciating that teaching is work that is suffused with relational and emotional, as well as intellectual, challenges is key to understanding why some teachers are willing and able to manage the demands of their work and achieve success, whilst others are not. Taken together, they provide clear indicators of the means through which quality may be built and sustained in all phases of their careers.

A recent report commissioned by CfBT identified eight main characteristics of inspiring (and effective) teachers:

- Having and transmitting enthusiasm
- Cultivating positive relationships with students
- Being flexible and adapting their practice
- Making learning purposeful and relevant for students
- Promoting a safe and stimulating classroom climate
- Establishing clear and positive classroom management

- Being reflective about their own practice and developing collaboratively
- Bringing innovation to the classroom

(Sammons et al.*, 2014:19)*

It found, also, that when these teachers were asked to identify what was most important for their practice, it was

- Enthusiasm for teaching
- Positive relationships with children
- High levels of motivation and commitment
- Confidence in the classroom

Ibid.

These findings confirm those of other research in the UK and internationally that highlight the cognitive, affective and practical knowledge, values, qualities and skills associated with 'effective' and 'inspiring' teachers (e.g. Kington *et al.*, 2014). Yet, as the chapters in this book have shown, there is abundant evidence that many teachers do not always sustain the levels of enthusiasm, passion and commitment with which they entered the profession, nor do they consistently demonstrate the qualities and skills listed by Sammons and her colleagues as being associated with the best teachers and the best teaching.

This chapter brings together the key themes of the previous chapters and the interactions between them. This holistic, nuanced conceptualization of the complexities of teachers' work and worlds and the influences on them suggests a movement by researchers away from generalized theoretical positions and atomistic empirical approaches that, taken singly, however well constructed, designed and conducted, are limited in their contributions to understandings of who teachers are, and what influences their willingness, capacities and abilities to teach to their best and well. Why some teachers remain passionate about what they do whilst others' commitment diminishes, why some stay whilst others leave, why some who stay are consistently effective whilst others are not, and why 'effectiveness' may fluctuate are key questions which this book has sought to address. The parts played in this by teachers' values and beliefs, school culture, PLD and external policy interventions are key issues for teachers themselves and all those with responsibilities for the quality of initial and in-service PLD, the leadership of schools, school improvement and classroom teaching and learning. The evidence in the chapters of this book points clearly to the need for teachers to think and plan in new ways that are more inclusive of the part played not only by the individual themes but also by the complex combinations and dynamic interactions that, together, influence teacher quality retention (see Figure 8.1):

- professionalism and professional identity
- commitment and resilience
- leadership and trust
- PLD
- teaching and emotions

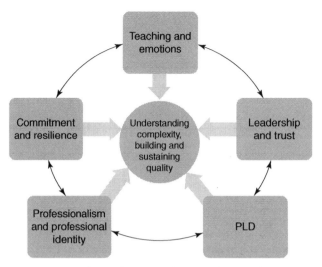

FIGURE 8.1   Understanding complexity, building and sustaining quality

Theme 1: teachers' professionalism and identity

The wise words of Whitty *et al.* (1998:65) continue to apply to the struggle for the collective 'soul' of teachers' professionalism:

> Whether or not what we are witnessing here is a struggle between a professionalising project or a deprofessionalising one, it is certainly a struggle among different stakeholders over the definition of teacher professionalism and professionality for the twenty-first century.

That the struggle continues is witnessed by the continuing flow of academic publications, for the most part critical of the 'performativity' agenda (Clarke and Newman, 1997; Ball, 2003b; Furlong *et al.*, 2000; Hargreaves and Fullan, 2012) and its effects on principals and teachers; and, alongside these, the exponentially increasing flow of detailed government policies and so-called 'evidence-based' documents (often commissioned by governments seeking short-term solutions to complex problems), many of which push forward agendas that continue to contribute to low-trust relationships between teachers and employers. They seem not to provide longer-term system improvements, perhaps because they fail to convince those on the ground. Hoyle and Wallace (2007:18) expressed teachers' and principals' responses to these as 'ironies of adaptation' versus 'ironies of representation':

> The former connotes the ways in which the practices of principals and teachers entail 'working around' prescriptions and expectations in order

better to meet the perceived needs of pupils in the contingent circumstances of a particular school. The latter connotes the ways in which principals and teachers represent their work to the agencies of accountability in order to appear to be meeting the requirements of these agencies.

(Hoyle and Wallace, 2007:18)

These 'ironies of adaptation' suggest a degree of autonomy that is asserted by teachers in the face of national policies which seek greater degrees of compliance, where such policies are not judged by them to be in the best interests of their students. Teachers' responses to policy imposition have also been described in terms of policy 'enactment'.

Our use of the term 'enactment' refers to an understanding that policies are interpreted and 'translated' by diverse policy actors in the school environment, rather than simply implemented. It is based on the related premise that 'policies do not normally tell you what to do, they create circumstances in which the range of options available in deciding what to do are narrowed or changed, or particular goals or outcomes are set' (Ball 1994:19).

Whilst these and other researchers have reported the effects of 'new public management' that seems to 'technicize' teachers' work (McNeil, 2000), and certainly causes a focus on the achievement of measurable academic attainment, much empirical research evidence points to a more nuanced and differentiated reality. Sloan, for example, has found that 'individual teachers actively read and respond to locally conceived accountability – explicit curriculum policies in varied, perhaps even unique ways' (Sloan, 2006:123). This in part echoes extensive research on teachers' work, lives and effectiveness (Day *et al.*, 2007) that found that teachers' sense of professionalism and professional identity construction can be positively or negatively influenced not only by their prior life and work experiences, but also by their sense of individual and collective efficacy and agency; that they are influenced by the strength of their 'call' to teach, the cultures of the schools in which they work and the vision, quality and actions of close colleagues and school leaders; and that these may have a greater influence on how external policy mandates are received (Day *et al.*, 2011b).

Much psychologically oriented research continues to characterize professional identity formation as being an individual property, a process through which individuals come to interact and adapt (or do not adapt) to the expectations of others in the environments that they experience (Erikson, 1959).

Developing an identity as a teacher is an important part of securing teachers' commitment to their work and adherence to professional norms ... the identities teachers develop shape their dispositions, where they place their effort, whether and how they seek out professional development opportunities, and what obligations they see as intrinsic to their role.

(Hammerness et al., 2005:383–384)

The process of identity development will have begun in the pre-service phase as student teachers and will have been influenced by the interactions between personal biographies (their own and their students' school, family and life experiences), particularities of the values and practices experienced during training and education programmes and experiences of the time spent in schools and classrooms during this phase, and, of course, the broader educational policy environments (Beijaard *et al.*, 2004; Beauchamp and Thomas, 2009; Akkerman and Meijer, 2011). However, such a process is unlikely to be complete at the time of qualification. Over the last 20 years, empirical research has found that identify formation is not linear (i.e. there is no guarantee that teachers' sense of professional identify or its stability, once achieved, will remain fixed). Levels of teacher motivation and commitment and components of professional identity have also been found to fluctuate according to the positive or negative impact of combinations of personal, workplace and external policy circumstances (see Chapter 2 for a more detailed discussion of identity scenarios). Managing oneself in one or all of these circumstances may cause teaching to become frustrating and ultimately debilitating.

It follows that the struggle to form a relatively stable sense of professional identity will continue through the early-career phase and beyond, and success in this regard will be likely to relate to how teachers are able to manage the interface between how they see themselves as professionals and how they respond to others' definitions. The forming, enactment and re-forming of professional identities, as Chapter 2 has demonstrated, cannot be described as an entirely rational process. Professional identities are suffused by emotion dynamics and played out in contexts of change.

> Change is complex because it is inextricably linked to our emotions. Imposed change can ball up a whole range of emotions: anger at the imposition and the denial of personal autonomy, sorrow at the sense of loss of the old, and anxiety at the uncertainties that the new will bring. Self-initiated change is also intertwined with emotion: excitement at the anticipation of the new, relief that the old will be left behind, and again anxiety because of the uncertainty and the unknown events that have been set in motion … The management of these non-rational responses to change, especially anxiety, is crucial to change management.
>
> *(James and Connolly, 2000:16–17)*

Thus, '… the teachers' creation of a professional self is formed as a result of the integration of, and conflict amongst, various subject positions and ideologies...' in which emotions play an important role (McDougall, 2010:682; Day and Leitch, 2001; Van Veen *et al.*, 2005).

Theme 2: teacher commitment and the capacity for resilience

Commitment to their profession generally and their identification with the values and practices of the school in which they work have been acknowledged in policy documents as being important factors in teacher retention (OECD, 2005). However, research has shown that the intensity and levels of teacher commitment are likely to vary (see Chapter 3 for a detailed discussion). As Choi and Tang stated, 'the interplay of the personal, workplace and systemic factors worked differently between the teachers who followed a positive and negative commitment trend' (2009:775).

Such variation is the result of their sense of professionalism and professional identity. There are associations between commitment and the capacity for resilience, and between these and the relative strength of their capacities to manage personal, professional life-phase, workplace and broader system-level challenges which themselves are likely to vary in intensity over time (Day *et al.*, 2011b; Smethem, 2007).

> The interaction between teachers' sense of efficacy, agency and emotional wellbeing on professional identities and their management of the interaction between these and the professional, workplace and personal influences which they experience during the different phases of their professional lives is a sophisticated process which contributes strongly to their commitment which is a necessary condition for their effectiveness.
>
> *(Gu and Day, 2007:1314)*

Pupils have a right to be taught by teachers who are more than competent, who care and who are passionately and knowledgeably committed to their well-being and achievement. Yet, teachers' continuing commitment to their students' learning and well-being, their subject discipline and the school in which they work cannot be taken for granted. It would be foolish to ignore the challenges at individual, school and system levels of recruiting and retaining highly qualified, high quality committed teachers who stay.

> Although teaching would appear to be an occupation considered central to a country's development and wellbeing, Australia, the US, Germany and Norway, among other countries including the UK and several European countries, report difficulties recruiting and retaining teachers …
>
> *(Watt* et al.*, 2012:791)*

Watt and her colleagues (2012) have provided in their research a reliable international comparison of the factors that influence students' motivations for choosing to teach. They found that the highest-rated motivations across Australia, the USA, Germany and Norway were 'intrinsic value, perceived teaching ability, the desire to make a social contribution, to work with children/adolescents, and having had a positive prior teaching and learning experiences', whereas 'the desire for job security, to enhance social equity, and for choosing teaching because of its provision for family time were rated consistently lower' (Watts *et al.*, 2012:804).

This reflects the research reported throughout this book that has shown, whether teachers view their work as a vocation, a career or 'just a job' (Seligman, 2002), their willingness and capacities to teach to their best and well may diminish where classrooms and schools are constant 'sites of struggle' in which different interests compete for attention, where they are subject to interventions in the form of unsought changing policy demands, parental expectations and student dispositions to engage in school-based learning. Some or all of these are likely to challenge teachers' conceptions of their roles, practices and sense of professionalism. When effective teachers become dissatisfied with their work environment, when they cease to feel that they are trusted to do a good job, even within the high visibility contexts in which they now find themselves, they either transfer or leave teaching, or remain with lower levels of commitment. As a result, their schools and students pay a price. Chronic disenchantment, emotional fatigue and turnover 'exacts instructional, financial, and organisational costs that can destabilise learning communities within schools, and compromise student learning … especially for low performing students' (Simon and Johnson, 2015:6).

To teach at one's best and well over time, then, requires a continuing commitment, and, as Chapter 4 has shown, a sustained capacity for resilience. While the concept of resilience elaborated in the discipline of psychology helps clarify the personal characteristics of trait-resilient people (the ability to bounce back in adverse circumstances), it fails to address how the capacity for resilience can be enhanced or inhibited by the nature of the external and internal environments in which they work, the people with whom they work and the strength of their beliefs, aspirations and moral/ethical purposes (Gu and Day, 2007:1305).

There is a large body of research that demonstrates that what teachers as individuals believe about the extent to which they can influence the learning and achievement of their students makes a significant difference in their teaching behaviours and outcomes.

> Teachers with strong efficacy beliefs are likely to be more enthusiastic, more organised, and devote more time in planning their teaching … In addition … [they] … are less likely to become angry, impatient, or frustrated with a student who is having difficulty; will stick with that student longer; and will try more strategies to help the student understand …
>
> *(Tschannen-Moran, 2004:128)*

The process of teaching, learning and leading requires of those who are engaged in them much more, then, than the ability to bounce back in adverse circumstances. It requires them to have a resolute persistence and commitment and to be supported in these by strong core values over three or more decades. A growing amount of research evidence suggests, also, that whilst there are generic qualities, strategies and skills which are common to all, teachers in schools that serve disadvantaged communities face a greater range of more persistent, intensive cognitive and emotional challenges than others and so not only need to possess these to a greater degree but may also need different qualities and skills which are specific to the social/ emotional contexts of their schools and their communities. Many of the students in these schools, along with their parents or carers, are likely to have had a history of failure and be alienated from school-based education. For those educators for whom equity, care and social justice are central to their educational commitment, it is particularly important, therefore, to examine conditions which may work to improve this because many of these students are at greater risk of underachieving in their personal, social and academic lives (Day, 2014:643).

Resilience in education, then, is not a quality that is innate. Rather, it is a construct that is relative, relational, developmental and dynamic (Rutter, 1990). Whilst it is both a product of personal and professional histories, and exercised through professional dispositions and values, these will be influenced positively and negatively by external policy, organizational and personal factors, and determined by individuals' willingness and emotional, as well as intellectual, capacities to manage these in a range of anticipated and unanticipated scenarios (Day 2014:641).

Finally, it is important to note that the amounts and degrees of internal, workplace and external support experienced at any one time, whilst helpful, may not always directly increase all teachers' longer-term capacities for resilience. For some resilience will grow, for others it may become fragile and for some it will erode. Teachers whose capacity for resilience is high are likely to be those whose individual strength of moral purpose and efficacy enables them to participate actively in shaping, building and sustaining their capacity for resilience. It is this active management, equated by some with 'agency' (Eteläpelto *et al.*, 2013), that may lead them to a strong, abiding sense of individual, relational and collective resilience. *It is also important to note that having the capacity for resilience does not, in itself, imply that teachers will teach well.* Without the required knowledge and classroom competencies and without strong moral and ethical values, 'resilience' may be used as a means only of survival or even a means of avoiding or resisting improvement.

Theme 3: leadership and trust

As previous chapters have shown, the nature and processes of teachers' work are subject to more nuanced, complex and contextual influences than previously proposed. Although it has been claimed that the room to manoeuvre for teachers and principals has been incrementally reduced over the last 20 years by the increasing dominance of the policy voice, empirical data from a recent project on policy enactment in English and Chinese schools judged to be successful (Gu *et al.*, 2014) revealed that enactment of policy in such schools results in actions which illustrate that head teachers, and other school leaders, are able to exercise a much greater degree of autonomy than was suggested by these previous analyses.

Rather than being dominated by external ideologies, the purposes, practices and identities of and relationships between teachers in successful schools are shaped and driven by the school principals' own core educational beliefs and values, and are played out through a complex set of interactions between school leaders, their staff members and the wider school community (Gu *et al.*, 2014). These are designed to build a collective sense of ownership, professional capital, and individual and organizational capacities for learning and well-being. In these schools, structures and cultures take account of external policies but are in line with identified school values and existing improvement priorities. Teachers in successful and improving schools have a sense of 'occupational' rather than 'managerial' professionalism and, within this, a positive and relatively stable sense of professional identity.

As earlier studies carried out in New Zealand and England have found (Timperley and Robinson, 2000; Day *et al.*, 2007), the extent to which commitment and the capacities for resilience grow and are sustained or decline is influenced significantly by the values and qualities of school leaders and their relations with colleagues. In all schools, principals have a prime responsibility for establishing ways of being and norms of behaviour among and between staff, students and external communities. As Chapter 7 has shown, the way they do so, their values, qualities, strategies, relationships and actions, will be reflected in existing power relations or dominant discourses (Tsang, 2013). They may, for example, result in indirect forms of control over, for example, the relative autonomy of teachers in the classroom (decisional capital), the kinds of and extent of leadership distribution, the strength of commitment to PLD and even the expression of emotions in classrooms and staffrooms (Zembylas, 2005b).

A key word that recurs in research reports about successful teachers and successful schools is 'trust':

> Why talk about trust? Not only because trust has long been neglected as an essential philosophical and ethical concept, but also because talking about trust is essential to building trust. Even if talking about trust can be awkward or uncomfortable, it is only by talking about trust, and trusting, that trust can be created, maintained and restored. Not talking about trust, on the other hand … can too easily betray a lack of trust, or result in continuing distrust. Trust … is, and must be made to be, a matter of conscious choice.
>
> *(Solomon and Flores, 2001:153)*

The nurturing and growth of social capital (trust) may be found in the way the everyday business and 'busyness' are conducted in schools. Reciprocity, respect and regard for others are essential characteristics. Teachers must '… trust each other, not just personally, but also in their ability to contribute to the enterprise of the community so that they feel comfortable addressing real problems together and speak truthfully' (Wenger, 2000:230).

Bryk and Schneider's (2002) seminal work on the key role played by *relational trust* in the improvement of academic achievement in elementary schools in Chicago provides empirical reinforcement to Seligman's (2011) association between positive relationships and well-being, They identified four qualities that are integral to relational trust: respect, competence, personal regard for others and integrity.

In investigating how trust affects teachers' willingness to work with innovations introduced by central office administrators' in the USA, Karen Seashore-Louis (2007) provided four messages which are particularly pertinent in assessing how improvements may be built and sustained through trust:

1. Trust is a critical factor associated with the effective response of school districts to demands for greater quality and accountability (ibid., p. 20).
2. Administrators (principals), particularly those who are appointed with a mandate to change a school's performance, must pay particular note to embedded cultures of distrust among the staff: if teachers cannot trust each other, they cannot work together effectively to create systemic change (ibid., p.19).
3. Administrators need to keep their fingers on the pulse of trust during a change process, and should not assume that their trustworthy reputation will persist (ibid., p. 18).
4. Trust cannot easily be separated from expanded teacher empowerment and influence. Teachers are not passive actors in the school, but co-constructors of trust. As active professionals, teachers who feel left out of important decisions will react by withdrawing trust, which then undermines change (ibid., pp. 18–20).

Reciprocity thrives as long as people trust one another. However, this takes time. As stated in Chapter 7,

> Trust is established through a commitment period during which each partner has the opportunity to signal to the other a willingness to accept personal risk and not to exploit the vulnerability of the other for personal gain … As participants begin to feel more comfortable with one another, there may be a tacit testing of the limits of trust and influence and attempts to arrive at a mutual set of expectations …
>
> *(Tschannen-Moran, 2004:42)*

In employing strategies that aim to build trust in the organization, successful leaders have been found to place trust in others. 'Relational trust' has been repeatedly reported to be a key contributing factor to whether teachers' sense of professionalism, professional identity and effectiveness is or is not built (Bryk and Schneider, 2002; Aelterman *et al.*, 2007). In a high trust, successful 'distributed leadership' organization, people are not merely seen as the means to an end. The person and task-centred approach to leadership is able to be identified by the

> … creation of an inclusive community; emphasis on relationships and ethic of care; creation of shared meanings and identities through the professional culture of the school; staff development programmes and arrangements for teaching; learning and assessment which encourage dialogue; a discourse of the personal; reciprocity of learning; encouraging new approaches to

learning; remaining restless about contemporary understandings of leadership and management.

(Day and Leithwood, 2007:184)

There will, thus, be a difference between those heads whose trust in staff is informed and ethically driven, aiming to develop individuals' motivation and commitment to their work and to the organization, and those for whom trust is a means to one end, as they aim to get tasks completed on a specific timescale regardless of the cost or longer-term benefit to the individual. Successful school principals are those who actively seek out new opportunities, experiences and challenges for their schools to improve staff and students' learning and achievement. To do so, like teachers, they need to be both committed and resilient, and to build and support these traits in others.

> Leaders are the stewards of organizational energy [resilience] ... they inspire or demoralize others, first by how effectively they manage their own energy and next by how well they manage, focus, invest and renew the collective energy [resilience] of those they lead.
>
> *(Loehr and Schwartz, 2003:5)*

If this is so, then all of those who prepare and support school leaders must take note for, arguably, it is resilience allied with moral purpose which is the key to the sustainability of school-wide cultures of PLD which support their teachers' commitment, efficacy, professional identities, well-being, resilience and continuing passion to teach to their best and well.

Theme 4: Professional Learning and Development (PLD)

> There is no developmentally attested evidence to prove that sticking around on the planet long enough to reach adult age always confers a corresponding capacity to learn from experience ... some of us are never able to learn from experience, others can only do it intermittently.
>
> *(Brookfield, 1998:286)*

There are at least five career-long challenges for teachers who wish to sustain or increase their perceived and evidence-informed classroom effectiveness in creating opportunities for learning and achievement for all their students:

1. the learning needs and motivations of students to engage in school-based learning led by teachers are likely to continue to change;
2. changes in government policies, with their increasing emphasis on promoting particular values, self-sufficiency and human capital (in terms of employment preparation and qualifications), are likely to affect the curriculum and how it is taught as the use of technology increases and its influence continues to grow;

3. the sustainment of teacher commitment to work engagement and continuing learning as workloads increase;
4. the nurturing and sustainment of their capacity for resilience;
5. teachers' willingness and ability to adapt to change, within strong and clearly articulated educational values.

Teachers are likely to be helped to meet these challenges effectively not only by their inner commitment to their profession but also by the provision of a range of fit-for-purpose PLD opportunities that are relevant to their *attitudinal* as well as *functional* needs. These will be mediated, positively or negatively, by the extent to which departments and schools nurture, challenge and support the development of their professional capital, and attend to their social and emotional competencies and capacities:

> Socially and emotionally competent teachers set the tone of the classroom by developing supportive and encouraging relationships with their students ... establishing and implementing behavioural guidelines in ways that promote intrinsic motivation, coaching students through conflict situations, encouraging cooperation among students and acting as a role model for respectful and appropriate communication and exhibition of prosocial behaviour ... When teachers lack the resources to effectively manage the social and emotional challenges within the particular context of their school or classroom, children show lower levels of on-task behaviour and performance.
>
> *(Jennings and Greenberg, 2009:492)*

Alvesson and Spicer offer a direct challenge to organizations which focus on the 'functional' at the expense of a broader learning agenda. They use the term 'functional stupidity', which they define as the 'inability and/or unwillingness [of the organization] to use cognitive and reflective capacities in anything other than narrow and circumspect ways. It involves a lack of reflexivity, a disinclination to require or provide justification, and avoidance of substantive reasoning' (Alvesson and Spicer, 2012:1201). They argue that 'functional stupidity' can have both positive and negative effects. Engaging staff in what they describe as 'a narrow and safe terrain' of, for example, reflection on the means of increasing the efficiency of the organization within existing boundaries of practice (in schools this might involve focusing only on improving test scores of students) can provide them with a sense of certainty of purpose and, in doing so, 'strengthen the organisational order', enabling the organization to function smoothly. It may 'motivate people, help them to cultivate their careers', but also 'subordinate them to socially acceptable forms of management and leadership'. They suggest that in the longer-term interests of organizational success, 'refusal to use the intellectual resources' of staff through 'organizationally-supported lack of reflexivity, substantive reasoning, and justification' is likely, also, to have 'negative consequences such as trapping individuals and organizations into problematic patterns of thinking, which engender the conditions for individual and organizational dissonance' (Alvesson and Spicer, 2012:1196). In short, 'functional stupidity' can stifle the intellectual curiosity, creativity and problem identification and problem-solving dispositions and abilities which are needed by all teachers, especially in times of change.

Chapters 5 and 6 provided a range of PLD approaches that emphasize PLD as a joint responsibility of the individual and the organization, as being based upon individual and organizational needs, as involving the interrogation, alone and with others, of values and practices and, alongside these, as involving the review and renewal of commitment, a sense of stable positive professional identity and the support and growth of a capacity for resilience.

Just as teachers who teach to their best and well identify and work to extend their pupils' learning orientations, so too those who plan and lead PLD in schools need to understand the complexities of teachers' learning. They need to 'understand and explain how teachers learn … how a teacher's individual learning orientation system interacts with the school's learning orientation system and how both of these systems together affect the activities' (Opfer and Pedder, 2011:393). In this respect, it is also worth noting Kennedy's (2016:974) recent message to researchers who seek to understand PLD and those who design formal activities and support informal learning that improves teaching:

> If we can tie our research designs and our PD (professional development) models more closely to underlying theories of teacher motivation and teacher learning, we will learn more from our studies. We need to replace our current conception of "good" PD as comprising a collection of particular design features with a conception that it is based on more nuanced understanding of what teachers do, what motivates them, and how they learn and grow … This is especially important in an era in which teachers receive numerous messages about what they should be doing and in which these messages compete for teachers' attention.

Opfer and Pedder have conceptualized teachers' professional learning as a 'complex system rather than an event' and suggested that there are 'various dynamics at work in social behaviour and these interact and combine in different ways such that even the simplest decisions can have multiple causal pathways' (Opfer and Pedder, 2011:378). In adopting complexity theory (Wheatley, 1999) as their frame of thinking, they challenged simple cause-and-effect relationships between the different forms of PLD and their relative impact on teachers' thinking and practices, and the levels of student attainment which it has become fashionable to adopt. The contents of this book have provided a range of research that supports their assertion that 'how these dynamics combine will vary for different people and even for the same person at different times of the day or in different contexts' (Opfer and Pedder, 2011:378). They suggest a dynamic model of teacher learning and change in which they identify three system levels of interaction:

1. The individual teacher system (including prior experiences, individual and collective beliefs, knowledge and practices, orientation to learning)
2. The school level system (cultures, collective norms of practice, beliefs about teaching and learning)
3. The learning activity system (tasks, practices, forms and relative intensity, length and locations of the activities)

(Opfer and Pedder, 2011)

Research reported in this book suggests a fourth system-level interaction:

4. The policy-level systems (e.g. curriculum reform, conditions for teaching and learning, conditions of service (e.g. performance management, Ofsted inspections)).

It is important to remember that it is not the interactions themselves but how these are managed within and between the four levels of system interaction that is likely to result in learning and that – because there are likely to be tensions between them – this is likely to be a complex process which requires considerable and continuing intellectual and emotional energy by the teacher. Two key factors need to suffuse each of these system-level interactions:

• the nurturing of teachers' professionalism, professional identities, commitment and capacities for resilience;
• the understanding of emotions in the management of the possibilities for change in beliefs and/or practices which learning activities present.

Most important is the understanding that such energy is finite and so needs to be renewed and enhanced.

Learning, defined as '… that reflective activity which enables the learner to draw upon previous experience to understand and evaluate the present, so as to shape future action and formulate new knowledge' (Abbott, 1994), is claimed to be

• An active process of relating new meaning to existing meaning, involving the accommodation and assimilation of ideas, skills, thoughts etc;
• Making connections between past, present and future which do not always follow in a linear fashion: un-learning and re-learning play a part;
• A process influenced by the use to which learning is to be put, and whether the learning may be effectively retrieved in future situations.

(NSIN:1)

If this is so, then it provides a useful starting point for the design of in-school learning opportunities especially. In order to engage in the processes, teachers will need to draw upon not only data from their own and others practices but also the educational values that are expressed in and through these, since there is always 'a self-consciously moral dimension to educational practice' (Brookfield, 1998:283).

Much has been written about the value of team-building as a key element in processes of capacity-building as a means of building 'bonding' social capital and establishing initial trust between key senior school-wide leaders and between departmental leaders, their teacher colleagues and others (e.g. classroom assistants). Nurturing, growing and establishing teamwork of different kinds is an important means of creating cultures of collegiality and is essential to achieving the 'deep learning' described by Hargreaves and Fink (2006).

Authentic collegiality is defined by 'evolutionary relationships of openness, trust, and support among teachers where they define and develop their own purposes and practices as a community'. It is different from contrived collegiality, defined as 'administratively contrived interactions among teachers where they meet and work to implement the curricula and instructional strategies developed by others' (Hargreaves and Dawe, 1990:227), and should not be confused with the dominance of the 'social' over the 'task'.

It is difficult to consider moving towards PLCs, for example, in the absence of team-building. It is an essential element of the deprivatization of practice, increasing the will for transparency between staff. It is a pre-requisite for 'opening' rather than 'closing' opportunities for sharing planning and practice. Sustained engagement in team-building requires a willingness to trust others, to make one's self vulnerable, to be prepared to share (hopes, fears) and to change.

For many years, academics have criticized what they have (correctly) identified as the predominant patterns of teacher-to-teacher collaboration in schools as being limited to the exchange of ideas or 'tricks of the trade' (Hargreaves and Dawe, 1990; Little, 1993). Yet, for as long as conditions of service in many countries dictate that teachers spend most of their time every day teaching and relatively little time planning, systematically reflecting upon and sharing practice, this situation is likely to prevail. In recent years, however, ironically in part as a result of government policy in England, collaboration and inquiry within and between schools have moved from being voluntary activities to ones in which teachers are expected to participate on a regular basis. Department meetings in secondary schools and key stage and curriculum development meetings in primary schools are now likely to include elements of 'lesson study' and other PD activities. Whole school PLD provision now, partly due to the government-inspired self-improving systems in which schools have been encouraged to form TSAs, Chains, Federations and MATs, includes forms of practitioner inquiry, school-to-school support and targeted provision for collaborative programmes of mentoring and coaching support for newly qualified teachers (NQTs), recently qualified teachers (RQTs), aspirational middle and senior leaders and many other subject- and phase-specific 'teacher leaders'.

In short, there is now considerably more differentiated provision for PLD across the system, led largely from within the system, than ever before. Although much of this has been described as 'instrumentally' harnessed to compliance with government targets for raising standards of school leadership and teaching and learning in the classroom (Spillane and Burch, 2006), this is a far too simplistic characterization. In educational systems in which more decision-making has been distributed to individual schools, it is schools themselves that now choose how they will interpret these demands. In improving and successful schools, as the evidence in this book shows, successful leaders continue to emphasize their broader moral and ethical purposes within these narrower agendas (Day *et al.*, 2016). (For an account of school–university partnerships which highlight the tensions between the partners in a climate of intensive, externally driven, reform, see Bartholemew and Sandholtz, 2009.)

Theme 5: teaching and emotions

> What matters is not what you learn, you can learn the same thing reading a book, but rather it is about seeing a real person talking about it and getting excited. Teaching in my opinion is not an intellectual thing, it's an emotional thing. If it was an intellectual thing, you could replace teachers with books … So if you want to communicate the beauty of a subject, you have to do it in person, and you have to remember that what you are really communicating is passion.
>
> *(Rovelli, 2016:8)*

These words, taken from an interview with a leading Italian theoretical physicist, inspirational teacher and author of the international best-selling book *Seven Brief Lessons in Physics*, highlight the important role that emotions play in teaching well. Perhaps more than those in any other profession, sustaining the personal and professional, intellectual and emotional health of teachers is important, if for no other reason than working every day with 30 children (or multiples of 30, if in a secondary school) who do necessarily want to be at school or learning, or who show little interest in what is being taught, is a largely complex process that demands considerable emotional as well as intellectual energy.

There are likely to be particular times when their work may become emotional labour rather than emotional work, when, for example, they need to (continue to) display enthusiasm for their work with students, avoid displaying extreme negative emotions, e.g. about student behaviour, or suppress their emotions about other personal or professional problems or setbacks. In a small-scale study of the positive and negative effects of the emotional labour of caring in enacting teaching in an inclusive classroom, Isenbarger and Zembylas (2006) sounded a warning that, whilst care was multi-faceted, mediated by the strength of teachers' vocation and moral purposes, caring relationships could also become 'a source of emotional strain, anxiety, disappointment' and have an impact on teachers' commitment, satisfaction and self-esteem (p.120). Such anxiety can grow where national policy changes challenge teachers' existing sense of stable, positive identities.

Positive support from school leaders has been claimed to contribute also to teachers' emotional well-being and sense of self-efficacy and accomplishment (Galand *et al.*, 2007; Näring *et al.*, 2006; Sarros, 1992; Day, 2014; MacDonald, 2004). As Dunlop and MacDonald found (2004:72), 'the principal's role in being approachable, offering sympathy and emotional support for teachers, and adopting a collegiate approach to proactive engagement with staff, was perceived as important by teachers'.

The most frequently reported causes for a decline in commitment and the capacity for resilience by teachers in England have been found to be excessive workload (68%), pupil behaviour (64%) and poor leadership (58%) (Day *et al.*, 2011b; Day and Gu, 2014). Yet, whilst the widespread existence of low teacher morale, disenchantment and stress as a result of the increased diversity of roles and policy agendas which have increased workloads and associated bureaucracy and its effects upon the quality of teaching and learning continues to be reported, a range of research internationally continues to demonstrate that this is not always the case. Many teachers sustain their commitment and passion for teaching throughout their careers. There are many improving and successful schools in different socio-economic contexts in different countries that are led by principals who place a priority on building teachers' professional capital and, as part of this, their emotional, social and intellectual well-being (e.g. Day and Leithwood, 2007; Bricheno *et al.*, 2009).

Teachers' dispositions to 'teach to their best and well' and associations between this and their sense of self-efficacy, agency, well-being and job fulfilment have also been increasingly asserted by research which has found that teachers' sense of meaning (Hostetler *et al.*, 2007; Osguthorpe and Sanger, 2013) is also associated with perceptions of more positive teacher–student relationships, increased engagement in work and higher levels of commitment and effectiveness (Maslach, 1993, 2001). Seligman (2012) identified 'meaningfulness' as a key element in his notion of 'human flourishing', particularly important for teachers since, as this and earlier chapters have shown, their work is inherently both emotionally and intellectually demanding.

Building and sustaining teacher quality: an agenda for the future

The complexities of teachers' work and worlds and the influences on these that have highlighted in this book suggest a need for a more nuanced conceptualization by policymakers, system leaders, teacher educators, principals and teachers themselves. Teacher educators will need to prepare teachers to meet and manage challenges to their sense of professionalism and professional identity, and school principals will need, if they are to recruit and retain the best teachers, to provide incentives and resources which acknowledge more explicitly, and are more finely tuned to meeting, teachers' core growth needs: their sense of moral purpose, professionalism, professional identities, commitment and capacities for resilience. For teachers to successfully meet the challenges that their work presents, they need to be willing to build and sustain high levels of *'professional capital'* – personal, social and decisional – in school cultures in which the complexities of their work and its challenges are embraced rather than ignored or dismissed as being too difficult to resolve, intractable or 'part of the job'. They will be seen as a values-driven framework for building and sustaining quality teaching, learning and achievement in which the care and achievement for all pupils is paramount. Teachers will be more likely to succeed if they have a strong, positive sense of professional identity and if they are led by leaders with high expectations, clearly articulated values, high levels of personal and interpersonal qualities, strategies and skills, and who exercise individual and collective trust – trust that is not blind or unconditional but based both on a combination of understandings of the complexities of their work and the positive and negative influences which mediate this, evidenced by its effects on the progress, well-being and achievements of students in their care.

Much previous research on teachers' lives and work in high-stakes contexts of performativity has tended to emphasize problems of professionalism and professional identity. The evidence in this book, whilst acknowledging these, suggests that it would be more productive to focus upon how teachers' willingness and abilities to teach to their best and well in meeting the challenges of different scenarios in their work and lives may be built, sustained and enhanced. Studies on teacher retention, for example, show that, as well as internally driven commitment, relationships with colleagues matter as they decide whether to stay in their school or transfer (Allensworth *et al.*, 2009; Guarino *et al.*, 2006; Johnson and Birkeland, 2003; Kardos and Johnson, 2007; Bryk and Schneider, 2002). Such relationships are likely to be a key factor in increasing teachers' engagement and influence their decisions about remaining committed to the school and to teaching as a profession for life: 'higher employee engagement in various fields has been found to predict greater motivation … increased productively … and higher rates of employee retention …' (Kirkpatrick and Moore-Johnson, 2014:233).

This aspect of retention has been termed *quality retention* (Gu and Day, 2007:1314), a conceptualization that is located essentially in teachers' values and their sense of professionalism, professional identity, commitment and capacities for resilience.

What is required by all concerned with recruiting, educating, employing and retaining the best teachers, then, is a better understanding of the factors that enable the majority of teachers to sustain their motivation, commitment and effectiveness in the profession. Research also has an important part to play. Research agendas for the future might, for example, involve a movement away from over-simplified ideological positions and discipline-limited atomistic empirical approaches. As stated earlier, taken individually, these have limited contributions to understanding of the complex interactions between the influences highlighted in this book, the energy and expertise required by teachers in managing these and the effects on who teachers are, and what influences their willingness, capacities and abilities to teach to their best and well. We do not yet know enough about why some teachers remain passionate about what they do whilst others do not, why some stay whilst others leave and why some are consistently effective whilst others are not. Understanding how some teachers in some schools manage to build and sustain a positive sense of professionalism, professional identity and classroom effectiveness in managing the sometimes conflicting combinations of personal, organizational, policy and social influences, whilst some do not, are key issues for teachers themselves and all those with responsibilities for the quality of initial and in-service PLD, the leadership of schools, school improvement and classroom teaching and learning.

For the future good of the teaching profession, employers, system leaders, teacher educators, principals and teachers themselves who, together, bear responsibility for professional growth, renewal and revitalization need to think, plan and act in new ways. Such ways would be more inclusive of the part played by the influences discussed and elaborated through the individual themes in the chapters of this book. They would acknowledge the complex combinations and dynamic intellectual, emotional and social interactions that, together, influence teachers' willingness and abilities to provide the best learning and achievement opportunities for all students in contexts of multiple change in classrooms and schools. Most of all, they would contribute to ensuring that all children and young people receive the best possible opportunities to learn and achieve from the best teachers.

REFERENCES

Aaronson, D., Barrow, L. and Sanders, W. (2003). *Teachers and Student Achievement in Chicago Public High Schools*. Chicago, IL: Federal Reserve Bank of Chicago.

Abbott, J. (1994). *Learning Makes Sense: Re-Creating Education for a Changing Future*. Letchworth, UK: Education 2000.

Acker, S. (1999). *The Realities of Teachers' Work: Never a Dull Moment*. London: Cassell.

Ackerman, R. and Goldsmith, M. (2011). Metacognitive regulation of text learning: on screen versus on paper. *Journal of Experimental Psychology: Applied*, 17, (1) 18–32.

Ackerman, B. P., Kogos, J., Youngstrom, E., Schoff, K. and Izard, C. (1999). Family instability and the problem behaviors of children from economically disadvantaged families. *Development Psychology*, 35 (1), 258–268.

Aeltermann, A., Engels, N., van Petegem, K. and Verheghe, J. P. (2007). The wellbeing of teachers in Flanders. *Educational Studies*, 33 (3), 285–297.

Ainscow, M., Hopkins, D., Southworth, G. and West, M. (1994). *Creating the Conditions for School Improvement*. London: Fulton.

Akkerman, S. F. and Meijer, P. C. (2011). A dialogical approach to conceptualizing teacher identity. *Teaching and Teacher Education*, 27 (2), 308–319.

Allensworth, B., Ponisciak, S. and Mazzeo, C. (2009). *The Schools Teachers Leave: Teacher Mobility in Chicago Public Schools*. Chicago, IL: Consortium on Chicago School Research, University of Chicago.

Alvesson, M. and Spicer, A. (2012). A stupidity based theory of organizations. *Journal of Management Studies*, 49 (7), 1194–1220.

Angelle, P. S., Nixon, T. J., Norton, E. M. and Miles, C. A. (2011). Increasing organizational effectiveness: an examination of teacher leadership, collective efficacy, and trust in schools. Paper presented at the annual meeting of the University Council for Educational Administration, Pittsburgh, PA, November 19, 2011.

Angle, H., Gilbrey, N. and Belcher, M. (2007). *Teachers' Workload Diary Survey*. March 2007. London: Office of Manpower Economics, School Teachers' Review Board.

Apple, M. W. (2006). *Educating the "Right" Way: Markets, Standards, God, and Education* (2nd ed.). New York, NY: Routledge.

Apple, M. W. (2008). Can schooling contribute to a more just society? *Education, Citizenship and Social Justice*, 3 (3), 239–261.

Argyris, C. and Schön, D. A. (1974). *Theory in Practice: Increasing Professional Effectiveness*. San Francisco, CA: Jossey-Bass.

Avey, J. B., Luthans, F. and Youssef, C. M. (2009). The additive value of positive psychological capital in predicting work attitudes and behaviors. *Journal of Management*, 36 (2), 430–452.

Bajorek, Z., Guilliford, J. and Taskila, T. (2014). *Healthy Teachers, Higher Marks? Establishing a Link between Teacher Health and Wellbeing, and Student Outcomes*. London: The Work Foundation.

Ball, S. J. (1994). *Education Reform: A Critical Post-Structural Approach*. Maidenhead, UK: Open University Press.

Ball, S. J. (2003a). The teacher's soul and the terrors of performativity. *Journal of Education Policy*, 18 (2), 215–228.

Ball, S. J. (2003b). Professionalism, managerialism and performativity. Keynote Address, Professional Development and Educational Change, a conference organized by The Danish University of Education, 14 May 2003.

Ball, S. J. (2012). *Global Education Inc: New Policy Networks and the Neo-liberal Imaginary*. London: Routledge.

Ball, S. J. and Goodson, I. (1985). *Teachers' Lives and Careers*. Lewes, UK: Falmer Press.

Ball, S. J., Maguire, M., Braun, A. and Hoskins, K. (2011). Policy actors: doing policy work in schools. Discourse. *Cultural Studies in the Politics of Education*, 32 (4), 625–639.

Bandura, A. (1982). Self-efficacy mechanism in human agency. *American Psychologist*, 37 (2), 122–147.

Bandura, A. (2000). Cultivate self-efficacy for personal and organizational effectiveness. In E. A. Locke (Ed.), *Handbook of Principles of Organization Behavior*. Oxford, UK: Blackwell, 120–136.

Barley, Z. and Beesley, A. (2007). Rural school success: what can we learn? *Journal of Research in Rural Education*, 21 (1), 1–15.

Barth, R. S. (2002). The culture builder. *Educational Leadership*, 59 (8), 6–11.

Bartholomew, S. S. and Sandholtz, J. H. (2009). Competing views of teaching in a school-university partnership. *Teaching and Teacher Education*, 25 (1),155–165.

Beatty, B. R. and Brew, C. R. (2005). Measuring student sense of connectedness with school: the development of an instrument for use in secondary schools. *Leading and Managing*, 11 (2), 103–118.

Beauchamp, C. and Thomas, L. (2009). Understanding teacher identity: an overview of issues in the literature and implications for teacher education. *Cambridge Journal of Education*, 39 (2), 175–189.

Beck, L. G. (1994). *Reclaiming Educational Administration as a Caring Profession*. New York, NY: Teachers College Press.

Beijaard, D., Meijer, P. C. and Verloop, N. (2004). Reconsidering research on teachers' professional identity. *Teaching and Teacher Education*, 20 (4), 107–128.

Beijaard, D., Verloop, M. and Vermunt, J. D. (2000). Teachers' perceptions of professional identity: an exploratory study from a personal knowledge perspective. *Teaching and Teacher Education*, 16 (7), 749–764.

Bell, M., Cordingley, P., Isham, C. and Davis, R. (2010). *Report of Professional Practitioner Use of Research Review: Practitioner Engagement in and/or with Research*. Coventry: CUREE, GTCE, LSIS and NTRP.

Benard, B. (1995). Fostering resilience in children. ERIC/EECE Digest, EDO-PS-99.

Benjamin, K. and Wilson, S. (2005). *Facts and Misconceptions about Age, Health Status and Employability*. Report HSL/2005/20. Buxton, UK: Health and Safety Laboratory.

Benner, P. E. (1984). *From Novice to Expert: Excellence and Power in Clinical Nursing Practice.* Menlo Park, CA: Addison-Wesley.

Bereiter, C. and Scardamalia, M. (1993). *Surpassing Ourselves: An Inquiry into the Nature and Implications of Expertise.* La Salle, IL: Open Court.

Biesta, G. and Tedder, M. (2007). Agency and learning in the lifecourse: towards an ecological perspective. *Studies in the Education of Adults*, 29 (3), 132–149.

Blasé, J. (2001). *Empowering Teachers: What Successful Principals Do.* Thousand Oaks, CA: Corwin Press.

Blau, P. M. (1964). *Exchange and Power in Social Life.* Piscataway, NJ: Transaction Publishers.

Bogotch, I., Miron, L. and Murry, J., Jr. (1998). Moral leadership discourses in urban school settings: the multiple influences of social context. *Urban Education*, 33 (3), 303–330.

Bolam, R. and McMahon, A. (2004). Literature, definitions and models: towards a conceptual map. In C. Day and J. Sachs (Eds.), *International Handbook on the Continuing Professional Development of Teachers.* Maidenhead, UK: Open University Press, 33–63.

Bolam, R., McMahon, A., Stoll, L., Thomas, S., Wallace, M., Greenwood, A. and Smith, M. (2005). *Creating and Sustaining Effective Professional Learning Communities.* Bath and London: University of Bristol/Institute of Education.

Bolger, N., DeLongis, A., Kessler, R. C. and Wethington, E. (1989). The microstructure of daily role-related stress in married couples. In J. Eckenrode and S. Gore, *Crossing the Boundaries: The Transmission of Stress between Work and Family.* New York, NY: Plenum Press, 95–115.

Bonanno, G.A. (2004). Loss, trauma, and human resilience: have we underestimated the human capacity to thrive after extremely aversive events? *American Psychologist*, 59 (1), 20–28.

Borman, G. D. and Dowling, N. M. (2008). Teacher attrition and retention: a meta-analytic and narrative review of the research. *Review of Educational Research*, 78 (3), 367–409.

Bottery, M. and Wright, N. (2000). The directed profession: teachers and the state in the third millennium. *Journal of In-Service Education*, 26 (1), 475–486.

Boyd, D. (2010). Social network sites as networked publics: affordances, dynamics, and implications. In Z. Papacharissi (Ed.), *Networked Self: Identity, Community, and Culture on Social Network Sites.* New York, NY: Routledge, 39–58. Available online at www.danah.org/papers/2010/SNSasNetworkedPublics.pdf (accessed 10 February 2012).

Boyd, D., Lankford, H., Loeb, S., Ronfeldt, M. and Wyckoff, J. (2010). *The Effect of School Neighborhoods on Teacher Retention Decisions.* (Working paper). Available online at www.stanford.edu/~sloeb/papers/Neighborhoods%2006Jan2010.pdf (accessed 24 February 2017).

Braun, A., Maguire, M. and Ball, S. (2010). Policy enactments in the UK secondary school: examining policy, practice and school positioning. *Journal of Education Policy*, 25 (4), 547–560.

Brennan, M. (1996). *Multiple Professionalisms for Australian Teachers in an Important Age.* New York, NY: American Educational Research Association.

Brewster, C. and Railsback, J. (2003). *Building Trusting Relationships for School Improvement: Implications for Principals and Teachers.* Portland, OR: Northwest Regional Educational Laboratory.

Bricheno, P., Brown, S. and Lubansky, R. (2009). *Teacher Wellbeing: A Review of the Evidence.* London: Teacher Support Network.

Bridwell-Mitchell, E. N. and Cooc, N. (2016). The ties that bind: how social capital is forged and forfeited in teacher communities. *Educational Researcher*, 45 (1), 7–17.

Britzman, D. P. (1991). *Practice Makes Practice: A Critical Study of Learning to Teach.* New York, NY: SUNY Press.

Brookfield, S. (1998). Understanding and facilitating moral learning in adults. *Journal of Moral Education*, 27 (3), 283–300.

Brunetti, G. (2006). Resilience under fire: perspectives on the work of experienced, inner city high school teachers in the United States. *Teaching and Teacher Education*, 22 (7), 812–825.

Bryk, A. S. and Schneider, B. L. (2002). *Trust in Schools: A Core Source for Improvement.* New York, NY: Russell Sage Foundation Publications.

Bryk, A. S., Sebring, P. B., Allensworth, E., Luppescu, S. and Easton, J. Q. (2010). *Organizing Schools for Improvement.* Chicago, IL: University of Chicago Press.

Burke, P. J. and Stets, J. E. (2009). *Identity Theory.* Oxford: Oxford University Press.

Butt, R. L. (1984). Arguments for using biography in understanding teacher thinking. In R. Halkes, and J. K. Olson (Eds.), *Teacher Thinking: A New Perspective on Persisting Problems in Education.* Tilburg, The Netherlands: Swets and Zeitlinger, 98–123.

Calabrese, R. L. (2006). Building social capital through the use of an appreciative inquiry theoretical perspective in a school and university partnership. *International Journal of Educational Management*, 20 (3), 173–182.

Campbell, A. (2003). Teachers' research and professional development in England: some questions, issues and concerns. *Journal of In-Service Education*, 29 (3), 375–388.

Campbell, S. (1997). *Interpreting the Personal: Expression and the Formation of Feelings.* Ithaca, NY: Cornell University Press.

Caprara, G. V., Barbaranelli, C., Steca, P. and Malone, P. S. (2006). Teachers' self-efficacy beliefs as determinants of job satisfaction and students' academic achievement: a study at the school level. *Journal of School Psychology*, 44 (6), 473–490.

Cardno, C. (2005). Leadership and professional development: the quiet revolution, *International Journal of Educational Management*, 19 (4), 292–306.

Castells, M. (1997). *Las Metamorfosis de la Cuestión Social [The Metamorphosis of the Social Question].* Buenos Aires: Paidós.

Castro, A. J., Kelly, J. and Shih, M. (2010). Resilience strategies for new teachers in high needs areas. *Teaching and Teacher Education*, 26 (3), 622–629.

Cefai, C. and Cavioni, V. (2014). *Social and Emotional Education in Primary School: Integrating Theory and Research into Practice.* London: Springer.

Certo, J. L. and Engelbright Fox, J. (2002). Retaining quality teachers. *The High School Journal*, 86 (1), 57–75.

Chapman, C. and Harris, A. (2004). Improving schools in difficult and challenging contexts: strategies for improvement. *Educational Research*, 46 (3), 219–228.

Cherubini, L. (2009). Reconciling the tensions of new teachers' socialisation into school culture: a review of the research. *Issues in Educational Research*, 19 (2), 83–99.

Chevalier, A. and Dolton, P. (Winter 2004). Teacher shortage: another impending crisis? *CentrePiece*, 15–21.

Choi, P. L. and Tang, S. Y. (2009). Teacher commitment trends: cases of Hong Kong teachers from 1997–2007. *Teaching and Teacher Education*, 25 (5), 767–777.

Chong, S. and Low, E. L. (2009). Why I want to teach and how I feel about teaching – formation of teacher identity from pre-service to the beginning teacher phase. *Educational Research Policy and Practice*, 8 (1), 59–72.

Cinamon, R. G. and Rich, Y. (2005). Work-family conflict among female teachers. *Teaching and Teacher Education*, 21 (4), 365–378.

Clandinin, J., Long, J., Schaefer, L., Downey, C. A., Steeves, P., Pinnegar, E., McKenzie Robblee, S. and Wnuk, S. (2015). Early career teacher attrition: intentions of teachers beginning, *Teaching Education*, 26 (1), 1–16.

Clarke, D. and Hollingsworth, H. (2002). Elaborating a model of teacher professional growth. *Teaching and Teacher Education*, 18 (8), 947–967.

Clarke, J. and Newman, J. (1997). *The Managerial State: Power, Politics and Ideology in the Remaking of Social Welfare*. London: Sage.

Claxton, G. L. (1997). *Hare Brain, Tortoise Mind: Why Intelligence Increases When You Think Less*. London: Fourth Estate; San Francisco, CA: HarperCollins.

Cochran-Smith, M. and Lytle, S. (2009). *Inquiry as Stance: Practitioner Research for the Next Generation*. New York, NY: Teachers College Press.

Cole, A. L. (1997). Impediments to reflective practice: toward a new agenda for research on teaching. *Teachers and Teaching: Theory and Practice*, 3 (1), 7–27.

Coleman, A. (2011). Towards a blended model of leadership for school based collaborations. *Educational Management Administration and Leadership*, 39 (3), 296–316.

Coleman, J. S. (1988). Social capital in the creation of human capital. *American Journal of Sociology*, 94 (Supplement: Organizations and Institutions: Sociological and Economic Approaches to the Analysis of Social Structure), S95–S120.

Collins, C. J. and Smith, K. G. (2006). Knowledge exchange and combination: the role of human resource practices in the performance of high-technology firms. *Academy of Management Journal*, 49 (3), 544–560.

Cooper, A. (2016). Open for business. *The Guardian*, 13 April 2016, 4.

Cordingley, P., Bell, M., Evans, D. and Firth, A (2005). The impact of collaborative CPD on classroom teaching and learning. Review: what do teacher impact data tell us about collaborative CPD? *Research Evidence in Education Library*. London: EPPI-Centre, Social Science Research Unit, Institute of Education, University of London.

Cowan, D'E., Fleming, G. L., Thompson, T. L. and Morrisey, M. S. (2004). Study description: investigating five PLC schools. In S. M. Hord (Ed.), *Learning Together, Leading Together: Changing Schools through Professional Learning Communities*. New York, NY: Teachers College Press and Oxford, OH: NSDC, 15–19.

Crippen, K. J., Biesinger, K. D. and Ebert, E. K. (2010). Using professional development to achieve classroom reform and science proficiency: an urban success story from Southern Nevada, USA. *Professional Development in Education*, 36 (4), 637–661.

Csikszentmihalyi, M. (1990). *Flow: The Psychology of Optimal Experience* (1st ed.). New York, NY: Harper & Row.

CUREE (2005). *National Framework for Mentoring and Coaching*. London: DfES.

Darling-Hammond, L. (1997). *Doing What Matters Most: Investing in Quality Teaching*. New York, NY: National Commission on Teaching & America's Future.

Darling-Hammond, L. (2000). Teacher quality and student achievement. *Educational Policy Analysis Archives*, 8 (1), 1 January 2000. Available online at http://epaa.asu.edu/ojs/article/view/392/515 (accessed 24 February 2017).

Darling-Hammond, L. and Richardson, N. (2009). How teachers learn. *Educational Leadership*, ASCD, 66 (5), 46–53.

Darling-Hammond, L., LaPointe, M., Meyerson, D. and Orr, M. T. (2007). *Preparing School Leaders for a Changing World: Lessons from Exemplary Leadership Development Programs*. Stanford, CA: Stanford Educational Leadership Institute.

Datnow, A., Hubbard, L. and Mehen, H. (2002). *Extending Educational Reform from One School to Many*. London: Taylor & Francis.

Davidson, R. J. and Begley, S. (2012). *The Emotional Life of Your Brain*. New York, NY: Hudson Street Press.

Davidson R. J. and McEwen, B. S. (2012). Social influences on neuroplasticity: stress and interventions to promote well-being. *Nature Neuroscience*, 15 (5), 689–695.

Day, C. (1999). *Developing Teachers: The Challenges of Lifelong Learning*. London: Falmer Press.

Day, C. (2002). School reform and transitions in teacher professionalism and identity. *International Journal of Educational Research*, 37 (8), 677–692.

Day, C. (2003). Transitions in teacher professionalism: identity, commitment and trust. In L. Moos and J. Krijsler (Eds.), *Professional Development and Educational Change – What Does It Mean to Be Professional in Education?* Copenhagen: Danish University of Education Press, 45–67.

Day, C. (2004). *A Passion for Teaching*. London: Falmer Press.

Day, C. (2009). Building and sustaining successful principalship in England: the importance of trust. *Journal of Educational Administration*, 47 (6), 719–730.

Day, C. (2014). Resilient principals in challenging schools: the courage and costs of conviction. *Teachers and Teaching*, 20 (5), 638–654.

Day, C. and Leitch, R. (2001). Reflective processes in action: mapping personal and professional contexts for learning and change. *Journal of In-service Education*, 27 (2), 237–259.

Day, C. and Sachs, J. (2004). Professionalism, performativity and empowerment: discourses in the politics, policies and purposes of continuing professional development. In C. Day and J. Sachs (Eds.), *International Handbook on the Continuing Professional Development of Teachers*. Maidenhead, UK: Open University Press, 3–32.

Day, C. and Gu, Q. (2007). Variations in the conditions for teachers' professional learning and development: sustaining commitment and effectiveness over a career. *Oxford Review of Education*, 33 (4), 423–443.

Day, C. and Leithwood, K. (Eds.) (2007). *Successful School Principal Leadership in Times of Change: International Perspectives*. Dordrecht Springer.

Day, C. and Johansson, O. (2008). Leadership with a difference in schools servicing disadvantaged communities: arenas for success. In K. Tirri (Ed.), *Educating Moral Sensibilities in Urban Schools*. Rotterdam: Sense Publishers, 19–34.

Day, C. and Kington, A. (2008). Identity, well-being and effectiveness: the emotional contexts of teaching. *Pedagogy, Culture and Society*, 16 (1), 7–23

Day, C. and Gu, Q. (2009). Veteran teachers: commitment, resilience and quality retention. *Teachers and Teaching*, 15 (4), 441–457.

Day, C. and Gu, Q. (2010). *The New Lives of Teachers*. Abingdon, UK: Routledge.

Day, C. and Gu, Q. (2011). Teacher emotions: well being and effectiveness. In P. A. Schutz and M. Zembylas (Eds.), *Advances in Teacher Emotion Research: The Impact on Teachers' Lives*. Dordrecht, The Netherlands: Springer, 15–31.

Day, C. and Gu, Q. (2014) *Resilient Teachers, Resilient Schools: Building and Sustaining Quality in Testing Times*. New York, NY: Routledge.

Day, C. and Gurr, D. (Eds.) (2014). *Leading Schools Successfully: Stories from the Field*. London: Routledge.

Day, C. and Hong, J. (2016). Influences on the capacities for emotional resilience of teachers in schools serving disadvantaged urban communities: challenges of living on the edge. *Teaching and Teacher Education*, 59 (October 2016), 115–125.

Day, C., Harris, A., Hadfield, M., Tolley, H. and Beresford, J. (2000). *Successful Leadership in Times of Change*. Buckingham, UK: Open University Press.

Day, C., Sammons, P., Stobart, G., Kington, A. and Gu, Q. (2007). *Teachers Matter: Connecting Lives, Work and Effectiveness*. Maidenhead, UK: Open University Press.

Day, C., Sammons, P., Hopkins, D., Harris, A., Leithwood, K., Gu, Q., Brown, E., Ahtaridou, E. and Kington, A. (2009). *The Impact of School Leadership on Pupil Outcomes: Final Report*. London: UK Department for Children, Schools and Families Research.

Day, C., Sammons, P., Hopkins, D., Harris, A., Leithwood, K., Gu, Q. and Brown, E. (2010). *10 Strong Claims about Successful School Leadership*. Nottingham: National College for Leadership of Schools and Children's Services.

Day, C., Sammons, P., Leithwood, K., Hopkins, D., Gu, Q., Brown, E. with Ahtaridou, E. (2011a). *Successful School Leadership: Linking with Learning and Achievement*. Maidenhead, UK: Open University Press.

Day, C., Sammons, P., Leithwood, K., Hopkins, D., Gu, Q., Brown, E. with Ahtaridou, E. (2011b). *School Leadership and Student Outcomes: Building and Sustaining Success*. Maidenhead, UK: Open University Press.

Day, C., Gu, Q. and Sammons, P. (2016). The impact of leadership on student outcomes: how successful school leaders use transformational and instructional strategies to make a difference. *Educational Administration Quarterly*. In Press.

DeConinck, J. B. (2010). The effect of organizational justice, perceived organizational support, and perceived supervisor support on marketing employees' level of trust. *Journal of Business Research*, 63 (12), 1349–1355.

Denicolo, P. and Pope, M. (1990). Adults learning-teachers thinking. In C. Day, M. Pope and P. Denicolo (Eds.), *Insights into Teachers' Thinking and Practice*. London: Falmer, 155–169.

Dewberry, C. and Briner, R. (2007). *Report for Worklife Support on the Relation between Well-Being and Climate in Schools and Pupil Performance*. London: Worklife Support.

Dewe, P. and Cooper, C. (2012). *Well-Being and Work: Towards a Balanced Agenda*. Houndmills, Basingstoke, UK: Palgrave-Macmillan.

Dietz, G. and Gillespie, N. (2011). *Building and Restoring Organisational Trust*. London: Institute of Business Ethics.

Dirks, K. T. and Ferrin, D. L. (2001). The role of trust in organizational settings. *Organization Science*, 12 (4), 450–467.

Dreyfus, H. L. and Dreyfus, S. E. (1986). *Mind over Machine: The Power of Human Intuition and Expertise in the Era of the Computer*. New York, NY: The Free Press.

Dunlop, C. A. and MacDonald, E. B. (2004). *The Teachers' Health and Wellbeing Study Scotland*. Edinburgh: NHS Health Scotland.

Earley, P. (2010). 'State of the nation', a discussion of some of the project's key findings. *The Curriculum Journal*, 21 (4), 473–483.

Earley, P. and Porritt, V. (2009). *Effective Practices in Continuing Professional Development: Lesson from Schools*. London: Institute of Education.

Earley, P. and Porritt, V. (2014). Evaluating the impact of professional development: the need for a student-focussed approach. *Professional Development in Education*, 40 (1), 112–129.

Ebbutt, D. (1985). Educational action research: some general concerns and specific quibbles. In R. Burgess (Ed.), *Issues in Educational Research: Qualitative Methods*. Lewes, UK: Falmer Press, 152–174.

Ebersohn, K., Loots, T., Eloff, I. and Ferreira, R. (2015). Taking note of obstacles research partners negotiate in long-term higher education community engagement partnerships. *Teaching and Teacher Education*, 45 (January 2015), 49–72.

Ehrich, L. C., Hansford, B. and Tennent, L. (2004). Formal mentoring programs in education and other professions: a review of the literature. *Educational Administration Quarterly*, 40 (4), 518–540.

Elbaz, F. (1990). Knowledge and discourse: the evolution of research on teacher thinking. In C. Day, M. Pope and P. Denicolo (Eds.), *Insights into Teacher Thinking and Practice*. London: Falmer, 15–42.

Elbaz, F. (1992). Hope, attentiveness, and caring for difference: the moral voice in teaching. *Teaching and Teacher Education*, 8 (5/6), 412–432.

Elbaz, R. (1991). Research on teacher's knowledge: the evolution of a discourse. *Journal of Curriculum Studies*, 23 (1), 1–19.

Elmore, R. F. (2000). *Building a New Structure for School Leadership*. Washington, DC: Albert Shanker Institute.

Elmore, R. F. (2002). *Bridging the Gap between Standards and Achievement: The Imperative for Professional Development in Education*. Washington, DC: Albert Shanker Institute.

Elmore, R. F. (2004). *School Reform from the Inside Out: Policy, Practice, and Performance*. Cambridge, MA: Harvard Education Press.

Elmore, R. F. (2008). Leadership as the practice of improvement. In D. Nusche, D. Hopkins and B. Pont (Eds.), *Improving School Leadership: Volume 2: Case Studies on System Leadership*. Lexington, KY: OECD, 37–67.

Emmet, D. (1958). *Function, Purpose and Powers*. London: Macmillan.

Engeström, Y. (1987). *Learning by Expanding: An Activity-Theoretical Approach to Developmental Research*. Helsinki: Orienta-Konsultit.

Engeström, Y. (2006). Development, movement and agency: breaking away into mycorrhizae activities. In K. Yamazumi (Ed.), *Building Activity Theory in Practice: Toward the Next Generation*. Osaka: Center for Human Activity Theory, Kansai University, 1–43.

Engeström, Y. and Sannino, A. (2010). Studies of expansive learning: foundations, findings and future challenges. *Educational Research Review*, 5 (1), 1–24.

England, P. and Farkas, G. (1986). *Households, Employment, and Gender. A Social, Economic, and Demographic View*. New York, NY: Aldine Publishers.

Eraut, M. (1991). *Education and the Information Society*. London: Cassell Education.

Eraut, M. (1995). Developing professional knowledge within a client-centred orientation. In T. R. Guskey and M. Huberman (Eds.), *Professional Development in Education*. New York, NY: Teachers College Press, 227–252.

Erikson, E. H. (1959). *Identity and the Life Cycle; Selected Papers, with an Historical Introduction by David Rapaport*. New York, NY: International University Press.

Eteläpelto, A. Vähäsantanen, K., Hökkä, P. and Paloniemi, S. (2013, Winter). What is agency? Conceptualizing professional agency at work. *Educational Research Review*, 10 (December 2013), 45–65.

Etzioni, A. (1969). *The Semi-Professionals and Their Organizations: Teachers, Workers, Social Workers*. New York, NY: Free Press.

European Commission (2007). *Improving the Quality of Teacher Education*. Available online at http://eur-lex.europa.eu/legal-content/EN/TXT/?uri=celex%3A52007DC0392 (accessed 10 July 2015).

Evans, G. W. (2004). The environment of childhood poverty. *American Psychologist*, 59 (2), 77–92.

Evans, L. (2008). Professionalism, professionality and the development of education professionals. *British Journal of Educational Studies*, 56 (1), 20–38.

Evans, G.W. and English, K. (2002). The environment of poverty: multiple stressor exposure, psychophysiological stress, and socioemotional adjustment. *Child Development*, 73 (4), 1238–1248.

Evetts, J. (2011). Professionalism in turbulent times: challenges to and opportunities for professionalism as an occupational value. Paper presented at the *NICEC National Network Meeting*, London, 21 March.

Fantilli, R. D. and McDougall, D. E. (2009). A study of novice teacher: challenges and supports in the first years. *Teaching and Teacher Education*, 25 (6), 814–825.

Farrell, T. S. (2003). Learning to teach English language during the first year: personal influences and challenges. *Teaching and Teacher Education*, 19 (1), 95–111.

Feinstein, L. (2000). The relative economic importance of academic, psychological and behavioural attributes developed in childhood. Centre for Economic Performance Discussion Paper, No. 443, February.

Fenstermacher, G. D. and Richardson, V. (2005). On making determinations of quality in teaching. *Teachers College Record*, 107 (1), 186–215.

Field, J. (2005). *Social Capital and Lifelong Learning*. Bristol: Policy Press.

Fielding, M. (2012). Education as if people matter: John Macmurray, community and the struggle for democracy. *Oxford Review of Education*, 38 (6), 675–692.

Flores, M. A. and Day, C. (2006). Contexts which shape and reshape new teachers' identities: a multi-perspective study. *Teaching and Teacher Education*, 22 (2), 219–232.

Forsyth, P. B. and Adams, C. M. (2014). The school principal and organizational predictability. *Trust Relationships and School Life*. New York, NY: Springer.

Fredrickson, B. L. (2001). The role of positive emotions in positive psychology: the broaden-and-build theory of positive emotions. *American Psychologist*, 56 (3), 218–226.

Frost, D. and Durrant, J. (2003). *Teacher-Led Development Work*. London: David Fulton.

Fullan, M. (1993). *Change Forces: Probing the Depths of Educational Reform*. London: Falmer Press.

Fullan, M. (2003). *The Moral Imperatives of School Leadership*. Thousand Oaks, CA: Corwin Press.

Fullan, M. (2007). *The New Meaning of Educational Change*. New York, NY: Teachers College Press.

Fullan, M. (2009). Large-scale reform comes of age. *Journal of Educational Change*, 10 (2–3), 101–113.

Furlong, J., Barton, L., Miles, S., Whiting, C. and Whitty, G. (2000). *Teacher Education in Transition: Reforming Professionalism?* Buckingham, UK: Open University Press.

Furu, E. M. (2007). Emotional aspects of action learning. In E. M. Furu, T. Lund and T. Tiller (Eds.), *Action Research. A Nordic Perspective*. Høyskoleforlaget: Norwegian Academic Press, 185–202.

Galand, B., Lecocq, C. and Philippot, P. (2007). School violence and teacher professional disengagement. *British Journal of Educational Psychology*, 77 (2), 465–477.

Gardner, H. and Davis, K. (2013). *The App Generation: How Today's Youth Navigate Identity, Intimacy, and Imagination in a Digital World*. New Haven, CT: Yale University Press.

Garet, M. S., Porter, A. C., Desimone, L., Birman, B. and Yoon, K. S. (2001). What makes professional development effective? Results from a national sample of teachers. *American Educational Research Journal*, 38 (4), 915–945.

Giddens, A. (1984) *The Constitution of Society: Outline of the Theory of Structuration*. Berkeley, CA: University of California Press.

Gladwell, M. (2008). Most likely to succeed: how can we hire teachers when we can't tell who's right for the job? *New Yorker*, 15 December. Available online at www.newyorker.com/magazine/2008/12/15/most-likely-to-succeed-malcolm-gladwell (accessed 6 January 2016).

Goddard, R. D. (2003). Relational networks, social trust, and norms: a social capital perspective on students' chances of academic success. *Educational Evaluation and Policy Analysis*, 25 (1), 59–74.

Goddard, R. D., Salloum, S. J. and Berebitsky, D. (2009). Trust as a mediator of the relationships between poverty, racial composition, and academic achievement evidence from Michigan's public elementary schools. *Educational Administration Quarterly*, 45 (2), 292–311.

Goe, L. (2007). The link between teacher quality and student outcomes: a research synthesis. Washington, DC: National Comprehensive Centre on Teacher Quality. Available online at http://files.eric.ed.gov/fulltext/ED521219.pdf (accessed 8 October 2015).

Goldstein, S. and Brooks, R. B. (2006). *Handbook of Resilience in Children*. New York, NY: Springer Science + Business Media.

Goodall, J., Day, C., Lindsay, G., Muijs, D. and Harris, A. (2005). *Evaluating the Impact of Continuing Professional Development (CPD) Research Report No. 659*. Nottingham: DfES.

Goodson, I. (Ed.) (1992). *Studying Teachers' Lives*. London: Routledge.

Goodson, I., Moore, S. and Hargreaves, A. (2006). Teacher nostalgia and the sustainability of reform: the generation and degeneration of teachers' missions, memory, and meaning. *Educational Administration Quarterly*, 42 (1), 42–61.

Gordon, K. A., Longo, M. and Trickett, M. (1999). Fostering resilience in children. *The Ohio State University Bulletin*, 875, 1–15.

Government Office for Science (2013). *GO-Science Annual Report 2013–14*. London: Government Office for Science.

Greenfield, S. (2015). *Mind Change: How Digital Technologies Are Leaving Their Mark on Our Brains*. New York, NY: Random House.

Greenhaus, J. H. and Beutell, N. J. (1985). Sources of conflict between work and family roles. *Academy of Management Review*, 10 (1), 76–88.

Griffiths, A. (2007a). Improving with age. *Safety and Health Practitioner*, 25 (4), 53–55.

Griffiths, A. (2007b). Healthy work for older workers: work design and management factors. In W. Loretto, S. Vickerstaff and P. White (Eds.), *The Future for Older Workers: New Perspectives*. Bristol: Policy Press, 121–137.

Gronn, P. (2008). *Hybrid Leadership*. In K. Leithwood, B. Mascall and T. Strauss, (Eds.), *Distributed Leadership According to the Evidence*. London: Routledge, 17–40.

Grootaert, C., Narayan, D., Nyhan Jones, V. and Woolcock, M. (2004). Measuring social capital: an integrated questionnaire. World Bank Working Paper No. 18. Washington DC: World Bank.

Grossman, P. L., Wineburg, S. S. and Woolworth, S. (2001). Toward a theory of teacher community. *Teachers College Record*, 103 (6), 942–1012.

Groundwater-Smith, S. and Mockler, N. (2009). *Teacher Professional Learning in an Age of Compliance: Mind the Gap* (Vol. 2). Dordrecht, The Netherlands: Springer.

Groundwater-Smith, S. and Mockler, N. (2012). Sustaining professional learning networks: the Australasian challenge. In C. Day (Ed.), *The Routledge Handbook of Teacher and School Development*. London: Routledge, 506–515.

Grundy, S. (1994). Action research at the school level. *Educational Action Research*, 2 (1), 23–38.

GTC. (2005). Research for teachers: teachers' professional learning. General Teaching Council. Available online at www.ntrp.org.uk/sites/all/documents/Teachers%20professional%20learning.pdf (accessed 6 May 2015).

Gu, Q. and Day, C. (2007). Teachers resilience: a necessary condition for effectiveness. *Teaching and Teacher Education*, 23 (8), 1302–1316.

Gu, Q. and Day, C. (2013). Challenges to teacher resilience: conditions count. *British Educational Research Journal*, 39 (1), 22–44.

Gu, Q. and Li, Q. (2013). Sustaining resilience in times of change: stories from Chinese teachers. *Asia-Pacific Journal of Teacher Education*, 41 (3), 288–303.

Gu, Q., Rea, S., Hill, R., Smethem, L. and Dunford, J. (2014). *The Evaluation of Teaching Schools: Emerging Findings from the First Phase Investigation*. London: Department for Education.

Guarino, C. M., Santibañez, L. and Daley, G. A. (2006). Teacher recruitment and retention: a review of the recent empirical literature. *Review of Educational Research*, 76 (2), 173–208.

Gudmundsdottir, S. (1990). Values in pedagogical context knowledge. *Journal of Teacher Education*, 41 (3), 44–52.

Guskey, T. (2000). *Evaluating Professional Development*. Thousand Oaks, CA: Corwin Press.

Guskey, T. R. (2002). Professional development and teacher change. *Teachers and Teaching: Theory and Practice*, 8 (3), 381–391.

Gutiérrez, K. D. (2008). Developing a sociocritical literacy in the third space. *Reading Research Quarterly*, 43 (2), 148–164.

Guttman, C. (2001). A hard sell for teaching. *The UNESCO Courier*, October.

Hakonen, J. J., Bakker, A. B. and Schaufeli, W. G. (2006). Burnout and work engagement among teachers. *Journal of School Psychology*, 43 (6), 495–513.

Hallinger, P. and Heck, R. H. (2010). Collaborative leadership and school improvement: understanding the impact on school capacity and student learning. *School Leadership and Management: Formerly School Organisation*, 30 (2), 95–110.

Halpern, D. (2009). Capital gains. London. *Royal Society of Arts Journal*, Autumn 2009, 10–15.

Hammerness, K., Darling-Hammond, L., and Bransford, J. (2005). How teachers learn and develop. In L. Darling-Hammond and J. Bransford (Eds.), *Preparing Teachers for a Changing World: What Teachers Should Learn and Be Able to Do*. San Francisco, CA: Jossy-Bass, 358–389.

Hammersley-Fletcher, L. (2015). Value(s)-driven decision-making: the ethics work of English headteachers within discourses of constraint. *Educational Management Administration and Leadership*, 43 (2), 198–213.

Handford, V. (2011). Why teachers trust school leaders. Unpublished thesis in Department of Theory and Policy Studies in Education, Ontario Institute for Studies in Education, University of Toronto.

Hannah, S. T., Woolfolk, R. L. and Lord, R. G. (2009). Leader self-structure: a framework for positive leadership. *Journal of Organizational Behavior*, 30 (2), 269–290.

Hansen, D. (1995). *The Call to Teach*. New York, NY: Teachers College Press.

Hanushek, E. A. (2011). The economic value of higher teacher quality. *Economics of Education Review*, 30 (3) (2011), 466–479.

Hargreaves, A. (1994). *Changing Teachers, Changing Times*. London: Falmer Press.

Hargreaves, A. and Dawe, R. (1990). Paths of professional development: contrived collegiality, collaborative culture, and the case of peer coaching. *Teaching and Teacher Education*, 6 (3), 227–241.

Hargreaves, A. and Fullan, M. (1992). *Understanding Teacher Development*. New York, NY: Teachers College Press.

Hargreaves, A. and Goodson, I. F. (1996). Teachers' professional lives: aspirations and actualities. In I. F. Goodson and A. Hargreaves (Eds.), *Teachers Professional Lives*. London: Falmer Press, 1–27.

Hargreaves, A. and Fink, D. (2006). *Sustainable Leadership*. San Francisco, CA: Jossey-Bass.

Hargreaves, A. and Fullan, M. (2012). *Professional Capital: Transforming Teaching in Every School*. New York, NY: Teachers College Press.

Hargreaves, L., Cunningham, M., Everton, T., Hansen, A., Hopper, B., McIntyre D., Maddock, M., Mukherjee, J., Pell, T., Rouse, M., Turner, P. and Wilson, L. (2006). The status of teachers and the teaching profession: views from inside and outside the profession: interim findings from the teacher status project. *Research Report 755*. London: DfES.

Hargreaves, L., Cunningham, M., Hansen, A., McIntyre, D. and Oliver, C. (2007). *The Status of Teachers and the Teaching Profession in England: Views from Inside and Outside the Profession*. Cambridge: University of Cambridge Faculty of Education.

Harris, A. (2008). Distributed leadership: the evidence. In *Distributed School Leadership: Developing Tomorrow's Leaders*, London: Routledge, 42–54.

Harris, A. and Jones, M. (2010). Professional learning communities and system improvement. *Improving Schools*, 13 (2), 173–182.

Hattie, J. A. C. (2009). *Visible Learning: A Synthesis of over 800 Meta-Analyses Relating to Achievement*. London: Routledge.

Healy, T. (2003). Social capital: challenges for its measurement at international level, paper presented at the conference on Sustainable Ties in the Information Society (March), Tilburg, The Netherlands: Tilburg University.

Heikkinen, H. L. T., Heikkinen, H., Jokinen, H. and Tynjala, P. (2012). Teacher education and development as lifelong and lifewide learning. In H. L. T. Heikkinen and P. Tynjala (Eds.), *Peer-Group Mentoring for Teacher Development*. London: Routledge, 3–30.

Heller, R., Calderon, S. and Medrich, E. (2003). *Academic Achievement in the Middle Grades: What Does Research Tell Us? A Review of the Literature*. Atlanta, GA: Southern Regional Education Board.

Helsby, G. and McCulloch, G. (1996). Teacher professionalism and curriculum control. In I. F. Goodson and A. Hargreaves (Eds.), *Teachers Professional Lives*. London and Washington DC: Falmer Press, 56–74.

Henry, G. T., Bastian, K. C. and Fortner, C. K. (2011). Stayers and leavers: early career teacher effectiveness and attrition. *Educational Researcher*, 40 (6), 271–280.

Hipp, K. K., Huffman, J. B., Pankake, A. M. and Olivier, D. F. (2008). Sustaining professional learning communities: case studies. *Journal of Educational Change*, 9 (2), 173–195.

Hobson, A. J., Malderez, A., Tracey, L., Homer, M. S., Tomlinson, P. D., Ashby, P., Mitchell, N., McIntyre, J., Cooper, D., Roper, T., Chambers, G. N. and Tomlinson, P. D. (2009). *Becoming a Teacher: Teachers' Experiences of Initial Teacher Training, Induction and Early Professional Development*. Research Report. DCSF Research Report No. RR115. Nottingham: DCSF.

Hochschild, A. R. (1983). *The Managed Heart: Commercialization of Human Feeling*. Berkeley, CA: University of California Press.

Hogan, D. and Donovan, C. (2005). The social outcomes of schooling: subjective agency among Tasmanian adolescents. *Leading and Managing*, 11 (2), 84–102.

Holstein, J. and Gubrium, J. (2000). *The Self That We Live By: Narrative Identity in the Postmodern World*. New York: Oxford University Press.

Hopkins, D. and Stern, D. (1996). Quality teachers, quality schools: international perspectives and policy implications. *Teaching and Teacher Education*, 12 (5), 501–517.

Hopmann, S. (2007). Epilogue: no child, no school, no state left behind: comparative research in the age of accountability. In S. Hopmann, G. Brinek and M. Retzl (Eds.), *PISA Zufolge PISA: PISA According to PISA*. Schulpädagogik und Pädagogishe Psykologie, Band 6. Münster: LIT Verlag, 363–416.

Hord, S. M. (1997). *Professional Learning Communities: Communities of Continuous Inquiry and Improvement*. Austin, TX: Southwest Educational Development Laboratory.

Hostetler, K., Macintyre Latta, M. A. and Sarroub, L. K. (2007). Retrieving meaning in teacher education: the question of being. *Journal of Teacher Education*, 58 (3), 231–244.

Howard, S. and Johnson, B. (2004). Resilient teachers: resisting stress and burnout. *Social Psychology of Education*, 7 (4), 399–420.

Hoy, W. K. and Tschannen-Moran, M. (1999). Five faces of trust: an empirical confirmation in urban elementary schools. *Journal of School Leadership*, 9 (3), 184–208.

Hoy, W. K., Tarter, C. J. and Kottkamp, R. B. (1991). *Open Schools, Healthy Schools: Measuring Organizational Climate*. Newbury Park, CA: Sage.

Hoyle, E. (1975). Professionality, professionalism and control in teaching. In V. Houghton, R. McHugh and M. Colin (Eds.), *Management in Education: The Management of Organizations and Individuals*. London: Ward Lock Educational in association with Open University Press, 314–320.

Hoyle, E. and Wallace, M. (2007). Educational reform: an ironic perspective. *Educational Management, Administration and Leadership*, 35 (1), 9–25.

Huberman, M. (1988). Teachers' careers and school improvement. *Journal of Curriculum Studies*, 20 (2), 119–132.

Huberman, M. (1989). The professional life cycle of teachers, *Teachers College Record*, 91 (1), Fall, 31–57.

Huberman, M. (1993a). *The Lives of Teachers*. London: Cassell.

Huberman, M. (1993b). The model of the independent artisan in teachers' professional relations. In J. W. Little and M. W. McLaughlin (Eds.), *Teachers' Work: Individuals, Colleagues and Contexts*. New York, NY: Teachers College Press, 11–50.

Huberman, M. (1995a). *The Lives of Teachers*. London: Cassell.

Huberman, M. (1995b). Professional careers and professional development: some intersections. In T. Guskey and M. Huberman (Eds.), *Professional Development in Education: New Paradigms and Practices*. New York, NY: Teachers College Press, 193–224.

Ingersoll, R. (2001). Teacher turnover, teacher shortages and the organization of schools. Center for the Study of Teaching and Policy, University of Washington, Seattle.

Ingersoll, R. (2003). Is there really a teacher shortage? Research report. The Consortium for Policy Research in Education and the Center for the Study of Teaching and Policy. Philadelphia, PA. Available online at http://repository.upenn.edu/gse_pubs/133/ (accessed 17 November 2016).

Ingersoll, R. (2004). Four myths about America's teacher quality problem. In M. Smylie and D. Miretzky (Eds.), *Developing the Teacher Workforce*. The 103rd Yearbook of the National Society for the Study of Education. Chicago, IL: National Society for the Study of Education, 1–33.

Ingersoll, R. (2011). Power, accountability, and the teacher quality problem. In S. Kelly (Ed.), *Assessing Teacher Quality: Understanding Teacher Effects on Instruction and Achievement*. New York, NY: Teachers College Press, 97–109.

Ingvarson, L. and Greenway, P. (1984). Portrayals of teacher development. *The Australian Journal of Education*, 28 (1), 45–64.

Isenbarger, L. and Zembylas, M. (2006). The emotional labour of caring in teaching. *Teaching and Teacher Education*, 22 (1), 120–134.

Jackson, D. (2000). School improvement and the planned growth of leadership capacity. Paper presented at BERA Conference, Cardiff, September 2000.

Jackson, P. W., Boostrom, R. E. and Hansen, D. T. (1993). *The Moral Life of Schools*. San Francisco, CA: Jossey-Bass.

James, C. and Connolly, U. (2000). *Effective Change in Schools*. London: Routledge.

James, C., Connolly, M., Dunning, G. and Elliott, T. (2006). *How Very Effective Primary Schools Work*. London: Paul Chapman.

James-Wilson, S. (2001). The influence of ethnocultural identity on emotions and teaching. Paper presented at the Annual Meeting of the American Educational Research Association, New Orleans.

Jeffrey, B. and Woods, P. (1996). Feeling deprofessionalised: the social construction of emotions during an OFSTED inspection. *Cambridge Journal of Education*, 26 (3), 325–343.

Jenkins, A. (2004). *A Guide to the Research Evidence on Teaching-Research Relationships*. York, UK: Higher Education Academy.

Jennings, P. A. and Greenberg, M. T. (2009). The prosocial classroom: teacher social and emotional competence in relation to student and classroom outcomes. *Review of Educational Research*, 79 (1), 491–525.

Jensen, E. (2009). *Teaching with Poverty in Mind: What Being Poor Does to Kids' Brains and What Schools Can Do about It*. Alexandria, VA: Association for Supervision and Curriculum Development (ASCD).

Jersild, A. (1995). *When Teachers Face Themselves*. New York, NY: Teachers College Press.

Johnson, S. M. and Birkeland, S. E. (2003). Pursuing a "sense of success": new teachers explain their career decisions. *American Educational Research Journal*, 40 (3), 581–617.

Johnson, S. M., Kraft, M. A. and Papay, J. P. (2012). How context matters in high-need schools: the effects of teachers' working conditions on their professional satisfaction and their students' achievement. *Teachers College Record*, 114 (10), 1–39.

Jordan, J. (2012). Relational resilience in girls. In S. Goldstein and R. B. Brooks (Eds.), *Handbook of Resilience in Children*, 2nd ed. New York, NY: Springer, 73–86.

Joyce, B. (2004). How are professional learning communities created? *Phi Delta Kappan*, 86 (1), 76–83.

Jugovi , I., Maruši , I., Pavin Ivanec, T. and Vizek Vidovi , V. (2012). Motivation and personality of preservice teachers in Croatia. *Asia-Pacific Journal of Teacher Education, Special Issue*, 40 (3), 271–287.

Kahneman, D. (2011). *Thinking, Fast and Slow*. New York, NY: Farrar, Straus and Giroux.

Kane, T. J., Rockoff, J. E. and Staiger, D. O. (2008). What does certification tell us about teacher effectiveness? Evidence from New York City. *Economics of Education Review*, 27 (6), 615–631.

Kardos, S. M. and Johnson, S. M. (2007). On their own and presumed expert: new teachers' experience with their colleagues. *Teachers College Record*, 109 (9), 2083–2106.

Kelchtermans, G. (1993). Getting the story, understanding the lives: from career stories to teachers' professional development. *Teaching and Teacher Education*, 9 (5–6), 443–456.

Kelchtermans, G. (1996). Teacher vulnerability: understanding its moral and political roots. *Cambridge Journal of Education*, 26 (3), 307–323.

Kelchtermans, G. (2009). Who I am in how I teach is the message: self understanding, vulnerability and reflection. *Teachers and Teaching: Theory and Practice*, 15 (2), 257–272.

Kemmis, S. (2006). Participatory action research and the public sphere. *Educational Action Research*, 14 (4), 459–476.

Kennedy, M. K. (2010). The uncertain relationship between teacher assessment and teacher quality. In M. Kennedy (Ed.), *Teacher Assessment and the Quest for Teacher Quality. A Handbook*. San Francisco, CA: Jossey Bass, 1–6.

Kennedy, M. (2016). How does professional development improve teaching? *Review of Educational Research*, 86 (4), 945–980.

Keyes, C. L. M. and Haidt, J. (Eds.) (2003). *Flourishing: Positive Psychology and the Life Well Lived. Special Issue: What is Positive Psychology?* Washington, DC: American Psychological Association.

Kington, A., Sammons, P., Brown, E., Regan, E., Ko, J. and Buckler, S. (2014). *Effective Classroom Practice*. Maidenhead, UK: Open University Press.

Kirkpatrick, C. L. and Moore-Johnson, S. (2014). Ensuring the ongoing engagement of second-stage teachers. *Journal of Educational Change*, 15 (3), 231–252.

Kirkwood, M. and Christie, D. (2006). The role of teacher research in continuing professional development. *British Journal of Educational Studies*, 54 (4), 429–448.

Kitching, K., Morgan, M. and O'Leary, M. (2009). It's the little things: exploring the importance of commonplace events for early-career teachers' motivation, *Teachers and Teaching: Theory and Practice*, 15 (1), 43–58.

Kohn, A. (1996). *Beyond Discipline: From Compliance to Community*. Alexandria, VA: ASCD.

Kouzes, J. M. and Posner, B. Z. (2007). *The Leadership Challenge* (4th ed.). San Francisco, CA: Jossey-Bass.

Kraft, M. A. and Papay, J. P. (2014). Can professional environments in schools promote teacher development? Explaining heterogeneity in returns to teacher experience. *Educational Evaluation and Policy Analysis*, 36 (4), 476–500.

Kremer-Hayon, L. and Fessler, R. (1991). The inner world of school principals: reflections on career life stages. Paper presented at Fourth International Conference of the International Study Association on Teacher Thinking, 23–27 September 1991, University of Surrey, UK.

Kruse, S. D. and Louis, K. S. (2007). Developing collective understanding over time: reflections on building professional community. In L. Stoll and K. Seashore-Louis (Eds.), *Professional Learning Communities: Divergence, Depth and Dilemmas*. Berkshire, UK: Open University Press, 106–118.

Ladd, H. F. and Sorensen, L. C. (2014). *Returns to Teacher Experience: Student Achievement and Motivation in Middle School*. Washington, DC: National Center for Analysis of Longitudinal Data in Education (CALDER).

Lai, E. (2014). Principal leadership practices in exploiting situated possibilities to build teacher capacity for change. *Asia Pacific Education Review*, 15 (2), 165–175.

Larson, M. S. (1977). *The Rise of Professionalism: A Sociological Analysis*. Berkeley, CA: University of California Press.

Lasch, C. (1991). *True and Only Heaven: Progress and Its Critics*. New York, NY: Norton.

Lasky, S. (2005). A sociocultural approach to understanding teacher identity, agency and professional vulnerability in a context of secondary school reform. *Teaching and Teacher Education*, 21 (8), 899–916.

Leana, C. R. (2011). The missing link in school reform. *Stanford Social Innovation Review*, 9 (4), 30–35.

Leana, C. and Pil, F. (2006). Social capital and organizational performance: evidence from urban public schools. *Organization Science*, 17 (3), 353–366.

Leicht, K. T. and Fennell, M. (2001). *Professional Work: A Sociological Approach*. Oxford: Blackwell.

Leiter, M. P. and Bakker, A. B. (Eds.) (2010). *Work Engagement: A Handbook of Essential Theory and Research*. New York, NY: Psychology Press.

Leithwood, K. (1990). The principal's role in teacher development. In B. Joyce (Ed.), *Changing School Culture through Staff Development*. Alexandria, VA: Association for Supervision and Curriculum, 71–90.

Leithwood, K. (2010). How the leading student achievement project improves student learning: an evolving theory of action. February 2010. Curriculum Org. Available online at www.curriculum.org/LSA/files/LSATheoryofAction.pdf (accessed 10 February 2012).

Leithwood, K. A. and Hallinger, P. (Eds.) (2012). *Second International Handbook of Educational Leadership and Administration (Vol. 8)*. Dordrecht: Springer Science & Business Media.

Leithwood, K. and Sun, J. P. (2012). The nature and effects of transformational school leadership: a meta-analytic review of unpublished research. *Educational Administration Quarterly*, 48 (3), 387–423.

Leithwood, K. I., Jantzi, D. and Steinbach, R. (1999). *Changing Leadership for Changing Times*. Buckingham, UK: Open University Press.

Leithwood, K., Day, C., Sammons, P., Harris, A. and Hopkins, D. (2006). *Seven Strong Claims about Successful School Leadership*. London: DfES and Nottingham: NCSL.

Leithwood, K., Harris, A. and Hopkins, D. (2008). Seven strong claims about successful school leadership. *School Leadership and Management*, 28 (1), 27–42.

Lemon, M., Jeffrey, P. and Snape, R. (2014). Levels of abstraction and cross-cutting skills: making sense of context in pursuit of more sustainable futures. In J. McGlade and M.

Strathern (Eds.), *The Social Face of Complexity Science*. Litchfield Park, AZ: Emergent Publications.

Lesser, E. L. and Storck, J. (2001). Communities of practice and organizational performance. *IBM Systems Journal*, 40 (4), 831–841.

Levinson, D. J., Darrow, C. N., Klein, E. B., Levinson, M. A. and McKee, B. (1978). *Seasons of a Man's Life*. New York, NY: Knopf.

Lewis, C. (2002). *Lesson Study: A Handbook of Teacher-Led Instructional Improvement*. Philadelphia, PA: Research for Better Schools.

Lewis, C., Perry, R. and Murata, A. (2006). How should research contribute to instructional improvement? The case of lesson study. *Educational Researcher*, 35 (3), 3–14.

Lichter, D. T., Shanahan, M. J. and Gardner, E. L. (2002). Helping others? The effects of childhood poverty and family instability on prosocial behavior. *Youth and Society*, 34 (1), 89–119.

Lieberman, A. (2010). Teachers, learners, leaders: joining practice, policy and research. *Educational Leadership*, 15 (67), 1–11.

Lieberman, A. and Miller, L. (2001). Introduction. In A. Lieberman and L. Miller (Eds.), *Teachers Caught in the Action: Professional Development That Matters*. New York, NY: Teachers College Press, vii–x.

Lieberman, A. and Wood, D. R. (2003). *Inside the National Writing Project*. New York, NY: Teachers College Press.

Lieberman, A. and Miller, L. (2004). *Teacher Leadership*. San Francisco, CA: Jossey-Bass.

Lieberman, A. and Mace, D. H. P. (2008). Teacher learning: the key to educational reform. *Journal of Teacher Education*, 59 (3), 226–234.

Lieberman, A. and Miller, L. (2008). *Teachers in Professional Communities: Improving Teaching and Learning*. New York, NY: Teachers College Press.

Lieberman, A. and Miller, L. (2011). Learning communities: the starting point for professional learning is in schools and classrooms. *Journal of Staff Development*, 32 (4), 16–20.

Lightfoot, S. L. (1983). *The Good High School*. New York, NY: Basic Books.

Lightfoot, L. (2016). Nearly half of England's teachers plan to leave in next five years. *The Guardian*, 22 March 2016. Available online at www.theguardian.com/education/2016/mar/22/teachers-plan-leave-five-years-survey-workload-england (accessed 22 March 2016).

Little, J. W. (1993). Teachers' professional development in a climate of educational reform. *Educational Evaluation and Policy Analysis*, 15 (2), 129–151.

Little, J. W. and Veugelers, W. (2005). Big change question: professional learning and school-network ties: prospects for school improvement. *Journal of Educational Change*, 6 (3), 277–291.

Loehr, J. and Schwartz, T. (2003). *The Power of Full Engagement*. New York, NY: Free Press.

Lortie, D. C. (1975). *Schoolteacher*. Chicago, IL: University of Chicago Press.

Louis, K. S., Marks, H. M. and Druse, S. (1994). Teachers' professional community in restructuring schools. Paper prepared for the American Educational Research Association, New Orleans, April.

Louis, K. S., Kruse, S. and Bryk, A. S. (1995). Professionalism and community: what is it and why is it important in urban schools? In K. S. Louis, S. Kruse and Associates, *Professionalism and Community: Perspectives on Reforming Urban Schools*. Thousand Oaks, CA: Corwin Press.

Lumby, J. and English, F. W. (2009). From simplicism to complexity in leadership identity and preparation: exploring the lineage and dark secrets. *International Journal of Leadership in Education*, 12 (2), 95–114.

Lundahl, L. (2002). Sweden: decentralisation, deregulation, quasi-markets – and then what? *Journal of Education Policy*, 17 (6), 687–697.

Luthans, F., Vogelgesang, G. R. and Lester, P. B. (2006). Developing the psychological capital of resiliency. *Human Resource Development Review*, 5 (1), 25–44.

Luthans, F., Youssef, C. M. and Avolio, B. J. (2007). *Psychological Capital: Developing the Human Competitive Edge*. Oxford: Oxford University Press.

Luthar, S., Cicchetti, D. and Becker, B. (2000). The construct of resilience: a critical evaluation and guidelines for future work. *Child Development*, 71 (3), 543–562.

MacBeath, J. (2008). *Distributed Leadership: Paradigms, Policy and Paradox*. In K. Leithwood, B. Mascall and T. Strauss (Eds.), *Distributed Leadership According to the Evidence*. London: Routledge, 41–58.

McCaffrey, D., Sass, T., Lockwood, J. R. and Mihaly, K. (2009). The intertemporal variability of teacher effect estimates. *Educational Finance and Policy*, 4 (4), 572–606.

McCann, T. M. and Johannessen, L. R. (2004). Why do new teachers cry? *The Clearing House*, 77 (4), 138–145.

MacDonald, S. (2004). *The History and Philosophy of Art Education*. Cambridge: James Clarke and Co. Ltd.

McDougall, J. K. (2010). A crisis of professional identity: how primary teachers are coming to terms with changing views of literacy. *Teacher and Teacher Education*, 26 (3), 679–687.

Macey, W. H., Schnieder, B., Barbara, K. M. and Young, S. A. (2009). *Employee Engagement: Tools for Analysis, Practice and Competitive Advantage*. Malden, MA: Wiley.

McLaughlin, M.W. and Talbert, J. E. (2001). *Professional Communities and the Work of High School Teaching*. Chicago, IL: University of Chicago Press.

McLaughlin, M. and Talbert, J. (2006). *Building School-Based Teacher Learning Communities*. New York, NY: Teachers College Press.

Maclean, R. (1992). *Teachers' Careers and Promotional Patterns: A Sociological Analysis*. London: Falmer Press.

MacLure, M. (1993). Arguing for your self: identity as an organising principle in teachers' jobs and lives. *British Education Research Journal*, 19 (4), 311–322.

McNeil, L.M. (2000). *Contradictions of School Reform: Educational Costs of Standardized Testing*. New York, NY: Routledge.

McNess, E., Broadfoot, P. and Osborn, M. (2003). Is the effective compromising the affective? *British Educational Research Journal*, 29 (2), 243–257.

Mansfield, C. F., Beltman, S., Price, A. and McConney, A. (2012). "Don't sweat the small stuff": understanding teacher resilience at the chalkface. *Teaching and Teacher Education*, 28 (3), 357–367.

Mansfield, C. F., Beltman, S. and Price, A. (2014). 'I'm coming back again!' The resilience process of early career teachers. *Teachers and Teaching*, 20 (5), 547–567.

Margolis, D. (1998). *The Fabric of Self: A Theory of Ethics and Emotions*. New Haven, CT and London: Yale University Press.

Margolis, J. (2008). What will keep today's teachers teaching? Looking for a hook as a new career cycle emerges. *Teachers College Record*, 110 (1), 160–194.

Marks, H. M. and Printy, S. M. (2003). Principal leadership and school performance: integrating transformational and instructional leadership. *Educational Administration Quarterly*, 39 (3), 370–397.

Marzano, R. J., Waters, T. and McNulty, B. A. (2005). *School Leadership That Works: From Research to Results*. Alexandria, VA: Association for Supervision and Curricula Development.

Mascall, B., Leithwood, K., Straus, T. and Sacks, R. (2008). The relationship between distributed leadership and teachers' academic optimism. *Journal of Educational Administration*, 46 (2), 214–228.

Maslach, C. (1993) Burnout: A multidimensional perspective. In W. B. Schaufeli, C. Maslach and T. Marek (Eds.), *Professional Burnout: Recent Developments in Theory and Research*. Washington, DC: Taylor & Francis, 19–32.

Maslach, C. (2001). What have we learned about burnout and health? *Psychology and Health*, 16 (5), 607–611.

Masten, A. S., Best, K. M. and Garmezy, N. (1990). Resilience and development: contributions from the study of children who overcome adversity. *Development and Psychopathology*, 2 (4), 425–444.

Matoba, M., Shibata, Y., Reza, M. and Arani, S. (2007). School-university partnerships: a new recipe for creating professional knowledge in school. *Educational Research, Policy and Practice*, 6 (1), 55–65.

Menter, I., Hulme, M., Elliott, D. and Lewin, J. (2010). *Literature Review on Teacher Education in the 21st Century*. Edinburgh: The Scottish Government.

Mintzes, J., Marcum, B., Messerschmidt-Yates, C. and Mark, A. (2013). Enhancing self efficacy in elementary science teaching with professional learning communities. *Journal of Science Teacher Education*, 24 (7), 1201–1218.

Mitchell, C. and Sackney, L. (2000). *Profound Improvement: Building Capacity for a Learning Community*. Lisse, the Netherlands: Swets & Zeitlinger.

Mockler, N. and Sachs, J. (2011). *Rethinking Educational Practice through Reflexive Inquiry: Essays in Honour of Susan Groundwater-Smith*. Dordrecht, The Netherlands: Springer.

Molina-Morales, F. X., Martínez-Fernández, M. T. and Torlo, V. J. (2011). The dark side of trust: the benefits, costs and optimal levels of trust for innovation performance. *Long Range Planning*, 44 (2), 118–133.

Moore-Johnson, S. (2015). Will VAMS reinforce the walls of the egg-crate school? *Educational Researcher*, 44 (2), 117–126.

Mourshed, M., Chijioke, C. and Barber, M. (2010). *How the World's Most Improved School Systems Keep Getting Better*. London: McKinsey & Company.

Mulford, B. (2008). *The Leadership Challenge: Improving Learning in Schools*. Camberwell, Victoria: Australian Education Review Number 53, Australian Council for Educational Research.

Näring, G., Briët, M. and Brouwers, A. (2006). Beyond demands–control: emotional labor and symptoms of burnout in teachers. *Work and Stress*, 20 (4), 303–315.

Nias, J. (1989). *Primary teachers talking. A Study of Teaching as Work*. London: Routledge.

Nias, J. (1996). Thinking about feeling: the emotions in teaching. *Cambridge Journal of Education*, 26 (3), 293–323.

Nias, J. (1999). Teachers' moral purposes: stress, vulnerability, and strength. In R. Vandenberghe and A. M. Huberman (Eds.), *Understanding and Preventing Teacher Burnout: A Sourcebook of International Research and Practice*. Cambridge: Cambridge University Press, 223–237.

Nias, J., Southworth, G. and Campbell, P. (1992). *Whole School Curriculum Development in the Primary School*. London: Falmer Press.

Ning, H. K., Lee, D. and Lee, W. O. (2015). Relationships between teacher value orientations, collegiality, and collaboration in school professional learning communities. *Social Psychology of Education*, 18 (2), 337–354.

Noddings, N. (1992). *The Challenge to Care in Schools: An Alternative Approach to Education*. New York, NY: Teachers College Press.

Nolder, R. (1992). Bringing teachers to the centre stage: a study of secondary school teachers' responses to curriculum change in mathematics. Unpublished PhD thesis. London: King's College, University of London.

Norman, S. M., Avolio, B. J. and Luthans, F. (2010). The impact of positivity and transparency on trust in leaders and their perceived effectiveness. *The Leadership Quarterly*, 21 (3), 350–364.

NSIN. *Research Matters*, No. 5, Summer 1996, 1. London: Institute of Education.

Oakes, J. and Rogers, J. (2007). Radical change through radical means: organizing for equitable schools. *Journal of Educational Change*, 8 (3), 193–206.

O'Connor, K. E. (2008). You choose to care: teachers, emotions and professional identity. *Teaching and Teacher Education*, 24 (1), 117–126.

OECD (2004). *Learning for Tomorrow's World: First Results from PISA 2003*. Paris: OECD.

OECD. (2005). *Teachers Matter: Attracting, Developing and Retaining Effective Teachers*. Paris: OECD.

OECD. (2008). *Education at a Glance 2008*. Paris: OECD.

OECD. (2009). *Creating Effective Teaching and Learning Environments: First Results from TALIS*. Paris: OECD.

Oja, E. (1989). Neural networks, principle components, and subspaces. *International Journal of Neural Systems*, 1 (1), 61–68.

Opfer, V. D. and Pedder, D. (2011). Conceptulisating teacher professional learning. *Review of Educational Research*, 81 (3), 376–407.

Orland-Barak, L. and Maskit, D. (2011). Novices "in story": what first year teachers' narratives reveal about the shady corners of teaching. *Teachers and Teaching: Theory and Practice*, 17 (4), 435–450.

Osguthorpe, R. and Sanger, M. (2013). The moral nature of teacher candidate beliefs about the purposes of schooling and their reasons for choosing teaching as a career. *Peabody Journal of Education*, 88 (2), 180–197.

Oswald, M., Johnson, B. and Howard, S. (2003). Quantifying and evaluating resilience promoting factors: teachers' beliefs and perceived roles. *Research in Education*, 70 (2), 50–64.

Oxford English Dictionary. (2006). Oxford: Oxford University Press.

Ozga, J. (2008). *Social Capital, Professionalism and Diversity: Studies in Inclusive Education* (with J. Allen, G. Smyth). Rotterdam: Sense Publishers.

Ozga, J. (2012). Governing knowledge: data, inspection and education policy in Europe. *Globalisation, Societies and Education*, 10 (4), 439–455.

Palmer, P. (1998). *The Courage to Teach*. San Francisco, CA: Jossey-Bass.

Palmer, P. J. (2007). *The Courage to Teach: Exploring the Inner Landscape of a Teachers's Life*. San Francisco, CA: Jossey-Bass.

Palmer, M., Rose, D., Sanders, M. and Randle, F. (2012). Conflict between work and family among New Zealand teachers with dependent children. *Teaching and Teacher Education*, 28 (7), 1049–1058.

Panatik, S. A. B., Badri, S. K. Z., Rajab, A., Rahman, H. A. and Shah, I. M. (2011). The impact of work family conflict on psychological well-being among school teachers in Malaysia. *Procedia – Social and Behavioral Sciences*, 29 (2011), 1500–1507.

Papatraianou, L. H. and Le Cornu, R. (2014). Problematising the role of personal and professional relationships in early career teacher resilience. *Australian Journal of Teacher Education*, 39 (1), 100–116.

Papay, J. P. (2011). Different tests, different answers: the stability of teacher value-added estimates across outcome measures. *American Educational Research Journal*, 48 (1), 163–193.

Parr, J. M. and Timperley, H. S. (2010). Multiple "black boxes": inquiry into learning within a professional development project. *Improving Schools*, 13 (2), 158–171.

Patoine, B. (2008). *Brain Development in a Hyper-Tech World*. Briefing Paper, 26 August 2008. The DANA Foundation. Available online at www.dana.org/Briefing_Papers/Brain_Development_in_a_Hyper-Tech_World/ (accessed 24 February 2017).

Patterson, J. M. (2002). Integrating family resilience and family stress theory. *Journal of Marriage and the Family*, 64 (2), 349–360.

Patterson, J. L. and Kelleher, P. (2005). *Resilient School Leaders: Strategies for Turning Adversity into Achievement*. Alexandria, VA: Association for Supervision and Curriculum Development (ASCD).

Payne, C. M. (2008). *So Much Reform, So Little Change: The Persistence of Failure in Urban Schools*. Chicago, IL: University of Chicago Press.

Pearson UK (2011). New campaign to help parents and teachers get children learning for life. Available online from https://uk.pearson.com/about-us/news-and-policy/news/2011/10/new-campaign-to-help-parents-and-teachers-get-children-reading-f.html (accessed 2 January 2015).

Pennings, J. M. (1975). The relevance of the structure-contingency model for organizational effectiveness. *Administrative Science Quarterly*, 20 (3), 292–410.

Polanyi, Michael. (1967). The growth of science in society. *Minerva* 5 (4), 533–545.

Pop, M. M. and Turner, J. E. (2009). To be or not to be… a teacher? Exploring levels of commitment related to perceptions of teaching among students enrolled in a teacher education program. *Teachers and Teaching: Theory and Practice*, 15 (6), 683–700.

Postman, Neil. (1992). *Technopoly: The Surrender of Culture to Technology*. New York, NY: Knopf.

Power, M. (2004). *The Audit Explosion*. London: Demos.

Pyhältö, K., Pietarinen, J. and Salmela-Aro, K. (2011). Teacher-working environment fit as a framework for burnout experienced by Finnish teachers. *Teaching and Teacher Education*, 27 (7), 1101–1111.

Raudenbush, S.W., Rowan, B. and Cheong, Y.F. (1992). Contextual effects on the self-perceived efficacy of high school teachers. *Sociology of Education*, 65 (2), 150–167.

Reio, T. G., Jr. (2005). Emotions as a lens to explore teacher identity and change: a commentary. *Teaching and Teacher Education*, 21 (8), 985–993.

Rhodes, S. (1983). Age-related differences in work attitudes and behaviour: a review and conceptual analysis. *Psychological Bulletin*, 93 (2), 328–367.

Rinne, R., Kivirauma, J. and Simola, H. (2002). Shoots of revisionist education policy or just slow readjustment? The Finnish case of educational reconstruction. *Journal of Educational Policy*, 17 (6), 643–658.

Rippon, J. H. (2005). Re-defining careers in education. *Career Development International*, 10 (4), 275–292.

Risley, T. R. and Hart, B. (2006). Promoting early language development. In N. F. Watt, C. Ayoub, R. H. Bradley, J. E. Puma and W. A. LeBoeuf (Eds.), *The Crisis in Youth Mental Health: Critical Issues and Effective Programs, Volume 4, Early Intervention Programs and Policies*. Westport, CT: Praeger, 83–88.

Rivers, J. C. and Sanders, W. L. (1996). *Cumulative and Residual Effects of Teachers on Future Student Academic Achievement*. Knoxville, TN: University of Tennessee Value-Added Research and Assessment Center.

Rivkin, S. G., Hanushek, E. A. and Kain, J. F. (2005). Teachers, schools and academic achievement. *Econometrica*, 73 (2), 417–458.

Robinson, V. M. J. (2007). *School Leadership and Student Outcomes: Identifying What Works and Why*. No. 41. October 2007. Melbourne: Australian Council for Educational Leaders.

Robinson, V. M. J. (2010). From instructional leadership to leadership capabilities: empirical findings and methodological challenges. *Leadership and Policy in Schools*, 9 (1), 1–26.

Robinson, V., Lloyd, C. and Rowe, K. (2008). The impact of leadership on student outcomes: an analysis of the differential effects of leadership types. *Educational Administration Quarterly*, 44 (5), 635–674.

Robinson, V., Hohepa, M. and Lloyd, C. (2009). *School Leadership and Student Outcomes: Identifying What Works and Why. Iterative Best Evidence Syntheses (BES) Programme.* Wellington: Ministry of Education, New Zealand.

Rockoff, J. E. (2004). The impact of individual teachers on student achievement: evidence from panel data. *American Economic Review,* 94 (2), 247–252.

Rose, N. (1990). *Governing the Soul: The Shaping of the Private Self.* London and New York: Routledge.

Rosenfeld, L. B. and Richman, J. M. (1997). Developing effective social support: team building and the social support process. *Journal of Applied Sport Psychology,* 9 (1), 133–153.

Rosenholtz, S. (1984). *Political Myths about Reforming the Teaching Profession.* Denver, CO: Education Commission of the States, July, 1984.

Rosenholtz, S. J. and Simpson, C. (1990). Workplace conditions and the rise and fall of teachers' commitment. *Sociology of Education,* 63 (4), 241–257.

Rovelli, C. (2016). A lesson from the world's most inspirational physics teacher, *The Telegraph,* cited in Boudicca Fox-Leonard. Available online at www.telegraph.co.uk/ education/2016/10/15/a-lesson-from-the-worlds-most-inspirational-physics-teacher/ (accessed 15 October 2016).

Rutter, M. (1990). Psychosocial resilience and protective mechanisms. In J. Rolf, A. S. Masten, D. Cicchetti, K. H. Nuechterlein and S. Weintraub (Eds.), *Risk and Protective Factors in the Development of Psychopathology.* New York, NY: Cambridge University Press, 181–214.

Ryan, R. M. and Deci, E. L. (Eds.) (2002). *Handbook of Self-Determination Research.* Rochester, NY: The University of Rochester Press.

Sachs, J. (2001). Teacher professional identity: competing discourses, competing outcomes. *Journal of Educational Policy,* 16 (2), 149–161.

Sachs, J. (2005). Teacher education and the development of professional identity: learning to be a teacher. In M. Kompf and P. Denicolo (Eds.), *Connecting Policy and Practice: Challenges for Teaching and Learning in Schools and Universities.* London and New York: Routledge, 5–21.

Sachs, J. (2016). Teacher professionalism: why are we still talking about it? *Teachers and Teaching: Theory and Practice,* 22 (4), 413–425.

Sachs, J. and Mockler, N. (2012). Performance cultures of teaching: threat or opportunity?' In C. Day (Ed.), *International Handbook of Teacher and School Development.* London: Routledge, 33–43.

Sammons, P., Kington, A., Lindorff-Vijayendran, A. and Ortega, L. (2014). *Inspiring Teachers: Perspectives and Practices.* Reading: CfBT Education Trust.

Sanger, M. N. and Osguthorpe, R. D. (2011). Teacher education, preservice teacher beliefs, and the moral work of teaching. *Teaching and Teacher Education,* 27 (3), 569–578.

Sarros, J. C. (1992). What leaders say they do: an Australian example. *Leadership and Organization Development Journal,* 13 (5), 21–27.

Scheffler, I. (1968). University scholarship and the education of teachers. *Teachers College Record,* 70 (1), 1–12.

Schön, D. (1983). *The Reflective Practitioner. How Professionals Think in Action.* New York, NY: Basic Books.

Schutz, P. A. and Zembylas, M. (2009). *Advances in Teacher Emotion Research: The Impact on Teachers' Lives.* Dordrecht, The Netherlands: Springer.

Schutz, P. A. and Zembylas, M. (Eds.) (2011). *Advances in Teacher Emotion Research. The Impact of Teachers' Lives.* Heidelberg: Springer.

Seashore-Louis, K. (2007). Trust and improvement in schools. *Journal of Educational Change,* 8 (1), 1–24.

Seashore-Louis, K. R., Anderson, A. R. and Riedel, E. (2003). Implementing arts for academic achievement: the impact of mental models, professional community and interdisciplinary teaming. Available online at http://conservancy.umn.edu/handle/11299/143717 (accessed 27 February 2017).

Sebring, P. B. and Bryk, A. S. (2000). School leadership and the bottom line in Chicago. *Phi Delta Kappan*, 81 (6), 440–443.

Seldon, A. (2009). *Trust: How we lost it and how to get it back*. London: Biteback Publishing.

Seligman, M. E. P. (2002). *Authentic Happiness*. New York, NY: Free Press.

Seligman, M. (2011). *Flourish: A New Understanding of Happiness and Well-Being*. New York, NY: Simon & Schuster.

Seligman, M. (2012). *Flourish: A Visionary New Understanding of Happiness and Well-Being*. New York, NY: Atria Books.

Senge, P. (1990). *The Fifth Discipline*. London: Century Business.

Shleifer, A. (2012). Psychologists at the gate: a review of Daniel Kahneman's *Thinking, Fast and Slow. Journal of Economic Literature*, 50 (4). Available online at https://dash.harvard.edu/handle/1/10735580 (accessed 24 February 2017).

Shoffner, M. (2011). Considering the first year: reflection as a means to address beginning teachers' concerns. *Teachers and Teaching: Theory and Practice*, 17 (4), 417–433.

Shulman, L. (1986). Those who understand: knowledge growth in teaching. *Educational Researcher*, 15 (2), 4–14.

Sikes, P., Measor, L. and Woods, P. (1985). *Teacher Careers: Crises and Continuities*. Lewes, UK: Falmer.

Simon, N. S. and Johnson, S. M. (2015). Teacher turnover in high-poverty schools: what we know and can do. *Teachers College Record*, 117 (3), 1–36.

Slater, H., Davies, N. and Burgess, S. (2009). Do teachers matter? Measuring the variation in teacher effectiveness in England. Centre for Market and Public Organisation Bristol Institute of Public Affairs, University of Bristol. Available from http://www.bristol.ac.uk/media-library/sites/cmpo/migrated/documents/wp212.pdf (accessed 7 February 2015).

Sloan, K. (2006). Teacher identity and agency in school worlds: beyond the all-good/all-bad discourse on accountability-explicit curriculum policies. *Curriculum Inquiry*, 36 (2), 119–152.

Smethem, L. (2007). Retention and intention in teaching careers: will the new generation stay? *Teachers and Teaching*, 13 (5), 465–480.

Smith, K. and Ulvik, M. (2014). Learning to teach in Norway: a shared responsibility. In O. McNamara (Ed.), *Workplace Learning in Teacher Education*. Dordrecht, The Netherlands: Springer Publishing Company, 261–277.

Smithers, A. and Robinson, P. (2000). *Coping with Teacher Shortages*. London: NUT.

Smithers, A. and Robinson, P. (2005). *Physics in Schools and Colleges: Teacher Deployment and Student Outcomes*. Buckingham, UK: Centre for Education and Employment Research, University of Buckingham.

Sockett, H. (1993). *The Moral Base for Teacher Professionalism*. New York, NY: Teachers College Press.

Soini, T., Pietarinen, J. and Pyhalto, K. (2016). What if teachers learn in the classroom? *Journal of Teacher Development*, 20 (3), 380–397.

Solomon, R. C. and Flores, F. (2001). *Building Trust: In Business, Politics, Relationships, and Life*. New York, NY: Oxford University Press.

Somekh, B. (1988). Action research and collaborative school development. In R. Mc Bride (Ed.), *The In-Service Training of Teachers*. London: Falmer Press, 160–176.

Somekh, B. (2006). *Action Research: A Methodology for Change and Development*. Buckingham, UK: Open University Press.

Southworth, G. (2011). Speech given at the Cambridge Teachers Conference on School Leadership.

Spillane, J. and Burch, P. (2006). The institutional environment and instructional practice: changing patterns of guidance and control in public education. In B. Rowan and H. Meyer (Eds.), *The New Institutionalism in Education*. Albany, NY: SUNY Press, 87–102.

Spillane, J. P. and Healey, K. (2010). Conceptualizing school leadership and management from a distributed perspective. *The Elementary School Journal*, 111 (2), 253–281.

Spillane, J. P., Camburn, E. M. and Pareja, A. S. (2007). Taking a distributed perspective to the school principal's workday. *Leadership and Policy in Schools*, 6 (1), 103–125.

Split, J. L., Koomen, H. M. U. and Thijs, J. T. (2011). Teacher wellbeing: the importance of teacher-student relationships. *Educational Psychology Review*, 23 (4), 457–477.

Sroufe, L. A. (2005). Attachment and development: a prospective, longitudinal study from birth to adulthood. *Attachment and Human Development*, 7 (4), 349–367.

Starratt, R. J. (1991). Building an ethical school: a theory for practice in educational leadership. *Educational Administration Quarterly*, 27 (2), 185–202.

Stenhouse, L. (1975). *An Introduction to Curriculum Research and Development*. London: Heinemann.

Stokking, K, Leenders, F. de Jong, J. and van Tartwijk, J. (2003). From student to teacher: reducing practice shock and early dropout in the teaching profession. *European Journal of Teacher Education*, 25 (3), 329–350.

Stoll, L. and Seashore-Louis, K. (2007). *Professional Learning Communities: Divergence, Depth and Dilemmas*. Maidenhead, UK: Open University Press.

Stoll, L., Bolam, R., McMahon, A., Wallace, M. and Thomas, S. (2006). Professional learning communities: a review of the literature. *Journal of Educational Change*, 7 (4), 221–258.

Sumsion, J. (2002). Becoming, being and unbecoming an early childhood educator: a phenomenological case study of teacher attrition. *Teaching and Teacher Education*, 18 (7), 869–885.

Sutton, R. E. (2004). Emotional regulation goals and strategies of teachers. *Social Psychology of Education*, 7 (4), 379–398.

Swann, M., McIntyre, D., Pell, T., Hargreaves, L. and Cunningham, M., (2010). Teachers' conceptions of teacher professionalism in England in 2003 and 2006. *British Educational Research Journal*, 36 (4), 549–571.

Szewczyk-Sokolowski, M., Bost, K. K. and Wainwright, A. B. (2005). Attachment, temperament, and preschool children's peer acceptance. *Social Development*, 3 (14), 379–397.

Talbert, J. E. and McLaughlin, M. W. (1996). Teacher professionalism in local school contexts. In I. Goodson, and A. Hargreaves (Eds.), *Teachers' Professional Lives*. London: Falmer Press, 127–153.

Thomson, M. M. and McIntyre, E. (2013). Prospective teachers' goal orientation: an examination of different teachers' typologies with respect to motivations and beliefs about teaching. *Teacher Development: An International Journal of Teachers' Professional Development*, 17 (4), 409–430.

Thomson, M. M. and Palermo, C. (2014). Preservice teachers' understanding of their professional goals: case studies from three different typologies. *Teaching and Teacher Education*, 44 (November 2014), 56–68.

Thomson, M. M., Turner, J. E., and Nietfeld, J. L. (2012). A typological approach to investigate the teaching career decision: motivations and beliefs about teaching of prospective teacher candidates. *Teaching and Teacher Education*, 28 (3), 324–335.

Timperley, H. (2008). *Teacher Professional Learning and Development*. Brussels: International Academy of Education and International Bureau of Education.

Timperley, V. and Robinson, V. (2000). Workload and the professional culture of teachers. *Educational Management and Administration*, 28 (1), 47–62.

Townsend, A. (2013). Rethinking networks in education: case studies of organisational development networks in neoliberal contexts. *Journal of Educational Change*, 43 (4), 343–362.

Tsang, K. K. (2013). Teacher emotions: sociological understandings. *Research Studies in Education*, 11, 127–143

Tschannen-Moran, M. (2004). *Trust Matters: Leadership for Successful Schools*. San Francisco, CA: Jossey-Bass.

Tschannen-Moran, M. (2014a). *Trust Matters: Leadership for Successful Schools* (2nd ed.). San Francisco, CA: Jossey-Bass.

Tschannen-Moran, M. (2014b). The interconnectivity of trust in schools. In *Trust and School Life*. Dordrecht, The Netherlands: Springer, 57–81.

Tschannen-Moran, M. and Hoy, W. K. (2000). A multidisciplinary analysis of the nature, meaning, and measurement of trust. *Review of Educational Research*, 70 (4), 547–593.

Tugade, M. and Fredrickson, B. L. (2004). Resilient individuals use positive emotions to bounce back from negative emotional arousal. *Journal of Personality and Social Psychology*, 86 (2), 320–333.

Van den Berg, R. (2002). Teachers' meanings regarding educational practice. *Review of Educational Research*, 72 (4), 577–625.

Vandenberghe, R. and Huberman, M. (Eds.) (1999). *Understanding and Preventing Teacher Burnout: A Sourcebook of International Research and Practice*. Cambridge: Cambridge University Press.

Van Maele, D., Van Houtte, M. and Forsyth, B.P. (2014). *Trust and School Life: The Role of Trust for Learning, Teaching, Leading and Bridging*. Dordrecht: Springer.

Van Veen, K. and Sleegers, P. (2006). How does it feel? Teachers' emotions in a context of change. *Journal of Curriculum Studies*, 38 (1), 85–111.

Van Veen, K., Sleegers, P. and van de Ven, P. (2005). One teacher's identity, emotions, and commitment to change: a case study into the cognitive–affective processes of a secondary school teacher in the context of reforms. *Teaching and Teacher Education*, 21 (8), 917–934.

Vermunt, J. D. and Verloop, N. (1999). Congruence and friction between learning and teaching. *Learning and Instruction*, 9 (3), 257–280.

Veugelers, W. M. M. H. (2005). Networks of teachers or teachers caught in networks. *Journal of Educational Change*, 6 (3), 284–291.

Villegas-Reimers, E. (2003). Teacher professional development: an international review of the literature. UNESCO: IIEP (International Institute for Educational Planning: 7). Available online at http://unesdoc.unesco.org/images/0013/001330/133010e.pdf (accessed 19 November 2015).

Waldman, D. and Avolio, B. (1986). A meta-analysis of age differences in job performance. *Journal of Applied Psychology*, 71 (1), 33–38.

Ware, H. and Kitsantas, A. (2007). Teacher and collective efficacy beliefs as predictors of professional commitment. *The Journal of Educational Research*, 100 (5), 303–309.

Warr, P. (1994). Age and job performance. In J. Snel and Cremer, R. (Eds.), *Work and Age: A European Perspective*. London: Taylor & Francis, 309–322.

Wasik, B. A. and Hindman, A. H. (2011). Improving vocabulary and pre-literacy skills of at-risk preschoolers through teacher professional development. *Journal of Educational Psychology*, 103 (2), 455–469.

Watt, H. M. G., Richardson, P. W., Klusmann, U., Kunter, M., Beyer, B., Trautwein, U. and Baumert, J. (2012). Motivations for choosing teaching as a career: an international comparison using the FIT-choice scale. *Teaching and Teacher Education*, 28 (6), 791–805.

Watts, A. G. (1981). Career patterns. In A.G. Watts, D. E. Super and Kidd, J. M. (Eds.), *Career Development in Great Britain*. Cambridge: Hobson's Press.

Webster-Wright, A. (2009). Reframing professional development through understanding authentic professional learning. *Review of Educational Research*, 79 (2), 702–739.

Welle-Strand, A. and Tjeldvoll, A. (2002). *Learning, ICT and Value Creation – Strategies Missing?* BI Research Report Series. Sandvika, Norway: BI.

Wenger, E. (1998). *Communities of Practice: Learning, Meaning and Identity*. Cambridge: Cambridge University Press.

Wenger, E. (2000). Communities of practice and social learning systems. *Organization*, 7 (2), 225–246.

Wenger, E. C. and Snyder, W. M. (2000). Communities of practice: the organizational frontier. *Harvard Business Review*, 78 (1), 139–145.

Wennergren, A. (2016). Teachers as learners – with a little help from a critical friend. *Educational Action Research*, 24 (3), 260–279.

Wertsch, J. V., Tulviste, P. and Hagstrom, F. (1993). A sociocultural approach to agency. In E. A. Forman, N. Minick and C. A. Stone (Eds.), *Contexts for Learning: Sociocultural Dynamics in Children's Development*. Oxford: Oxford University Press, 336–356.

Wheatley, M. J. (1999). *Leadership and the New Science: Discovering Order in a Chaotic World*. San Francisco, CA: Berrett-Koehler Publishers.

Wheatley, M. (2001). Restoring hope for the future through critical education of leaders. *Vimut Shiksha*, March.

Whitty, G., Power, S. and Halpin, D. (1998). *Devolution and Choice in Education: The School, the State and the Market*. Buckingham, UK: Open University Press.

Williams, J., Ryan, J. and Morgan, S. (2014). Lesson study in a performative culture. In O. McNamara, J. Murray and M. Jones (Eds.), *Workplace Learning in Teacher Education: International Practice and Policy*. Dordrecht, The Netherlands: Springer, 141–157.

Wong, J. L. N. (2010). What makes a professional learning community possible? A case study of a Mathematics department in a junior secondary school of China. *Asia Pacific Education Review*, 11 (2), 131–139.

Woolfolk Hoy, A., Hoy, W. K. and Kurz, N. (2008). Teacher's academic optimism: the development and test of a new construct. *Teaching and Teacher Education*, 24 (4), 821–834.

Wright, M. O. and Masten. A.S. (2006). Resilience processes in development. In S. Goldstein and R. Brooks (Eds.), *Handbook of Resilience in Children*. New York, NY: Springer, 17–37.

Yamagata-Lynch, L. C. and Smaldino, S. (2007). Using activity theory to evaluate and improve K-12 school and university partnerships. *Evaluation and Program Planning*, 30 (4), 364–380.

Youngs, P. and King, M. (2002). Principal leadership for professional development to build school capacity. *Educational Administration Quarterly*, 38 (5), 643–670.

Zeichner, K. (1993). *Educating Teachers for Cultural Diversity*. Special Report. East Lansing, MI: Michigan State University, National Center for Research on Teacher Learning.

Zeichner, K. (2010). Rethinking the connections between campus courses and field experiences in college and university-based teacher education. *Journal of Teacher Education*, 61 (1–2), 89–99.

Zeichner, K. and Liston, D. (1996). *Reflective Teaching: An Introduction*. Mahwah, NJ: Lawrence Erlbaum Associates.

Zembylas, M. (2003). Interrogating "teacher identity": emotion, resistance, and self-formation. *Educational Theory*, 53 (1), 107–127.

Zembylas, M. (2005a). *Teaching with Emotion: A Postmodern Enactment*. Greenwich, CT: IAP.

Zembylas, M. (2005b). Discursive practices, genealogies, and emotional rules: a poststructuralist view on emotion and identity in teaching. *Teaching and Teacher Education*, 21 (8), 935–948.

INDEX

Page numbers in italic refer to figures and in bold refer to tables.